ACHIEVEMENT AND INEQUALITY IN EDUCATION

This reader is one part of an Open University integrated teaching system and the selection is therefore related to other material available to students. It is designed to evoke the critical understanding of students. Opinions expressed in it are not necessarily those of the course team or of the University.

ACHIEVEMENT AND INEQUALITY IN EDUCATION

A Reader edited by June Purvis and Margaret Hales
for the course
Conflict and Change in Education: A Sociological Introduction
at the Open University

Routledge & Kegan Paul
London, Melbourne and Henley
in association with
The Open University

First published in 1983
by Routledge & Kegan Paul plc
39 Store Street, London WC1E 7DD, England
464 St Kilda Road, Melbourne,
Victoria 3004, Australia and
Broadway House, Newtown Road,
Henley-on-Thames, Oxon RG9 1EN, England
Set in Times Roman by Input Typesetting Ltd, London
and printed in Great Britain by
T. J. Press (Padstow) Ltd,
Padstow, Cornwall

Selection and editorial material
copyright © The Open University 1983

British Library Cataloguing in Publication Data

Achievement and inequality in education.

1. Educational sociology—England
I. Purvis, June   II. Hales, Margaret
370.19'0942   LC191.8.G7
ISBN 0–7102–0010–2

Contents

Personnel associated with OU Course E205

Course team

Jim Burge (BBC)
Ben Cosin (Chairman/unit author)
Brian Davies (Course assessor)
Rosemary Deem (Unit author)
Chris Gravell (Editor)
Margaret Hales (Course co-ordinator)
Martyn Hammersley (Unit author)
Audrey Lambart (Staff tutor)
Roger Lowry (Editor)
Maggie Lawson (Project control)
Donald MacKinnon (Unit author)
Caroline Morrow-Brown (Editor)
June Purvis (Unit author)
Anne Diack (BBC)
Patti Langton (BBC)
Sally Baker (Library)
Pam Higgins (Designer)

Consultant authors

Stephen Ball
Kevin Brehony
Sara Delamont
James Donald
Mary Fuller
Andy Hargreaves
Anthony Heath
David Rubinstein
Peter Woods

Secretaries

Meryl Baker
Laurily Dellaway (Course secretary)
Stella Riches
Lilian Walsh

Block assessors

Sandra Acker
Paul Atkinson
Tessa Blackstone
Colin Lacey
Brian Simon
Dennis Smith

Preface

This collection of articles is the second of two volumes[1] that are required reading for an Open University course, entitled E205, *Conflict and Change in Education: A Sociological Introduction*. This new course has been made as a replacement for E202 *Schooling and Society*, which first appeared in 1976. Though the two collections of readings have been compiled for use by Open University students, it is hoped that they will be of interest to a much wider audience of people, especially those concerned about and interested in educational issues.

Conflict and Change in Education outlines a wide range of theoretical approaches to the study of education as well as providing detailed investigation of several key issues: comprehensive education, progressive teaching; gender, race and education; educational policy and ideology; schooling, work and unemployment; and education, leisure and the family. The two set books for the coursework are *Beachside Comprehensive* by Stephen Ball (1981) and *Gender and Schooling* by Michelle Stanworth (1982).[2]

It is not necessary to become an undergraduate of the Open University in order to take E205. Further information about the course may be obtained by writing to: The Admissions Office, The Open University, PO Box 48, Walton Hall, Milton Keynes, MK7 6AB.

Notes

1 The other volume is Cosin, B. R. and Hales, M. (eds) (1983), *Education, Policy and Society: Theoretical Perspectives*, London, Routledge & Kegan Paul.
2 Ball, S. (1981), *Beachside Comprehensive*, Cambridge, Cambridge University Press; Stanworth, M. (1983), *Gender and Schooling*, London, Hutchinson.

Acknowledgments

The Open University and the publishers would like to thank the following for permission to reproduce copyright material. All possible care has been taken to trace ownership of the selections included and to make full acknowledgment for their use.

Chapter 1 By permission of the author and Nafferton Books 1978.
Chapter 2 Copyright © Temple University Press 1977.
Chapter 3 By permission of Heinemann, 1978.
Chapter 4 Copyright © Berkeley Journal of Sociology 1963.
Chapter 5 © Routledge & Kegan Paul, 1976.
Chapter 6 By permission of Croom Helm 1983.
Chapter 7 By permission of the author and The Women's Press, 1980.
Chapter 8 By permission of the author and the Carfax Publishing Company, 1981.
Chapter 9 © Routledge & Kegan Paul 1980.
Chapter 10 By permission of Croom Helm, 1979.
Chapter 11 By permission of Società Editrice il Mulino 1982.
Chapter 12 By permission of the author and A. D. Peters & Co., 1973.

Introduction

June Purvis and Margaret Hales

Debates about achievement and inequality in education have been a persistent theme in British sociology of education as it developed as a systematic field of enquiry after the Second World War. Two particularly influential forces helping to shape the early development of the sociology of education in the 1950s were the political arithmetic tradition within British sociology and the structural-functionalist theoretical perspective that dominated American sociology.

As its name implies, political arithmetic was 'arithmetical' in that it was concerned with providing a quantitative picture of British society. It was 'political' in that the collection of such information was often associated with the advocacy of certain reforms in the British educational system that would help to bring about greater equality of educational achievement between children of different social classes. As Heath (1980) argues, political arithmeticians tackled questions such as injustice and social waste in education – in particular the social 'waste' of able children who failed to gain access to secondary and higher education – and the unjust distribution of opportunities for educational advancement granted to children from different social classes.[1] In particular, those working within the political arithmetic tradition argued that the tripartite system of secondary schooling (the division into grammar, secondary modern and technical high schools), established after the 1944 Education Act, was both 'unjust' and 'inefficient' since it failed to tap a large pool of working-class talent. The intelligence and attainment tests in English and arithmetic that were used to select those children who could attend grammar school were, it was claimed, not only imprecise but biased towards the cultural attributes of middle-class children. While grammar school pupils might seek higher education and enter white-collar, professional jobs, the bulk of secondary school children, the 'unselected' majority who attended the secondary modern schools, left school at the earliest available opportunity to enter a variety of skilled and unskilled jobs that were of low status, comparatively poorly paid and offered few chances for further educational study. The political arithmetic tradition within British sociology of education helped, therefore, to place the issues of achievement and inequality in education, especially between the various social classes, firmly on the agenda within the sociology of education as it developed in the 1950s and 1960s.

Alongside the impact of the political arithmetic tradition within British sociology of education at this time, was the force of that theoretical perspective called 'structural functionalism', a perspective that was dominant within American sociology but which also exercised considerable influence upon British sociology. Functionalism claims that social phenomena may be explained in terms of their 'functions' for a social group, social structure or the wider society. In particular, structural-functionalism sees society as a social system with a number of inter-related parts or subsystems that perform functions for the whole society. Thus, for example, the family and educational subsystems socialize people into the norms and values of the wider society in such a way that people are able and motivated to play that wide variety of social roles which are necessary if society is to persist.[2]

A number of writings within the sociology of education in the 1950s and 1960s adopted a functionalist or weak structural-functionalist framework. For example, two of the most popular textbooks of the time – those by Peter Musgrave and Olive Banks[3] – were written from a functionalist perspective. In 1959, the main exponent of structural-functionalism, the American sociologist Talcott Parsons,[4] published an influential article on the school class as a social system. In this article, Parsons gave central importance to the way the process of socialization both differentiates and integrates the school class. Schools socialize their pupils into the value of achievement and also teach them that it is fair to give differential rewards for different levels of achievement, provided there has been fair access to educational opportunities. While the value of achievement thus differentiates pupils, it also performs an important integrative function since those pupils who do not do well academically, accept the situation. Parsons's analysis of the school class had an important impact upon the way that the school was perceived by sociologists of education. Two influential studies of boys' schools, those by David Hargreaves of 'Lumley' secondary modern (1967) and by Colin Lacey (1970) of 'Hightown' grammar, drew heavily upon Parsons's notion of differentiation, though they did not adopt his functionalist framework.[5]

During the 1960s, sociology courses expanded in institutions of higher education. And as the sociology of education became an option on sociology degree courses and a part of teacher training, the scope of the field began to broaden and diversify. At the same time, the political arithmetic and the structural-functionalist perspectives came under increasing criticism. Other theoretical perspectives, such as interactionism, phenomenology, ethnomethodology and various forms of Marxism came to the fore.[6] These developments had a major impact on the sociology of education.

In 1971, M. F. D. Young edited *Knowledge and Control*, a book which had as its subtitle 'New Directions for the Sociology of Education'.[7] In his introduction to this book, Young criticized earlier work in the sociology of education which had focused on the social class determinants of educational opportunity on the grounds that it had never treated as problematic 'what it is to be educated' (p. 2). Young argued that sociologists of education should begin to look at how school knowledge is socially constructed, selected and transmitted. This emphasis upon the social construction of knowledge within educational institutions was echoed by other contributors to this volume. The links that were suggested between the sociology of education, cultural transmission and the sociology of education in *Knowledge and Control* were further strengthened by the writings of the French sociologist Pierre Bourdieu.[8]

The so-called 'new' sociology of education drew its intellectual stimulation from a variety of sources that included Marx, Mead, Schutz, Berger, Blumer, Cicourel, Garfinkel and Becker.[9] Whereas the structural functionalist perspective had stressed the relationship between education and the wider social structure of society, and had seen men and women as rather passive beings who were largely 'determined' by the social system, the perspectives comprising the 'new' sociology of education stressed that people were active individuals, continually constructing their own reality as they made sense of the world. In particular, studies of the classroom within the 'new' sociology of education stressed that teachers and pupils were actors negotiating and interpreting meanings rather than puppets operated by the social system. As Banks (1978) has noted, the interest in classroom interaction which the 'new' sociology of education had stimulated, sometimes meant the abandonment of the concepts of 'system' and 'structure' and an emphasis upon 'process and interaction'.[10]

While some sociologists of education in the 1970s moved towards detailed analyses of face-to-face interaction within classrooms, others began to be concerned much more with the old question of the determining effects of the social system of society upon education. The renewed interest in this topic came not from any revival of structural-functionalism but from those utilizing Marxist and neo-Marxist perspectives within the sociology of education.[11] Particularly influential was Bowles and Gintis's *Schooling in Capitalist America* (1976) (a book that was adopted as a set book for the OU course *Schooling and society*[12]), Bowles and Gintis related the educational system to the social structure of North American society and argued that the form the educational system took was determined by the function it performed for the economy – of preparing an appropriately socialized, differentially skilled and stratified workforce. At the heart of their analysis was the 'correspondence principle', the argument that there were important parallels between the educational system and the economic system and that through socialization in schools, the hierarchical divisions within the economy were replicated.[13]

These two main strands of thought in the sociology of education in the 1970s – the so-called 'micro' analysis of classroom interaction and the 'macro' analysis of the relationship between education and the wider society – were both to be found in the OU course *Schooling and Society*, first offered in 1976. Since that date, criticisms of and reflections about both strands of thought have been made, including pleas for integration of the two levels of analysis.[14] Bowles and Gintis, for example, have been criticized for presenting an over-simplified view of the relationship between education and the economy, and have attempted to answer some of the criticisms in a paper (1980) elaborating further on their views.[15] Nevertheless, the discussion which the initial book provoked opened up a range of questions about the relationship between education and the economy in a capitalist society. In particular, consideration of such 'macro' issues has included discussion about the state as the key provider of education in a capitalist society. This focus is the theme of another OU course that first appeared in 1981 – *Society, Education and the State*.[16]

However, developments were occurring in the 1970s other than the so-called 'micro' and 'macro' directions within the sociology of education. The most important of these developments was the contribution made by feminist[17] sociologists who focused on the way that girls and women were disadvantaged within the educational system in comparison with boys and men.[18] Such an intervention illustrated only too well that in the past, sociologists of education had frequently ignored girls and women as a topic of study. For example, Sandra Acker (1980), in an analysis of articles on education published between 1960 and 1979 in three major sociology journals, suggested that a Martian coming to Britain and relying on these articles for information about British society and its educational system would conclude that:

> numerous boys but few girls go to secondary modern schools; that there were no girls' public schools; that there are almost no adult women influentials of any sort; that most students in higher education study science and engineering; that women rarely make a ritual transition 'from school to work' and never go into further education colleges. Although some women go to university, most probably enter directly into motherhood, where they are of some interest as transmitters of language codes to their children. And except for a small number of teachers, social workers and nurses, there are almost no adult women workers in the labour market.[19]

The feminist intervention in the sociology of education, then, has raised many additional dimensions to the debate about the social construction of knowledge within the sociology of education itself. In particular, it has exposed the fact that much of our academic knowledge, as well as many of our academic practices, have patriarchal[20] and sexist biases which favour boys and men. The integration of considerations about sex and gender[21] into mainstream sociology of education still has a long way to go, however. We do include in this Reader, though, some articles written from a feminist perspective which highlight not only the inequalities that girls and women may experience in education but also the inadequacies of many gender-blind conceptualizations within the sociology of education.

The readings in the first section of this Reader examine *teachers' perspectives* within the classroom. In his paper, Andy Hargreaves (1.1) argues that 'structural' (or 'macro') questions and 'interactionist' (or 'micro') questions should be linked together rather than dealt with as separate issues. What happens in the classroom, he continues, may relate to the nature of the socio-economic and political structure of the wider society and the functions which the educational system performs for that structure. Sociologists of education can attempt, he argues, to fuse a Marxist analysis of contemporary society and the role of education in that society with an investigation of classroom processes that is informed by phenomenological and interactionist perspectives. Hargreaves himself proposes to link the 'interactional' questions about the classroom to the 'structural' questions about society through conceptualizing teachers' classroom practices in terms of 'coping strategies' that represent adaptations to various constraints that are imposed by the wider society.

The paper by Sussman (1.2) provides a descriptive account of two classrooms that exemplify – at polar ends of a continuum – the two most common ways that 'open education', sometimes called 'progressive' or 'child-centred' education, is being implemented in the United States. In theory, as Sussman points out, the 'open classroom' structures space strongly but destructures time. For example, children are not supposed to move from tasks such as reading or arithmetic according to the time on the clock but according to how long an activity absorbs them. However, both classrooms described here – the 'structured' open classroom of Natalie Roseman and the 'unstructured' open classroom of Abe Winner – deviated from this ideal. Such variability in the implementation of open education is, Sussman suggests, due to many factors, such as the vagueness of open education philosophy.

The final paper in this section on teachers' perspectives looks at a comprehensive school that is part of the Abraham Moss Community Centre in Manchester. Edwards and Furlong (1.3) focus on the teaching of humanities in the lower school, looking in particular at the structure of classroom talk. They found that teachers assumed that pupils would not know what the material for a lesson meant until they had been taught – until, for example, the pupils had had a lead lesson or had been told what to look out for in the booklets. Pupils are likely to hold the same assumptions, too, and until they have been taught, they suspend anything they already know about the subject matter. Pupils thus assume that they are 'ignorant' until they take over the teacher's system of meanings. Being taught then, usually means withholding your own interpretations of the lesson material and searching for what the teacher means. The general conclusion that Edwards and Furlong come to is that even in the 'more open environment' being developed at the Abraham Moss Community Centre, the learning process for pupils involves moving towards the teacher's meanings.

The second section of this Reader is concerned with *pupils' perspectives* and contains articles by Werthman (2.1), Willis (2.2), Fuller (2.3) and Payne (2.4). One of the effects of the emphasis given in the 'new' sociology of education to the fact that people construct their own understandings of the world and, on the basis of such meanings, act in the world, was that more attention was given to the active potential of men and women. As Hammersley and Woods (1976) have pointed out, from the perspective of the 'new' sociology of education, all beliefs and actions, including the beliefs and actions of those considered 'deviant' or 'weird', were now assumed to be rational: pupils' views could no longer be dismissed as a product of unintelligence, home background or even pupil subcultures when they differed from official school views.[22] The four papers in this section all illustrate these points.

Traditionally within the sociology of education it has been male, rather than female, pupils who have been seen as 'deviant' or 'troublesome' within the classroom. And the papers by Werthman and Willis provide now classic accounts of such deviance amongst working-class boys.

Werthman (2.1) notes that many sociological accounts of working-class male delinquency characterize the school as a major stimulus for such behaviour. The school is depicted as a middle-class institution within which many working-class males fail and against which they react. Using data collected on working-class boys who were members of gangs in an inner-city area in the USA, Werthman suggests that such sociological accounts are simplistic. Amongst other things, he points out that members of gangs include not only those boys who do poorly in school but also boys who pass and some who do well. Werthman looks at how the boys respond to the authority claims made by teachers and specifically at the criteria by which they judge the legitimacy of those claims. He argues that the behaviour of the boys in lessons varies from conformity to direct challenge according to the demands that teachers make on the pupils and the pupils' assessments of the legitimacy of these demands. Thus gang members are frequently 'delinquent' in one class and 'ordinary students' in another.

Willis's paper (2.2) focuses upon the anti-school culture of some working-class male pupils – 'the lads' – in an industrial area of England. Like the papers of Fuller and Payne that follow, Willis relates pupils' evaluations of the experience of schooling to social and cultural factors outside the school. He argues that there is a direct relationship between the main features of working-class culture in the wider society, especially the 'shop-floor' culture of factory work, and the counter-school culture adopted by 'the lads'. Both share, for example, various strategies for dealing with things such as boredom, blocked opportunities, alienation and lack of control. The similarities between the two cultures accomplish a continuity between school and work. In particular, the culture of 'the lads' supplies a set of 'unofficial' criteria by which the individual can judge what kind of working situation is going to be most relevant. For Willis, then, the social class location of 'the lads' and their realistic assessment of their own position within a capitalist society are crucial for an understanding of their deviance in school.

Fuller (2.3) points out that most of the research on deviant youth has been on boys. In addition, most of the researchers have been male, and have not made sexism problematic – their own or that within the institutions or cultures they write about. And when these researchers define male pupil experience as the most interesting, the most important, and the most worthy of explanation and description, they are taking on, and working within, teachers' definitions of deviant pupils rather than engaging in the task of defining deviance themselves. Other forms of deviance which may be more common amongst girls, such as indifference and instrumentalism, have received little attention. Indeed, such forms of deviance cannot be neatly fitted into conceptualizations of deviance that focus on 'the flashy, visible and physically confrontational'. Drawing upon data collected in a large, co-educational, multi-racial comprehensive school in the London borough of Brent, Fuller shows that fifth-form girls may be actively critical and contemptuous of much that is going on in and outside the school – though not in ways that appear to be so obviously 'oppositional' in the terms that are used to describe troublesome male pupils. Some Afro-Caribbean girls, for example, were prepared to conform minimally within the classroom and maximally when completing work set by teachers. Forms of deviance included such things as being late for lessons – simply because one chatted to a friend. Nevertheless, these girls were also high attainers within the school, and saw education in instrumental terms as the passport to paper qualifications that could get one a 'good' job. As Fuller points out, such attitudes must be linked to issues in the wider society outside the classroom, especially the experience of sexism and racism.

Finally in this section, we look at one ex-pupil's evaluation of her grammar school education – that by Payne (2.4). Payne believes that our educational system maintains the existing social divisions within society, especially the social divisions based on social class and gender. As a working-class girl in a single-sex grammar school in the 1960s, she felt that the school attempted to impose on her certain middle-class values and ideas about gender that were often in conflict with the values and practices of her working-class neighbourhood. It was, she says, like leading a double life. Overall she concludes that the curriculum, the careers advice and the construction of a particular form of femininity in the school – the 'young lady' – all served to reproduce the sexual division of labour.

Section three of this Reader looks at *sexual inequalities in educational provision*. The articles by Purvis, Clarricoates and Okely, like those of Fuller and Payne in the previous sections, are written from a feminist perspective. Many of our educational theories and practices today have their origins in the pattern of education that was established in the nineteenth century, and in the paper by Purvis (3.1) we read about some of the inequalities in the provision and content of education that were experienced by working-class and middle-class women in nineteenth-century Britain. A major theme of the article is that we cannot understand class and sex inequalities in such provision unless we examine economic, social, cultural and ideological factors outside the educational field. In particular, Purvis highlights two key factors. First of all, she stresses the importance of what has been called the 'domestic ideology' i.e. the idea that a woman's primary role is in the home, as a wife and mother. Secondly, she also emphasizes the importance of class-specific ideals of femininity within that ideology, ideals that helped to shape both the form and content of education for women and to pose contradictions for them.

Even though girls and women won many gains in regard to access to various kinds of educational provision in the nineteenth and twentieth centuries, they still remain unequal in our present-day educational system, in comparison with boys and men, especially in regard to educational achievement. Clarricoates documents (3.2), through her observations on four state primary schools, some of those processes that help to maintain inequalities between boys and girls in the classroom.

In all four schools that she studied – urban traditional, suburban middle class, council estate and village schools – she suggests that the social construction of femininity and masculinity for girls and boys may be related to the value structure of the school and the value structure of the wider community in which the school is located. Despite the variations in the social construction of femininity, variations which differ especially according to social class, the subordination of girls is, she claims, always maintained. Girls internalize beliefs that they are inferior to boys and are pressurized towards a stereotypical feminine role. For working-class girls, this process begins earlier than for middle-class girls, since the former are not encouraged by the school or by their neighbourhood community to seek educational achievement.

The final paper in this section is by Okely (3.3). Like Payne, Okely provides an ethnographic account of schooling that is largely autobiographical. In particular, the account relates to her nine years of education in a girls' boarding school in the 1950s.

The majority of pupils in our fee-paying boarding schools come from middle-class and upper-middle-class backgrounds. Though there are similarities between boarding education for boys and girls, especially in regard to the containment and development of social class consciousness, Okely concentrates upon some of the differences for girls. For girls, she claims, marriage and not a career is seen as the ultimate vocation. She has no recollection of the word 'equality' ever being used in regard to the educational achievements and occupations of girls and their brothers who were also in private schools.

It is the theme of the social control of girls, through what Okely call 'spiders' webs of fine rules and constraints' that forms the focus of her article. While their brothers are schooled for independence and power, girls are schooled for dependence. Thus they learn not only about the hierarchy between the social classes but also about the hierarchy between men and women. In particular, they learn that women are subordinate to, and dependent on, men. Such girls are, continues Okely, protected for a future marriage contract within an elite whose biological and social reproduction they ensure.

The final section of the Reader is titled *education and qualifications*. In the first paper, Heath and Ridge (4.1) attempt to relate two main studies in which they were involved – *Origins and Destinations* (1980) and *Social Mobility and Class Structure in Modern Britain* (1980).[23] Their information refers to a survey (begun in 1972) of 10,000 adult men resident in England and Wales and aged between 20 and 64. The failure to include women attracted much criticism.[24] Despite such a limitation, *Origins* and *Social Mobility* are regarded as important empirical studies, within the political arithmetic tradition, that aid our understanding of educational opportunity, educational achievement and social mobility.

Heath and Ridge compare the educational and occupational experience of older respondents (born between 1913 and 1932) with younger respondents (born between 1933 and 1947) who attended one of the tripartite schools established after the 1944 Education Act. Their main conclusion is that service-class boys attending grammar schools from 1944 actually increased rather than diminished their advantages over working-class boys. Post-war economic expansion made it easier for the service-class to strengthen its hold – despite the spread of credentialism (undue emphasis on paper qualifications) as a means for the selection and promotion of people in the labour market. In times of expansion, the rigours of competition are less. Appointments and promotion do not need to be justified quite so carefully. Thus there are 'many easy pickings' to be gained by those who are 'well-placed in society'.

Whereas the issues that Heath and Ridge discuss – educational achievement, educational qualifications, inequalities between the social classes – have been traditional concerns within the sociology of education, the theme of Jary's paper (4.2) is not. Sociology of education has frequently been identified with the sociology of schooling and Jary looks at a sector of education that has been given little attention by sociologists – the 'liberal adult education' provided by such bodies as university extra-mural departments and the Workers' Educational Association.

Jary stresses that writers about liberal adult education often under-emphasize the leisure functions it may perform for its participants. Liberal adult education is often described in rather lofty terms as education for 'individual development' or education for 'democracy' rather than as a leisure activity. He cites a study of his own where he found that 80 per cent of liberal adult education students in social science showed little or no vocational purpose and few signs of a specific 'social' purpose, such as contributing to a healthy, democratic society. Most students saw adult education as an opportunity for reflection, self-expansion and sociability. In addition, Jary suggests that a kind of 'cultural activism' pervades adult education students in that they make a differentially large use of libraries, theatres, 'quality' newspapers and the like, and a much smaller than average use of the mass media.

Though this Reader is primarily intended for OU students, we hope that it will be of interest to a wider range of people. The 1980s will be critical years for the future development of the sociology of education, especially if further cutbacks are experienced in higher education. Yet, as this Reader and its accompanying volume show, the sociology of education can illuminate many educational processes. The knowledge base that has been accumulated must not be allowed to wither away but must be consolidated and further extended.

Acknowledgments

We would like to express our grateful thanks to those people who have given considerable help and support in the compilation of this Reader, especially Martyn Hammersley, Rosemary Deem, Ben Cosin and Donald MacKinnon. Laurily Dellaway maintained, as usual, a high standard of secretarial assistance.

References

1 Heath, A. 'Class and meritocracy in British education', in Finch, A. and Scrimshaw, P. (eds) (1980), *Standards, Schooling and Education*, London, Hodder & Stoughton.
2 The main exponent of structural functionalism was the American sociologist Talcott Parsons (1902–79). His output includes such works as the following: *The Structure of Social Action* (1937), New York, McGraw-Hill, *The Social System* (1951) London, Routledge & Kegan Paul and *Societies: Evolutionary and Comparative Perspectives* (1966), Englewood Cliffs, NJ, Prentice-Hall.
3 Musgrave, P. W. (1965), *The Sociology of Education*, London, Methuen; and Banks, O. (1968), *The Sociology of Education*, London, Methuen. Both books were revised and reprinted in the second half of the 1970s.

4 Parsons, T. (1959), 'The school class as a social system: some of its functions in American society', reprinted in Cosin, B. R. and Hales, M. (eds) (1983), *Education, Policy and Society: Theoretical Perspectives*, London, Routledge & Kegan Paul.
5 Hargreaves, D. H. (1967), *Social Relations in a Secondary School*, London, Routledge & Kegan Paul; Lacey C. (1970), *Hightown Grammar: The School as a Social System*, Manchester, University of Manchester Press.
6 Hammersley, M. and Woods, P. (eds) (1976), *The Process of Schooling*, London, Routledge & Kegan Paul, offer, in their introduction to this book, the following useful footnote (pp. 8-9) defining these perspectives:

Interactionism is a sociological tradition, American in origin, dating from the early twentieth century, and deriving particularly from the work of G. H. Mead. It was further developed by the Chicago School of the 1930s and 1940s, notably in their ethnographic studies of various aspects of Chicago life. There was a resurgence of interest in America in this perspective in the 1960s, again focused on the University of Chicago. The stress here is on the partial independence from social structural, cultural and psychological forces of the sense people make of the world and of action based on such perspectives (G. H. Mead, *Mind, Self and Society*, University of Chicago Press, 1934. For a description of the original Chicago School from a neo-Chicagoan position see D. Matza, *Becoming Deviant*, Prentice-Hall, 1969). Sociological work inspired by phenomenology, a philosophical tradition founded by Edmund Husserl, is a fairly recent phenomenon of which the best-known exponents are Alfred Schutz and Berger and Luckmann. These authors are concerned with the knowledge and assumptions which must be possessed and acted on by people in order for the social world to exist. Their project is to explicate this knowledge, which is not given in consciousness but rather is taken for granted by all of us in our everyday lives (see for instance A. Schutz, *Collected Papers*, Martinus Nijhoff, 1971, vols 1 and 2, and P. L. Berger and T. Luckmann, *The Social Construction of Reality*, Penguin, 1967). Ethnomethodology is in one sense a brand of phenomenological sociology since it has certainly drawn on phenomenology, though there are other important sources in Goffman's interactionism and the work of the philosopher Wittgenstein. However, in other ways ethnomethodology constitutes a much more radical break with previous sociology than do other forms of phenomenological sociology. Thus the latter see themselves as providing a sounder basis for the investigation of the traditional sociological issues, whereas ethnomethodology proposes an entirely different sociological enterprise: the study of the methods by which people interpret and display the social world as having the recognisable features it appears obviously to have. As in phenomenological sociology and interactionism, there is a focus on the ways in which people construct the social world through their interpretations and actions, but here the stress is on the discovery of methods, formal devices which it is argued must underlie this construction, rather than on substantive, context-bound knowledge (see R. Turner (ed.), *Ethnomethodology*, Penguin, 1974). There are almost as many versions of Marxism as there are of sociology, and this tradition also has its origins in the nineteenth century. Like ethnomethodology, Marxism partly stands outside of sociology as an alternative enterprise, despite many attempts to incorporate it into sociology. The tradition stems of course from the work of Karl Marx and much Marxist work has been devoted to close study of his writings. Marx

stresses the dialectical nature of the development of societies, which he sees
as leading to the realisation of man's species-specific nature; that is, the
realisation of the ideals of the French Enlightenment. The motor of
societal development is a struggle between social classes which are integral
to particular modes of production. Class conflict is caused by
contradictions between developing forces of production and the continued
existence of social relations of production once suited to but now
hampering the further development of the forces of production. However
there have been important disagreements over the interpretation of Marx's
work among Marxists, the most significant contemporary one being over
the extent to which the Hegelian philosophy of history forms the basis for
Marx's later work. The neo-Hegelians such as the Frankfurt School believe
that it does, the Althusserians see a break in Marx's work which divides his
Hegelian early work from his later scientific writings. (For an account of
Marx (and Durkheim and Weber), see A. Giddens, *Capitalism and
Modern Social Theory*, Cambridge University Press, 1971. On the
Frankfurt School, see M. Jay, *The Dialectical Imagination*, Heinemann,
1973. For the Althusserian approach to the study of educational
institutions, see L. Althusser, 'Ideology and ideological state apparatuses',
in B. R. Cosin (ed.), *Education: Structure and Society*, Penguin, 1972.)

7 Young, M. F. D. (ed.) (1971), *Knowledge and Control: New Directions
for the Sociology of Education*, London, Collier-Macmillan.
8 See, for example, his article, 'Intellectual field and creative project', in
Young (ed.) (1971), op. cit.; and Bourdieu, P. and Passeron, J. C. (1977),
Reproduction in Education, Society and Culture, London, Sage
Publications.
9 Gorbutt, D. (1972), 'The new sociology of education', *Education for
Teaching*, Autumn 1972, p. 6.
10 Banks, O. (1978), 'School and society' in Barton, L. and Meighan, R.
(eds),
Sociological Interpretations of Schooling and Classrooms: A Reappraisal,
(1978), Driffield, Nafferton Books, p. 40.
11 For an account of these shifts in direction in the sociology of education at
this time see Banks (1978), op. cit.; and Reynolds, D. and Sullivan, M.
(1980), 'Towards a new socialist sociology of education' in Barton, L.,
Meighan, R. and Walker, S. (eds), *Schooling, Ideology and the Curriculum*,
Lewes, Falmer Press.
12 Open University (1976), *Schooling and Society* (E202), Milton Keynes,
Open University Press.
13 Bowles, S. and Gintis, H. (1976), *Schooling in Capitalist America*, London,
Routledge & Kegan Paul, p. 131.
14 See, for example, Banks (1978), op. cit.; Hargreaves, A. (1980), 'Synthesis
and the study of strategies: a project for the sociological imagination' in
Woods, P. (ed.) *Pupil Strategies*, London, Croom Helm; and Hammersley,
M. (1980), 'Classroom ethnography', *Educational Analysis*, vol. 2, no. 2,
Winter.
15 One of the most lucid and thorough of the critiques is provided by the
American historian of education, David Hogan, in his review article,
'Capitalism, liberalism, and schooling' in *Theory and Society*, November
1979. In his conclusion, Hogan suggests that *Schooling in Capitalist
America* is characterised by an 'ahistorical treatment of the functions of
education, an economic conception of social structure, an inadequate
theory of reproduction and contradiction, and a seriously inaccurate

account of educational politics' (p. 408). Nevertheless, Hogan also points out that *Schooling* is a very important and valuable work. See also Tunnell, D. R. (1978), 'An analysis of Bowles's and Gintis's thesis that schools reproduce economic inequality', *Educational Theory*, Fall. The views expressed in *Schooling* were further elaborated upon in Gintis, H. and Bowles, S. (1980), 'Contradictions and reproduction in educational theory' in Barton, L., Meighan, R. and Walker, S. (eds), *Schooling, Ideology and the Curriculum*, Lewes, Falmer Press.

16 Open University (1981), *Society, Education and the State*, (E353), Milton Keynes, Open University Press. This is a third-level course produced by the Faculty of Educational Studies. The two collections of readings to accompany the Course are Dale, R., Esland, G., Fergusson R. and MacDonald, M. (eds) (1981a), *Education and the State Vol. 1: Schooling and the National Interest* and (1981b), *Education and the State, Vol. 2: Politics, Patriarchy and Practice* both Lewes, Falmer Press. The theme of the state and education is also the subject of another recent collection of articles edited by Michael W. Apple (1982), *Cultural and Economic Reproduction in Education*, London, Routledge & Kegan Paul.

17 Many definitions have, and could be offered, of feminism. Oakley, A. (1981), *Subject Women*, Oxford, Martin Robertson, suggests, amongst other things, that feminism involves judging women's interests (however defined) to be important and to be insufficiently represented and accommodated within mainstream politics/academia. This position allows, she continues, a wide range of stances, theories, practices and recommendations to be selected. The main division is between *socialist feminists* and *radical feminists*. While the former implicate capitalism as the perpetrator of women's oppression, the latter see men as the main source and beneficiaries of women's oppression (pp. 337–8). Some feminist writers, however, locate women's oppression within both capitalism and patriarchy (see, for example, the articles by Purvis (3.1) and Payne (2.4) in this Reader). As Oakley observes, within each of the two main categories of feminism there is a variety of opinion.

18 The literature here is quite extensive. See, for example, Wolpe, A. (1977), *Some Processes in Sexist Education*, London, Women's Research and Resources Centre; Wolpe, A. (1978), 'Education and the sexual division of labour' in Kuhn, A. and Wolpe, A. (eds), *Feminism and Materialism*, London, Routledge & Kegan Paul; Deem, R. (1978), *Women and Schooling*, London, Routledge & Kegan Paul; Byrne, E. (1978), *Women and Education*, London, Tavistock; Delamont, S. (1981), *Sex Roles and the School*, London, Methuen; Deem R. (ed.) (1980), *Schooling for Women's Work*, London, Routledge & Kegan Paul; David, M. E. (1980), *The State, the Family and Education*, London, Routledge & Kegan Paul; Acker, S. (1980), 'Women, the other academics', *British Journal of Sociology of Education*, vol. 1, no. 1; Spender D. and Sarah, E. (eds) (1980), *Learning to Lose*, London, the Women's Press; MacDonald, M. (1980), 'Schooling and the reproduction of class and gender relations' in Barton, L., Meighan, R. and Walker S. (eds), *Schooling, Ideology and the Curriculum*, Lewes, Falmer Press; Arnot, M. (1981), 'Culture and political economy: dual perspectives in the sociology of women's education' in Davies, B. (ed.), *The State of Schooling* being vol. 3, no. 1 of *Educational Analysis*, Lewes, Falmer Press; Stanworth, M. (1981), *Gender and Schooling: A Study of Sexual Divisions in the Classroom*, London, Women's Research and Resources Centre; Spender D. (1982), *Invisible Women: The Schooling Scandal*, London, Writers' and Readers'

Publishing Cooperative Society; Mahony, P. (1982), ' "Silence is a woman's glory": the sexist content of education', *Women's Studies International Forum*, vol. 5, no. 5; and the papers in Walker, S. and Barton, L. (eds) (1983), *Gender, Class and Education*, Lewes, Falmer Press.

19 Acker, S. (1981), 'No-woman's land: British sociology of education 1960–1979', reprinted in Cosin, B. R. and Hales, M. (eds) (1983) op. cit.

20 Patriarchy is a problematic concept. One common usage is that suggested by Beechey, V. (1970), 'On patriarchy', *Feminist Review*, vol. 3, p. 66, that patriarchy refers to male domination and to the power relationships by which men dominate women. Within this Reader, 'patriarchy' is used by those authors who write from a feminist perspective (see note 17).

21 A distinction is often made between sex and gender. Sex usually refers to the biological categories of male and female and, for most people, is fixed throughout their lives. Gender, on the other hand, refers to learnt behaviour and is often categorised broadly as masculinity and femininity. The integration of considerations about sex and gender into mainstream sociology of education need not necessarily imply the integration of a feminist perspective. One may write about sex and gender differences *without* adopting a feminist perspective.

22 Hammersley and Woods (1976), op. cit., p. 2.

23 Halsey, A. H., Heath, A. F. and Ridge, J. M. (1980), *Origins and Destinations: Family, Class, and Education in Modern Britain*, London, Oxford University Press; and Goldthorpe, J. H. (in collaboration with C. Llewellyn and C. Payne) (1980), *Social Mobility and Class Structure in Modern Britain*, London, Oxford University Press.

24 See, for example, the review of *Origins* by Tessa Blackstone in *The Times Higher Education Supplement*, 18 Jan. 1980.

Part one
Teachers' perspectives

1.1
The significance of classroom coping strategies†

Andy Hargreaves*

Much of what has passed for sociology of education has either failed
to grasp the consciousness of those about whom it claims to theorise,
or else it has over-optimistically celebrated the seemingly limitless
power of the individual to define, make and remake his own world. In
taking the first line, the old sociology of education failed to treat people
seriously. In taking the second, the 'new' sociology of education and
the studies of classroom interaction which it has spawned have insulated
the classroom encounter from wider and extremely urgent social, economic and political concerns. If the 'Great Debate' *was* little more
than carefully directed political drama (or farce – depending on your
perspective!) it did at least teach one important lesson; that education
and society cannot be so studied in isolated realms.

The message for sociologists of education should be clear. 'Structural'
questions and 'interactionist' questions should no longer be dealt with
as separate 'issues', each to be covered in their respective fields. Such
a false fragmentation and dichotomisation of an educational and social
whole will lead to nothing more than a continuation of what has been
a sad trend in the sociology of education; that of a wild oscillation
between two poles of sociological explanation. From systems theories
to interpretive brands of sociology and back again to a structurally-
based Marxism; almost no time has been spent in taking the opportunity
to analyse how classroom matters may relate to the nature of the socio-
economic and political structure and the functions which the educational
system performs within that structure. Like the gymnast on the trampo-
line, movement has tended to be up and down between ground level

† Source: L. Barton and R. Meighan (1978) (eds), *Sociological Interpretations of
Schooling and Classrooms: a Reappraisal*, Nafferton Books, Driffield, pp. 73–100.
* I would like to thank the S.S.R.C. for funding the research from which this article
has arisen.

and the dizzy structural heights and has rarely provided any degree of forward momentum.

We certainly need to know what goes on in our classrooms. But at the same time we need to question, not just in passing but with commitment and with rigour, just what sort of society it is that we live in. We cannot assume that our society is characterised by democratic pluralism even though this might 'fit' nicely with the view that classroom realities are the product of a democratically-based negotiation process.[1] Rather, in a society where wealth is socially produced yet privately appropriated, where increased economic prosperity is paralleled by decreased humanity,[2] and where increased levels of qualification are accompanied by greater opportunities for unemployment,[3] there are grounds for seriously considering or at least confronting a Marxist analysis of contemporary British society.

Whilst it is true that most Marxist explanations of education have ignored detailed interpretations of classroom life and have instead talked of assumed 'correspondences' between the social relations of the classroom and the workplace, this should not deter any attempts to progress through a fusion of a Marxist analysis of contemporary society and the role of education in that society with a phenomenologically and interactionally informed investigation of classroom processes. The basic point of this paper is that such a fusion will provide more hope for theoretical advance and for discovering the possibilities for change than will any romantically retrospective glance to unfulfilled sub-specialisms within the sociology of education, whether these take the form of an 'old-style' educational sociology[4] or a 'new-style' symbolic interactionism.[5]

The remainder of the paper constitutes an attempt to provide a framework which might link structural questions to interactionist concerns. The concept of coping strategy will be the important bridging point here.[6] Some empirical support for such an approach will be provided through drawing upon data gathered in a case study of two middle schools which I shall call Riverdale and Moorhead.[7] These neighbouring schools are situated some two miles apart on the commuter fringe of a large northern conurbation. Both schools contain a large proportion of parents of professional and managerial status, though each is not without its children of working class council tenants, even though these are somewhat under-represented.

At first glance, Moorhead is a traditional school and Riverdale a progressive one; indeed these features were of major importance in their selection for case study. Moorhead School is a 10–13 middle school housed in converted post-war secondary modern premises. Its staff comprises ex-primary and ex-secondary school teachers who were drawn into Moorhead on reorganisation without necessarily having any definite commitment to the aims and purposes of middle school education in general. These staff have been supplemented and are increasingly being replaced by teachers drawn from other schools and direct from training (a few having followed some course which was organised explicitly on middle-school lines). Moorhead is relatively traditional in character. Much of the teaching is class teaching in isolated classrooms dotted along floor-tiled corridors, though this pattern holds less true for the 10–11 age group.

Riverdale school is a smaller 9–13 school, with only a two-and-a-half form entry, though this too creates problems in terms of lack of career opportunities for staff *within* the school. The school is also newer, being of a purpose-built open plan design. There are few corridors here, only class spaces and work areas. There are also very few doors, though this is something which staff and pupils do not always appreciate, frequently finding that curtains serve as a poor screen when noise and activity threaten to penetrate their own work. In general the atmosphere at Riverdale appears much more informal, there being much pupil movement and activity in an open-plan environment.

Each area of discussion, the polemical introduction, the development of the concept of coping strategy, and the provision of empirical illustrations, points to urgent and extremely contentious areas of debate, yet each can be treated only briefly here. Hopefully, further investigation and argument may be stimulated by the raising of these issues.

Coping strategies – a conceptual framework

In linking features of the social structure to issues in the classroom, and in noting how the former impinge upon or even shape the latter, there are good reasons for selecting the teacher as the starting point of investigation.[8] The grounds for such a choice can be justified sociologically. The teacher is the immediate processor of the curriculum for the child. She is the evaluator of his academic work and the assessor of his overall ability. She is the immediate adjudicator of his moral worth and the direct arbiter of the 'appropriateness' of his everyday behaviour. It is she most immediately and perhaps most significantly who therefore creates, transmits and attempts to impose definitions of the child as success or failure, ideal pupil or deviant.[9]

How the teacher organises pupil learning experiences and evaluates those experiences would seem to be an important topic for investigation. *Why* the teacher organises and evaluates pupil learning and behaviour in one way rather than another would also seem to qualify as a question worth asking. If we pursue this latter question then we need to explore how the pedagogical strategies which the teacher employs are meaningful responses to experienced problems, constraints and dilemmas. We need to consider the possibility that teachers construct the world of the classroom through the employment of different teaching styles but that this process of construction occurs perhaps in situations not of their own choosing and that there are a set of constraints in play which require some sort of resolution through the decisions that teachers are daily and repeatedly called upon to make.

The teacher is thus a crucial linch pin in the wheel of causality that connects structural features of the society to interactional patterns in the classroom and back again, thereby reproducing those structural arrangements. Coping with society in its institutionally mediated forms as a set of ongoing and perplexing 'problems' provides teachers with the important yet frequently taken-for-granted challenge to devise and enact, creatively and constructively a set of teaching strategies which will make life bearable, possible and even rewarding as an educational practitioner. By focussing on the teacher, the dilemmas she faces and her attempts to resolve them, we might be able to connect within one framework, the *how* and the *what* questions (previously the major preserve of 'interpretive' sociology) with the '*why*' questions (over which Marxists and functionalists have thus far exercised a considerable monopoly).

In summary form, the salient characteristics of coping strategies can be itemised as follows:–

1. *Coping strategies are the product of constructive and creative activity on the part of teachers*. The concept of coping strategy thus lends weight to the view that teachers respond to the 'demands' of their world not in the 'thoughtless' manner of Skinnerian rats or programmed role-players but as constructive meaning-makers. Consequently the use of the concept of coping strategy involves the recognition of man's essential humanity as a creature of consciousness. A basic and important principle of symbolic interactionism is that such constructiveness is a universal feature of human action. It is a core element of man's being-in-the-world. This point has not always been appreciated by those who observe and document the everyday world of the school. Some researchers of varied theoretical affiliations, from the 'new' sociology of education through to various brands of Marxism, have tended to give a privileged purchase on creativity to selected protagonists in the educational arena, whether these are the traditional pupil elite or the subcultural underdogs. Although Nell Keddie, for example, has cogently argued the case that much 'conventional' educational research has treated the disadvantaged child as if he were a deficit system, a thin cultural shadow of his rational and articulate middle class counterpart,[10] elsewhere she herself commits a very similar error. In her study of an urban secondary school, Keddie portrays the working class lower stream pupils as *more* rational and accurate interpreters of the absurd requirements placed upon them by middle class teachers, than the conformist middle class cultural dopes of the 'A' stream.[11]

More recently, Paul Willis in a generally stimulating attempt to combine ethnography with Marxism, in a study of twelve working class 'lads' in the secondary modern school and on the shopfloor, unfortunately falls into the same trap as Keddie, though somewhat less consistently so. Willis' adherence to an inverse deficit theory which celebrates the superior insight of the deviant underdog is clearly shown in the following extract where he is discussing the non-conformist grammar school group:

> Despite even their origins and anti-school attitude, the *lack of* a dominant working class ethos within their (grammar) school culture profoundly separates their experience from 'the lads'. It can also lead to *artificial attempts* to demonstrate solidarity on the street and with street contacts. That the *working class cultural forms* of school opposition *are creative*, specific, borne and reproduced by particular individuals and groups from afresh and in particular contexts – though always within a class mode – is shown by the *cultural awkwardness and separation of such lads*.[12]

Here the yardstick has changed from a middle-class to a working class one but a yardstick remains nevertheless. Whereas deficit theories falsely presented middle-class values as 'accepted' societal values, Keddie and Willis convert working-classness into working classiness though Willis plants his feet a little more firmly on the ground insofar as he recognises that this power of insight and the forms of opposition which it generates may eventually prove self-defeating in the long term.

If a model is to be developed which sensitively appreciates the meanings that different groups (pupils and teachers, working-class pupils and middle class pupils etc.) attach to their experience and situation, then it is necessary to abandon theoretical attachments to the cultural superiority of any one group over another. A good model should be like a cubist painting and present different perspectives simultaneously, equally and appreciatively. If, as researchers, we fail to do this then we will deride the perspectives of those whom we should instead be seeking to understand.

The essence of a model organised around the concept of coping strategy is thus that all actors whether working-class or middle-class, pupil or teacher, act meaningfully and creatively in response to their experienced world. [. . .]

2 The addition of the word 'coping' to that of 'strategy' implies that there are limits to the variety of styles which teachers may adopt in the classroom. Styles will be generated and sustained only insofar as they enable successful coping with experienced constraints. *Coping strategies are therefore not only constructive but also adaptive*. They are creatively articulated solutions to recurring daily problems. The more these solutions 'work' and the more will they become institutionalised, routinised and hence, ultimately, taken for granted as the definition not of a version of teaching but of teaching itself. It is at this point, where coping strategies become institutionally and professionally embedded as accepted, legitimate pedagogical forms, that they can come to resist demands for innovation generated by emergent sets of new constraints. The 'persistence of the recitation' in the face of pressures for progressive educational reform is just one example of this process.[13]

3 Following from (2), it should be clear that *coping strategies refer to very generalised definitions of teaching behaviour which cannot be reduced to a simple set of alternative teaching and control techniques.* The latter can be more conventionally regarded as constitutive of a Goffmanesque model of strategic interaction where the actor tries to gain and maintain advantage over his rival. Disciplinary techniques and the second-by-second decisions which they imply could be included in this lower-level category, which I have elsewhere called 'negotiative strategies'.[14] Coping strategies subsume and establish the parameters for the range of employed negotiative strategies in any instance, though clearly, at their inception they are themselves partly the outcome of classroom and organisational negotiations and to some extent depend on the successful daily accomplishment of such negotiations for their continued existence i.e. once they fail to 'work' then the time is ripe for change.

4 The view that teachers seek to cope or 'survive' is not a particularly novel one. Becker pointed out that the behaviour of the slum school teacher is a response to the 'problems' presented by the slum school child. It has also been argued at different levels by Westbury[15] and by Sharp and Green[16] for example, that in part, teaching strategies such as the 'recitation' or 'busyness' emerge in response to a set of immediate material pressures such as large class sizes and building restrictions. As Sharp and Green put it,

> we need to develop some conceptualisations of the situations that individuals find themselves in, in terms of the structure of opportunities the situations make available to them and the kinds of constraints they impose. The actors may be conscious of these constraints but need not necessarily be so. They may be subconsciously taken for granted or unrecognised, but the situation will present them with contingencies which affect what they do irrespective of how they define it.[17]

The concept of coping strategy becomes a truly radical one only when one re-poses the question of what it is that teachers have to cope with. Such a view involves awareness of the fact that constraints like class-sizes, building limitations or the problems of teaching slum-school children are themselves the immediate institutional expression of wider social-structural and historical forces which also require investigation and analysis. It is in their failure to articulate connections between these levels that the promise of Sharp and Green's Marxist synthesis is unfulfilled. They do not make the vital link between the presence of material constraints at the institutional level and the generation of structural constraints within the wider society. How then might these different levels be connected?

5 At the most general level, the nature of the constraints which produce institutional problems that the teacher must resolve would appear to fall into at least three broad categories:

(a) Following Bowles and Gintis it can be argued that *in contemporary capitalist society the goals of the educational system are fundamentally contradictory*. Liberals and reformers frequently seek to promote egalitarianism and to foster personal development (the education of the 'whole' child) whilst at the same time they also recognise the need to prepare the child for the position he will be expected to occupy in the social, occupational and political order. At the classroom level, this contradiction often comes to present itself as a wish to educate and relate to children in the spirit of liberal individualism, counter-balanced by a necessity to select and socialise children for a class-stratified society (the latter being a point of which functionalists have always been astutely aware).[18]

Managing the pedagogical paradox known as 'guided discovery' is one common solution which teachers have devised and which has become embedded in professional subcultures that now seek to resist the intrusions of the Great Debaters. Guided choice as a somewhat wider pedagogic principle than 'guided discovery' tends to permeate all levels of the education system, even through to the point of occupational choice.[19] It is perhaps this principle which most broadly encapsulates the dilemmas and tensions contained in processes of 'democratic' participation and decision-making in educational and other institutions. The aptness and wider applicability of this notion is well summarised by a group of Riverdale teachers discussing the organisation of the curriculum for the following academic year:

Mr. Button   In particular I notice (name of school) do CSE work with children and they had to choose topic work. Well very often they . . . they would choose any old thing and very soon they . . . they would realise that what they've chosen is beyond them or is . . . not interesting enough for them.

Mr. Kitchen   (Headmaster). So it's got to be guided.

Mrs Arrow   Yes,

Mr. Kitchen   It's like choosing a career, isn't it?

Mr. Button   Yeah (sharp).

Mr. Kitchen   In . . . exactly the same things apply in this case.

The logic of nominal democracy at the entry point of production where allocation of the individual into the occupational structure occurs on lines very different from official conceptions of open and free choice in an equal contest for work opportunities in the job market, is therefore recognised by teachers of middle school children; children who have still some years of schooling to complete before they become directly and explicitly involved in the process of occupational choice. The one-dimensional manner in which participation is conventionally conceived as token participation and the nominal forms which 'democracy' usually takes are pervasive features of economic and political life in advanced capitalist society.[20] Choice as 'guided' choice is a definition available and taken for granted within the dominant social democratic hegemony, and is also a practice which best resolves the dilemmas that teachers confront. These dilemmas take the form of reconciling a desire to give pupils a measure of choice and freedom in the interests of their personal development, with the necessity to impose work requirements in order to fulfil the integrative demands of required sets of knowledge, skills and competences derived externally from the wider society and internally (within the education system) from the secondary or upper school. 'Guided' choice' is thus the outcome of both pragmatic response and available ideology, but is most essentially the product of the inter-section of these two.[21]

At other age levels, the strategy varies from that of 'busyness' in the infant school to the employment of a Dalton-plan block timetable approach in some progressively organised middle schools, like River-dale,[22] both of which reconcile to some extent the contradictory forces generated in advanced capitalist society. The 'Crisis' in education and the airing of the Great Debate through their increased emphasis on 'standards', the core curriculum and the relationship between education and industry, should not be seen as removing the contradiction or as tolling the death-knell of parting progressivism. Instead, the emergence of such concerns can be viewed as highlighting the problems of manage-ment in the increasingly complex systems of control characteristic of advanced capitalist societies[23] and as instancing the fact that the achiev-ement of any appearance of social democratic 'balance' in educational practice is becoming ever more tenuous.

(b) *The second general area of constraints upon teaching activity can be given the broad label 'material'.*

In this sense, material constraints such as school buildings resources and class sizes are not the result of randomness in educational planning nor of administrative and political short sightedness and incompetence. There is instead a definite connection between the magnitude and variety of these constraints, and a characteristic pattern and orientation of educational and social change, which one might call both reformist and centripetal. The story of educational and social reform in British society is one of ad hoc adjustment and piecemeal change. Ever since the State included the large-scale provision and organisation of educa-tion within its orbit of influence, educational change has been character-ised not by a radical reform of contemporary arrangements in the light of a rigorous analysis of the educational and social whole but, in the words of Forster at the time of the 1870 Act, by an inclination to 'fill up the gaps' which could be identified in the existing range of provision using the minimum possible amount of expenditure.[24] Gradualism, pragmatism and economy are the characteristic stamp of the British approach, an approach which accepts unquestioningly the legitimacy of a capitalist society based on the private appropriation of socially produced wealth, and which assumes that an educational system which selects and socialises for such a class-divided society is both desirable and necessary.

Such pragmatic underpinnings of educational reform have usually resulted in a style of policy making based on administrative convenience and economic expediency. In recent times, comprehensive reorganisation has frequently taken place within tight budgetary restrictions and where a three-tier middle school system has been chosen, for example, this has invariably been 'because the buildings fitted'.[25] As a result, teachers now work within widely variant architectural constraints; some in old 1870 buildings and others, who are fortunate enough to be working in areas of expanding population, in modern open-plan units. It is this pragmatic tradition which is as much responsible for the wide and bewildering variety of educational provision as is the devolution of considerable decision-making power to local authorities. That many teachers, especially those middle school teachers who subscribe to the central tenets of 'progressive' Plowden ideology, find themselves teaching in buildings totally unsuited to such an educational approach (many middle schools have been set up in old secondary-modern school buildings), can also be traced to the pragmatic orientations of educational reformers.

The assumption that current provision is adequate, in the main, coupled with the fact that available expenditure for education is maintained at an 'acceptable' level, can also be held jointly responsible for the failure to significantly reduce class-sizes when the opportunity has presented itself in the form of falling birth rates. In consequence, no progress has been made in relieving the 'immediacy' of the teacher's role: the necessity to make a large number of decisions with a large number of pupils in a short space of time.

The most interesting case, though, is not where idealistic teachers become frustrated by material constrictions but where building constraints combine with a set of other factors to produce and shape a generalised type of coping strategy which admits of some but only a limited amount of internal variation from teacher to teacher. An example of the range of styles produced by this combinatory effect is the teaching in the upper years of Moorhead School.

Moorhead is one of many middle schools sited in converted secondary modern school premises. The architecture of the post-war secondary school is hardly conducive to the growth of non-specialist co-operatively based teaching so often advocated in documents prescribing curriculum change for 'the middle years'. The presence of corridors with classrooms leading off as a set of disparate, physically autonomous units offers few opportunities for innovatory progressive teaching practice. The very nature of the building, then, suggests a style of teaching practice which is directed more to the secondary than the primary school tradition. Where adaptations have been made to the building in the provision of an open-plan wing, it is hardly surprising and perfectly reasonable that this should be allocated to the lower age groups in the school. Even architecturally, then, there is the suggestion of a split at the 11+ dividing line, the conventional watershed between primary and secondary education.

These architectural restrictions are exacerbated by overcrowding. Philip Jackson has emphasised how 'crowds' are a pervasive feature of all classroom life though his stress, perhaps, is on the consequences this has for pupils rather than for teachers. The lack of sufficient expenditure for extra school building and the tardiness of the local authority in providing a new school at Millbeck which would considerably relieve the pressures on Moorhead have meant that Moorhead is an overcrowded institution. So many additional 'temporary' classrooms have been installed that, from the air, the main building would no doubt appear as an island stranded in a sea of terrapins. The large pupil roll and the shortage and unsuitability of existing accommodation also mean that several valued educational activities cannot be provided for large groups of children. One example of this is that heavy craft and science facilities are confined within the same room such that, in any one period, the pursuit of one activity automatically excludes anyone from engaging in the other.[26]

That such constraints obviate the development of favoured educational programmes and elicit a consciously adaptive response, at least on the part of the headmaster, is illustrated by the comments of the head, Mr. Butcher, in interview:

> *Mr. Butcher* The timetable ought not to be regarded in the middle school as it is in the secondary school and which unfortunately it sometimes is this year for all sorts of other reasons which aren't necessarily educational . . . organisational and which is dependent on the buildings available and so on . . . There are factors which are restricting. In fact, there are many factors which have made it impossible for me to put my educational philosophy which I . . . uh . . . had when we were established, into practice . . . um . . . Those are mainly areas of accommodation, overcrowding, desperate shortage of specialist facilities. I'm not suggesting dual purpose rooms are not suitable in other schools. I *am* saying that in this situation which we find ourselves in, they are certainly most unsuitable . . .[27]

In time, it is conceivable that a short term pragmatic response of the realist to a set of overwhelming and frustrating constraints, shifts to an acceptance of those very constraints such that ad hoc measures become accepted and defined as educational goals. That constraints not only determine possible educational policy as a set of mere pragmatic responses with which the practitioner need not necessarily agree in principle, but that they also lead to a broader shaping of educational goals and desirable definitions of teaching itself, is the essence of coping strategies and their institutionalisation. Mr. Butcher seems to be partly aware of this in his own case.

Mr. Butcher   I suppose . . . um . . . I might have modified my philosophy to some extent after five years of operation in that . . . um . . . there is a greater need for structure than I had originally anticipated there would be . . . and . . . since the system itself has demanded; the situation itself has demanded, that I should structure things – obviously to cope with these large numbers of children that we have and the inadequate facilities – to some extent perhaps, that's made me realise that . . . uh . . . there may well be something to be said for structure – and it isn't the dirty word that I originally thought it was.

A.H.   So you find yourself having to operate in certain ways out of necessity and, sort of, have come to appreciate their value . . . having carried them out?

Mr. Butcher   Yes! Undoubtedly! So that it was necessity which . . . uh . . . it was necessity in the first place which was the reason why we introduced things . . . but after five years of operation now we've decided that these are desirable as educational aims anyway.

Experience is a great teacher. Where constraints persist, the unwilling adaptation becomes the unwitting educational goal. Practitioners 'discover' that a way of coping might be educationally desirable after all. Necessity can indeed be the mother of both invention and intention.

A further effect of the organisation of educational reform on economic and expediential grounds has been upon the organisation of staffing in middle schools. Many middle schools utilise not only existing buildings but also existing local pools of teaching labour. In this sense the evolution of a new educational concept is fettered by the legacy of inherited buildings and staff. Many staff work in middle schools not to implement educational goals as 'middle years' teachers but because employment in such a school is a marginally better prospect than employment in any other of the institutions created by reorganisation. Mr. Butcher articulately encapsulates the extent and effects of such difficulties.

Mr. Butcher   Staff, I think, can teach most efficiently when they are teaching the way with which they themselves are most familiar and it's nonsense to think that you can . . . uh . . . change a teacher who has been teaching for many years in a particular way into an entirely different way of teaching without allowing him or her time to develop. And therefore, initially, I think,

> we had one year or so of the primary school and
> two years in the secondary school here . . . (he goes
> on to argue that with some redeployment of staff
> the situation has changed somewhat since) . . . We
> inherited staffs who . . . uh . . . almost entirely were
> either primary trained and experienced or secondary
> trained and experienced and uh . . . since the
> introduction of comprehensive education in this area,
> they've not really evolved . . . uh . . . apart from
> marginally, the need for more teachers . . . We
> simply had to use the teachers who were available.
> So those who opted to come to the middle school
> either opted to do so from the primary school on
> the one hand or from the secondary schools on the
> other and eighty-per-cent of our staff were recruited
> in this way. They didn't necessarily have a burning
> desire to teach in middle schools, the burning desire
> being in fact to remain in Moorhead (the town) . . .
> uh . . . and it may well have been and certainly was
> the case that these . . . um . . . in some cases they
> just wanted a job and they found themselves
> becoming redundant in the primary schools . . . or
> else they found themselves unable to get the sort of
> jobs which they wanted in the upper schools and so
> they had no alternative . . . and certainly there were
> members of staff who came here . . . uh . . . not out
> of choice but out of necessity. (Then he states that
> there are some exceptions).[28]

This extract is worth quoting at some length since it expresses very
clearly the problems of which the headmaster was aware on re-organisa-
tion and renders intelligible his tendencies to deploy ex-secondary
teachers in the upper years and ex-primary teachers in the lower school
thus reinforcing the traditional split between primary and secondary
stages of schooling. In consequence, without any clear intentions or
manipulations to perpetuate 'valued' educational traditions, staffing and
material constraints and the headmaster's response to these tend to
produce and reproduce the schizoid identity of the middle school which
diverges somewhat from the notion of a unique identity of the middle
school which has been ideologically propounded elsewhere.[29] Although
these constraints produce *generational* effects in terms of a separation
between primary and secondary stages, they are nevertheless rooted in
a pragmatic style of educational policy making characteristic of and
acceptant of the dominant assumptions of a class-divided capitalist
society. The immediate material constraints of architecture and class
sizes can therefore be connected to deeper issues embedded in a pragmatic approach to educational reform which rests on the premise that

fundamental change in educational arrangements and in the society which such arrangements serve, are neither necessary nor desirable.

Partly through the mediating influence of Mr. Butcher's emergent but stabilising educational philosophy and partly through the direct effect which material constraints exert in shaping, facilitating or inhibiting different patterns of teaching, Moorhead's siting in a converted secondary modern school has led to a limited range of variation in fourth-year teaching styles. Although there are real and considerable differences between, say, Mr. Bird whom his headmaster regarded as 'a bit of a tartar' and Mrs. Close who views herself as 'firm but approachable', these differences are, even for teachers at the extremes of the continuum of teaching styles constructed and enacted in the fourth-year at Moorhead, differences of degree rather than of kind. The styles of fourth-year Moorhead teachers are all contained within a dominant model of secondary-orientated teaching. This also includes those teachers such as Mr. Bird and Mrs. Close who are not themselves secondary trained and experienced but whose conceptions of teaching and learning are nevertheless skewed in a 'secondary' direction. Mr. Bird, for example, was a teacher in one of the reorganised primary schools but his at least partial attachment to a tradition other than primary is revealed by his statement that he enjoyed teaching the 'A' class most of all and that 'the years that I was interested in were the top end'. Similarly, Mrs. Close, though specifically and recently middle-school trained, holds a firm subject identity which she sums up through a rather coy admission that 'here you've got what might be termed specialist teaching which I have to confess I enjoy because I am still interested in English as a subject'. There is thus no necessity that middle schools will blur or dissolve existing educational categories. In the case of Moorhead for instance, reorganisation has facilitated a pattern of teacher redeployment to upper and lower years which in many ways has purified the separate primary and secondary stages of education by reallotting teachers who were previously 'misplaced'[30] to more appropriate niches in the educational system. Variations in fourth year teaching styles are thus variations on a theme – a predominantly 'secondary' one reinforced by the constraints of building, crowding and head-teacher policy.

Two examples must suffice. On the one hand, there is Mr. Bird, a teacher nearing retirement, who operates a typical 'recitation' style of teaching where he throws out a stream of questions and demands immediate, sharp and correct responses. Although, as Westbury has pointed out, this interactional structure maintains the attention and participation of the pupils and although it achieves the simultaneous transmission of any given content, this occurs at the expense of the growth of conceptual understanding for which is substituted a stock of 'right' answers.[31] Such a situation arises in Mr. Bird's 'B' set where pupils experience some difficulty in producing the answers he requires.

> *T.* There's no difference, just bigger numbers that's all. We'll be all day if we do it like this (child using long method). Read the first number. Two . . .
>
> *P.* Thousand (quietly).
>
> *T.* *Again.*
>
> *P.* Two thousand.
>
> *T.* Yeah. Read the second number.
>
> *P.* Five thousand.
>
> *T.* What is the common factor?
>
> *P.* (No reply).
>
> *T.* You've just told me! Read them again and put the accent on the last word.
>
> *P.* Two thousand.
>
> *T.* Two ...
>
> *P.*
> *T.*   Thousand.
>
> *T.* That's putting the accent on, yes? Read the second number.
>
> *P.* Five thousand.
>
> *T.* Yes. So what's the common factor?
>
> *P.* (inaudible).
>
> *T.* What was the word you said both times? You didn't say two both times. You didn't say five both times. What did you say both times?
>
> *P.* A thousand.
>
> *T.* That's the common factor isn't it? (raised voice) Eh? If it happens that it's common to both it's the common factor. A thousand is a number, isn't it? Isn't it? (louder). Divide by a thousand is just the same as divide by two. We've done it before, you know.
>
> *P.* (Nods).

Mr. Bird and his class here engage in an uneasy collusion to produce the 'right' answer irrespective of the methods used. Hence it is possible for pupils and teacher to exchange mathematical comprehension for an exercise in word-repetition and still produce the required response.

The fall of reasoning and the decline of conceptual understanding which such a 'direct' teacher here produces, would be something to be abhorred by many educational researchers who would instead prefer the approach of a more 'indirect' teacher like Mrs. Close.[32] Mrs. Close organises some of her lessons on discussion principles. In these lessons, pupils submit topics of interest which are then randomly selected from a hat and discussed by the class as a whole, the teacher taking on the role of neutral chairperson who guides and assists pupils in their pursuit of solutions to *their own* problems. Yet Mrs. Close's strong 'subject' attachment and her formal control over the interaction process, even as chairperson, provides her with the opportunity and the temptation to convert pupil concerns into teacher concerns. As a result a 'right-answer' structure is reinserted into a 'democratic' discussion lesson. For example, in a discussion of whether a fee should be charged for the loan of library books in order to provide income for authors, when a pupil raises the intriguing 'economic' point that certain popular writers like Enid Blyton would 'make a bomb', Mrs. Close exploits this opportunity to substitute her own problem of how far and why, many pupils *still* read Enid Blyton books.

> *T.*   In fact, of course, the sale of Enid Blyton's books do run into millions and are there any of you who still read Enid Blyton? Let's have a look. Don't be ashamed. You're usually very honest . . . Put your hands down. Yes, Richard, do you read any other author as well?
>
> *P.*   Not . . . uh . . . I read some of them. I look at a book and . . . uh . . .
>
> *T.*   What appeals to you about Enid Blyton's books? Why do you like them? Those of you who in fact . . . Let's just have hands up again 'cos this is actually an interesting sideline. Hands up again. Just put your hands up. Now, why Richard, why are you still reading Enid Blyton?

In consequence, the exploratory talk of discussion centred around pupil concerns is transformed into a series of verbally defensive attempts by pupils to parry the teacher's thrusting inquiry as to why they *still* read Enid Blyton. Such responses range from the pragmatic and apologetic.

> *P.*   I don't really know . . . I mean . . . well . . . my younger brother's always reading them . . . and they're really the only books we ever have in the house.

to the cultural critic's more comic response of

> *P.*   I don't like her very much but a lot of my books are by her and I like criticising (giggles).

'Direct' and 'indirect' teaching in this context are alternatives within a set of limits which define the core of secondary-oriented teaching as explicitly teacher-dominant in a way which is directly expressed through the asymmetric structure of the interactional exchange.[33] In this scheme of classroom life, pupil participation is nominal and passive, for it is the teacher who controls and evaluates both the quality and quantity of contributions.[34]

The circumscribing factors which define the limits of alternative teacher coping strategies as a set of teaching styles, can thus be partly identified in material terms as the pressures exerted by buildings and crowding and the way in which these shape at the same time as they are mediated by headteacher policy and his engineering of a 'fit' between a teacher's orientation and the year-group with which that teacher will work. However, such an analysis, though correct at one level, is somewhat incomplete.

It should further be remembered that at all times such factors are themselves the immediate expression at the institutional level of much deeper forces at work in the wider society. Classroom and society are inextricably bound together in the tangled web which ad hoc reformism weaves around the enduring centre of hierarchical social relations in British capitalist society. It is the purpose of both critical social theory (in the widest sense) and political action to isolate the separate strands which comprise the entanglements of social democracy and its institutions. In this way, we may catch a glimpse of the organising centre of such a society and of the centripetal tendencies of wider social, educational and political changes which serve, ultimately, to sustain and reproduce fundamental stability in its existing order.

(c) *One important constraint which appears to exert some considerable influence on the emergence, maintenance and eclipse of different coping strategies is the generation and proliferation of differing educational ideologies.*

At any point in time, certain ideologies in education gain popularity and receive support from key personnel in the education system. Insofar as these ideologies, such as the progressive Plowden ideology or the Great Debate, contain definitions of 'correct' practice and provide routes for career advancement for those who attach themselves to such a body of ideas and approaches, then they can provide a clear-cut constraint to which teachers feel they must respond through their construction and maintenance of appropriate displays of educational imagery. The reasons for the emergence of particular ideologies about education[35] are complex, though it is usually possible to identify a set of socio-economic factors which appear to be of some importance – progressivism and the cult of the individual, for example, seem to flourish in times of economic prosperity when new kinds of 'adaptable' men are felt to be required in the workplace under new conditions of supervision, (as was the case for the United States in the 1920s and for Britain in the 1960s).[36] Whatever their origin, the important point is that such ideologies and those who support them stand as constraints to which teachers and headmasters respond. It is therefore possible for teachers to create an image of individualistically-based teaching for the benefit of interested 'outsiders' whilst maintaining either a rigid system of setting or streaming, or a carefully monitored scheme of individual learning programmes.

An illustration is provided by Riverdale which, in contrast to Moorhead, is situated within and circumscribed by the ideological constraints of Plowden as they are borne by their messengers and friends in the inspectorate, the advisory service, etc. In this context, the progressive image as a public one, must be displayed consistently for all interested 'outsiders' who may pass comment and judgement upon the school. One such group of outsiders is the governing body.

In the headteacher's report presented to the joint governing body of Moorhead and Riverdale, for example, Mr. Kitchen (Riverdale) makes no mention of the extensive setting practices which are implemented in the third and fourth-years of his school. By contrast, Mr. Butcher (Moorhead) in a separate report at a separate meeting explicitly refers to the existence of setting in his school when he states that 'In previous years we have deliberately inflated the numbers in the *more able sets* in order to create a small group of remedial children'. According to one informant, the governing body were unaware that setting took place at Riverdale. This view would be considerably enhanced by the photographic display of the school and its activities which confronted governors when they convened there one evening to hold a meeting. Some photographs in this display portrayed the school as an idyllic rural enclave, surrounded by trees and bathed in sunlight; a paradise for the educational romantic. The remaining photographs of indoor and outdoor educational activity reinforced this romanticism with their images of individuals or small groups of children working in creative and expressive arts; of teachers crouching with pupils as they engage in seemingly cooperative and egalitarian discussion, etc. Through these photographs, nature and human nature are symbolically brought together in the portrayal of the individual child at one with a supportive, nurturant environment which he constantly seeks to explore and discover with the teacher's helpful support, guidance and co-operation.

The idyll is at once appealing and convincing yet also one-sided and partial. There are no photographs of other facets of school life in Riverdale; of formal French being taught to different ability sets, or of science 'lectures' where pupils take down dictated notes as a way of digesting not only 'scientific knowledge' but also 'appropriate' terminology as in the following extract from a lesson on plant cells.

e.g. 'It couldn't divide like an animal cell because of the rigid cell wall. Use the word *rigid* because it really is the operative one'.

In this sense the refraction of educational reality occurs through a photographic reflection of institutional assumptions about what counts as good and favoured educational practice.[37] In reflecting, communicating and reinforcing these assumptions, the messages communicated by photographic displays are at one with messages communicated through the open-plan architecture of the school, through its internal organisation in the form of 'shared areas' and desks organised in groups rather than rows, and through the patterns of pupil movement and activity in that part of the curriculum devoted to the block-timetable which these arrangements facilitate. Openness, movement and diversity and the dissolution of curricular and pedagogic boundaries are the 'progressive' messages conveyed by these institutional features. For the educational voyeur who looks upon the school and its activity for a day or even less, the plausibility of such an appealing representation is difficult to refute and extremely tempting to accept. In consequence, it is hardly surprising if groups and individuals other than the governing body are also largely unaware of practices such as setting and tend to define the middle school in terms of its public image.[38]

At Riverdale the contradictions of progressivism and the constraints of ideology and architecture serve to produce a range of coping strategies which lock together in the form of a juxtaposition of block-timetable teaching with more formal teaching in ability sets. At Moorhead, since the architectural and staffing constraints are of a different kind and since, partly because of this, the progressive ideology has been somewhat less influential in patterns of teaching and learning, the dominant theme of teaching in the upper years is an explicitly 'secondary' one. In the sense of contradictory demands, of material constraints and of ideological constraints, teachers are thus presented with a series of problems and dilemmas with which they must attempt to cope. The outcomes, even in the limited case of Moorhead and Riverdale, are varied and depend upon the manner in which such constraints combine and exert themselves in any particular situation. But these constraints, it has been argued, originate not within the school itself but within the wider society, though they are usually experienced in a way which renders their societal origin obscure.

6. *Societal constraints are institutionally mediated.* In other words, the same societal constraint will be expressed differently in different kinds of educational institutions according to factors such as the age-level being taught and the social-class background of the school intake. The further away any group of children is from the *formal* point of selection and examination (which has become increasingly delayed in British society), the less specific are the knowledge demands made upon the children and the more diffuse are the criteria for achievement. At the middle school level, for example, the use of the block timetable for part of the school day enables teachers to sustain an image of progressivism and pupil choice whilst in the remainder of the curriculum they can transmit a required curriculum as a basis for 'O' level work in the upper school. In contrast, within the infant school, knowledge demands take the more diffuse form of literacy and numeracy levels which some children are expected to attain. The reconciliation of these with the child-centred approach embodied in the 'theology' of the infant school[39] is achieved through the coping strategy of 'busyness'.[40]

In addition to the mediating factor of age-level, the social-class background of pupils would also seem to be of some importance. Schools below the secondary level frequently draw upon a relatively homogeneous catchment area. Under these circumstances, where working-class children are concerned, there may be some difficulty in meshing the 'new' modes of control characteristic of progressive education with the socialisation practices that the child experiences in the home. Such a child may be unused to subtle and indirect forms of speech and social control, and find it difficult to respond as a result. Maintaining a progressive image with large numbers of pupils often in unsuitable buildings whilst retaining control over learning and behaviour might then be achieved through rigidly organised and carefully broken down work programmes which are evaluated systematically and at regular intervals under a bureaucratised system of individual supervision.[41]

The age and social class background of pupils would thus seem to be two mediating factors which might lead to a variety of responses by teachers to the same general constraint.

7. *The notion of institutional mediations prevents the concept of coping strategy from being employed in an over-simplistic manner.* It enables a bridge to be built between features of the society and issues in the classroom without *reducing* statements about structure to statements about action. The minimal requirement is only that observations of interaction can and must be explained within this framework.[42] Furthermore the creation of such a bridging point in explanation leads to an understanding of the fact that teaching styles are a response, albeit a creative and personal one, to a set of institutional and societal constraints. In consequence, injunctions to teachers to change their style or to cease engaging pupils in 'mere' busyness[43] are unlikely to be heeded unless due attention is paid to the *reasons* why teachers employ such styles and to the *pressures* which necessitate their use.

8. *Whether coping strategies persist and become institutionalised depends, in part, on the response of pupils.* The personal effort and social costs of management and control in some progressivist coping strategies, for example, are great. In this respect, Antonio Gramsci once offered some interesting observations on the difficulty of administering a Dalton Plan block-timetable approach to the curriculum:

> the pupils are free to attend whichever lessons (whether practical or theoretical) they please, provided that by the end of each month they have completed the programme set for them: discipline is entrusted to the pupils themselves. The system has a serious defect: the pupils generally postpone doing their work until the last days of the month, and this detracts from the seriousness of the education and represents a major difficulty for the teachers who are supposed to help them but are overwhelmed with work . . . .[44]

At a Riverdale curriculum meeting, Mr. Button provides some concrete grounding for Gramsci's rather generalised comments, though Mr. Kitchen then guides the discussion away from what appears to be a central staff concern –

Mr. Button   One of the things which I think are . . . One of the things that we fall down very badly is having the children organise their own time during the day when they have choices. We are . . . I mean . . . we do give them choice now in . . . in . . . what work they do and when they do it . . . well not so much what work but when they do the work. They're given a lot of free time and there are many, many children who cannot organise themselves well enough to

	appreciate . . . well they can't see more than a little time ahead and I think this is something that we . . . we've really got to work at . . . is how they organise their time. I mean, there's some children . . . I know when I was in the third year, we literally had to write out timetables for one or two because they just couldn't do it.
Mr. Banks	Umhum . . . And some in the fourth year can't do it either.
Mr. Button	Yeah and . . . and they are the problem children because even . . . even within that situation, if other children see them doing nothing, there . . . there is a certain . . . um . . .
Mr. Kitchen	Yes. Well can we take, what steps do we take in the first year for example that leads on to an improvement throughout the school. There's this way of looking at it . . .

The situation which third and fourth year Riverdale pupils encounter and which they themselves partly construct is a rich and complex one. A few extracts and quotations from informal discussions with different pupils during lesson time will provide at least a sense of some of the difficulties.

Firstly, although it is recognised by teachers such as Mr. Button that the opportunity for pupils to make choices is largely in the realm of how they organise their time, even this appreciation of the rather limited nature of pupil choice is not shared by the pupils themselves. For them, school time is teachers' time, not pupils' time and as one pupil complained, teachers 'are always dragging us off to do something'. Another pupil expressed it as follows:

> *P.*   You're just getting in your flow, then you get dragged off somewhere. It's better not to start anything at all . . . just to play noughts and crosses (which he had been doing) ready for when anybody comes.

At this point, with an immaculate sense of timing, a teacher walked across to the pupil and his group and asked them to clear up the neighbouring Art area. With a shrug of the shoulders and a 'knowing' look the pupil muttered resignedly 'See what I mean?'

Given their recognition that school time is teachers' time but that there is a low predictability of how this time will be apportioned by teachers, some pupils express a desire for a more rigidly compartmentalised timetable which will maximise the predictability of imposed schedules. Two third year pupils stated a preference for this kind of organisation.

> P_1 You think, 'I'll leave that till tomorrow', and then when tomorrow comes you find you have a film and you don't know

about it, then you . . . you can't get it done. But if your work's
. . . um . . . you know . . . you have set periods to do
everything . . .

P₂   Yeah.

P₁   . . . you do get it done.

In addition to the unpredictable nature of time allocation, some
pupils also suggested that the amount of blocked time made available
to complete set tasks was insufficient. Rather melodramatically, one
pupil estimated that 'we get three months work a week'. Time is thus
experienced by pupils as externally controlled by the teaching staff who
manipulate it, extend it or contract it at their will.

It is not only time that pupils experience as an imposition, however.
As Mr. Button himself recognised, such imposition also applies to the
content of school work. Occasionally, this is described explicitly by
pupils in terms of lessons being boring,[45] but more usually it is the
taken-for-granted style of their speech which betrays the fact that work
is imposed work and that knowledge is produced for others rather than
for themselves. Thus, when pupils discuss any work in which they are
currently engaged, their remarks are almost always prefaced with
phrases such as 'We've got to . . .', 'We have to . . .' 'She said we had
to . . .' etc.

Other constraints make the completion of imposed work an especially
arduous task for many pupils. The level of noise is a pervasive problem
and many believe that 'There's too much racket in here'. For some the
burden of blame for the generation of noise is placed upon other pupils
i.e. 'It's people like *them* being silly', but for others the open-plan
architecture of the school creates a situation where noise and even
odour can be either an unpleasant obstructive barrier or an appealing
distraction. Three comments illustrate the range of perceptions here:

'They should have doors on the classrooms.'
'In the cookery area you have woodshavings from the craft area and
also in the library you get smells from the cookery area.'
'I mean, they've got the woodwork area next to the library area.
You can't think.'

Open-plan design allows movement and flexibility but where work is
imposed and perceived as alien and where pupils engage in the inevitable side-activities as a result, the facilitating effects of such architecture are transferred into a perceived oppressive constraint. Noise is not
only generated but also more effectively transmitted within such an
environment.

Tensions like these may threaten the stability of the system as a
whole, for there is a very real danger that at the end of the week,
teachers will be confronted by a long queue of children holding out
their uncompleted assignments. An emphasis on individual direction
and cajoling, as Mr. Button suggests, may partly resolve these tensions,

but, as Gramsci pointed out, because teachers are overwhelmed with work, individual direction can only be given to a few. How then, is the survival of the block-timetable system guaranteed?

Under such alienating conditions for the production of knowledge where work is imposed but time is allowed for avoiding it (as a means of reconciling the contradictory demands for integration in the form of fulfilling given knowledge requirements, and personal development in the form of allowing some space for the existence and visibility of freedom of choice), the maintenance of any kind of managerial equilibrium and the teacher coping strategies which constitute it, are together heavily dependent upon the creative ingenuity of pupils in coping with the dilemmas *they* face, and upon the ability of teachers to create spaces where such pupil ingenuity will be allowed to develop. 'Homework', defined as 'taking work home' because it is presented as a freely chosen extension of schoolwork (i.e. it can be justified ideologically), frequently provides such a safety valve. The persistence of complex coping strategies depends upon the efficiency of such safety valve mechanisms.

These mechanisms might be viewed as engendering a peculiar form of compensatory education where the home compensates for the 'deficient' experiences which the child receives in school. The reasons for coping in this way, through homework, are clearly stated by some pupils:

P.   I prefer working at home. It's quiet and I've got my own room.

AH. Do you usually finish all your work during the week?

P_1 Sometimes.

P_2 But I always take my English home and do it on a Tuesday night. (Many pupils have mentioned that since English requires high levels of concentration, it is best completed at home where there is no noise and general interference).

AH   So is that the only thing you take home then? English?

P_2 Sometime you take topic home.

AH   Um hum. That's when you're getting really keen, is it? Really interested?

P_1 Or when we've got too much to do!

In a third-year class, a small group of pupils attempted to define for me the very fine distinctions between having homework set and having its existence recognised.

AH   How do you go on for taking work home? Do you take it home?

P.   Yes.

P.   I do.

P.   I do sometimes.

P.   You're allowed to. You don't have to.

P.   Mrs. Speaker won't set homework.

AH   Well, do you want her to?

P.   No. (laughing).
P.   We take a lot home, though.
P.   You take homework if you haven't finished anything . . . like
     . . . you take it home over the weekend or something and
     then if it's done on Monday morning, you're O.K.

The collusion that exists on homework is revealed somewhat uninten-
tionally in the following pupil's remark:

AH   Is it easy to avoid working?
P.   Oh yeah.
P.   Oh yeah. Yeah, it's easy to avoid it because *you can keep
     saying you left it at home*. (my emphasis).
P.   Yeah.

In summary, there is a mutual recognition on the part of both teacher
and pupil of the existence and necessity of homework, though its specifi-
cation as an official category of 'set' work is avoided, presumably
because it would run counter to the expected practices of a relatively
'progressive' institution. Instead of set *homework*, there is instead, the
available legitimation that in progressive forms of teaching pupils can
take work home if they choose, as a way of breaking down the barriers
between home and school. As Riverdale's headmaster puts it:

Mr. Kitchen   Quite frankly, I think that children have had enough
                at this age with school alone, but I would encourage
                children if they wish to take work home . . .[46]

'Homework', for the upper-middle school teacher, is as central an
organising category for structuring the teaching role as is 'busyness' for
the infant school teacher. For this very reason, it is just as difficult to
eliminate or 'take the steam out of' (in Mr. Kitchen's words). In each
case, the respective principle serves as an organising category for
teachers' responses to organisational and societal constraints and cannot
be readily removed unless the institutional conditions which make such
coping strategies necessary are themselves transformed. It is upon these
material supports and also upon the creative response of pupils in
themselves coping with *their* experienced constraints that the persistence
of teacher coping strategies depends. If these material supports were
to be removed or if pupil responses were to prove inadequate and
inefficient, then some degree of change, no matter how limited, would
be expected.
    9. *The claimed effectiveness of coping strategies* (and hence the
grounds for their institutionalisation) *are ultimately validated in teacher
'experience'*. Experience should be viewed not as a basis of judgement
superior to all others (as with Saville's rigid and authoritarian headmaster in David Storey's novel of that title),[47] nor as an obstructive
force to the achievement of rational decision-making (which Philip

Jackson implies that *his* 'experienced' teachers are incapable of making).[48]

Instead, in a tightly constraining environment where few opportunities are provided for individual or collective reflection, experience should be viewed as an organising mechanism for proceeding routinely yet accountably within the work situation. It is 'experience' that tells teachers which particular teaching styles have proved 'effective'. In interview, for example, when asked about the source of their ideas on various educational matters, the majority of both Riverdale and Moorhead teachers cited 'experience' as their mentor. When experience is used as the yardstick, effectiveness and efficiency are determined and assessed with reference to the teacher's explicit and tacit subscription to personal and institutional goals and to a set of mediated constraints. Rarely is the problem of efficiency translated into one of what efficiency might be for. The use of 'experience' as the dominant organising category of teachers' thought and everyday actions thus ensures that coping strategies are essentially adaptive in character, that their institutionalisation fosters the perpetuation of structures rather than their transformation and that they serve to produce stability regarding the major functions of education, rather than radical social change.

10. Following from the previous point, it should be stressed that *although coping strategies are constructive and creative in character, nevertheless they are also based upon a set of tacitly accepted and taken for granted assumptions* about schooling, children and learning. In other words, it should be emphasised that coping strategies are not created in a vacuum but are constructed within a set of definite parameters so that the scope for creativity is limited. These assumptions about, for instance, the 'needs' of working class children and the deficiency of their home backgrounds; about the distribution of natural, hierarchically ranked ability; about the compulsory nature of education and the benevolent role of the State in providing for this; about the role of the teacher as the controller and evaluator of the acquisition of knowledge by pupils; about the compatibility of individual needs with the requirements of the society; all of these constitute a range of taken-for-granted ideas which form the building blocks out of which 'experience' is constructed and validated but only insofar as such ideas provide a plausible interpretation of everyday practice. Such assumptions also serve as parameters within which coping strategies are constructed. Furthermore as constituent features of a dominant social democratic hegemony which stresses individualism, gradualism, reasonable balance and State benevolence, they also guarantee the non-radical character of teacher coping strategies.

Conclusion

In this paper, I have attempted to provide a rather sketchy model of

As a rather crude diagrammatic summary, the model of coping strategies may be expressed as follows:

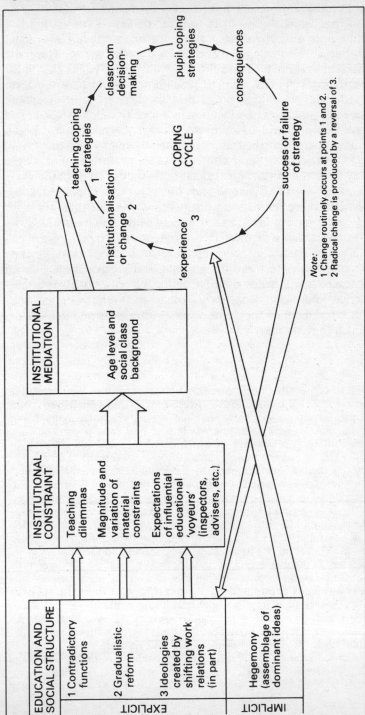

Figure 1 coping Strategies – a model

classroom and school-based coping strategies in order to provide a bridge not only between classroom and society but also between inter-pretive and Marxist approaches in the study of education. Some illustra-tive material has been drawn from the middle school which holds a central position not only chronologically in the hierarchy of educational institutions but also sociologically as a focal point for studying the dilemmas which teachers face and the constraints with which they must cope in the British school system. If teaching styles *do* take the form of coping strategies as in the model presented here, then, given the present goals and functions of education in a society which can be called capitalist, the prospects for fundamental change are not great. Coping strategies may change as constraints themselves change, or they may, over time, as teacher and pupil strategies react to one another, begin to drift away from the initial constraints: in this sense, the coping cycle itself contains an internal dynamic and, like a bicycle wheel, advances as it rotates. But there seems little prospect, at present, that strategies for *coping* with society and its problems and constraints will be converted into strategies for *transforming* it, unless, that is, ways can be found of easing daily classroom pressure on teachers (smaller class sizes, more free time, etc.) and invigorating staffroom culture in such a way that teachers will become active collective critics of their educa-tional practice and also, along with other men and women, self-conscious co-producers of the frameworks – the goals and constraints – within which they do their vital work.

Notes

1 This is not to suggest that all researchers who have focused upon classroom processes assume that negotiations between teachers and pupils are based on an equal distribution of power resources and interactional skills. More usually, the model is a pluralist one where society is seen as constituted by different interest groups each of which exerts pressure and attempts to have its definitions accepted in a process of open, observable conflict. In such a model, the school is an arena where pressure is exerted by teachers, pupils, parents, governors and so forth in a process of conflict-ridden but democratic decision-making. Under this view then, conflict is central and essential to the democratic process in society; its influence is beneficial. By comparison, all Marxist approaches contain the central assumption that in capitalist societies conflict is not only permanent, but also irresolvable. Problems are conceived not as isolated, unconnected and temporary difficulties but as the expression of an enduring contradiction between the interests of capital and labour. The absence of overt conflict does not necessarily indicate a natural shared consensus for such consensus may be engineered through ideological and political means with only minor residual issues being legitimate subjects for conflict and debate. A sensitive Marxist approach at least offers the hope that the observable and the non-observable can be recognised, distinguished and related.
For an extended account of the different approaches to 'conflict' see Ralph Miliband, *Marxism and Politics*, Oxford University Press, London, 1977, especially Chapter 2.

2 On the degradation of work in contemporary capitalist society see H. Braverman *Labour & Monopoly Capital*, Monthly Review Press, New York and London, 1974. Further support for this thesis is provided by T. Nichols and H. Beynon in *Living with Capitalism*, Routledge & Kegan Paul, London, 1977, where considerable attention is given to workers' own accounts and perceptions of the work process.

3 For a challenge to the conventional wisdom that improved qualifications lead to better jobs, see, for example, I. Berg, *Education and Jobs: the Great Training Robbery*, Penguin, Harmondsworth, 1970 and S. Bowles & H. Gintis, *Schooling in Capitalist America*, Routledge & Kegan Paul, London, 1976.

4 See B. Williamson, 'Continuities and discontinuities in the sociology of education' in M. Flude and J. Ahier, *Educability, Schools & Ideology*, Croom Helm, London, 1974.

5 The most disturbing example of entrapment within the 'interpretive' web has been provided by those researchers who suspend all questions about the constraints which bear down upon the classroom. Instead, in an egocentric and esoteric form of theorising they analyse only how educational theorists construct their theories and render them accountable and how they (the authors) then construct their own theories about such theorists' theorising. Examples of such an approach can be found in C. Jenks (ed.), *Rationality, Education and the Social Organisation of Knowledge*, Routledge & Kegan Paul, London, 1977. Although we must constantly seek to encourage reflexivity in our theorising, at a time when there is truly a 'crisis' in education, this relativist snare seems a particularly vicious one.

6 There have been few attempts to provide such forms of inclusive explanation to date, but some recent movements in this area *can* be detected, though the precise nature of the model varies in each case. See especially R. Sharp & A. Green, *Education & Social Control*, Routledge & Kegan Paul, London 1975; P. Willis *Learning to Labour*, Saxon House, Farnborough, 1977 and M. Ginsburg et al., *The Role of the Middle School Teacher*, Aston Educational Enquiry Monograph No. 7, University of Aston, 1977.

7 For a more extensive discussion of these schools and of middle-school ideology and practice in general see A. Hargreaves, *The Sociology of the Middle School*, Routledge & Kegan Paul, London, forthcoming.

8 Pupils' definitions are also, of course, extremely important and will receive some consideration here.

9 This does not mean that the actual way in which teachers type pupils is necessarily in terms of such categories, as David Hargreaves has pointed out in 'The process of typification in classroom interaction: models and methods', *British Journal of Educational Psychology*, November, 1977.

10 N. Keddie (ed.), *Tinker, Tailor . . ., the Myth of Cultural Deprivation*, Penguin, Harmondsworth, 1973 (Introduction).

11 N. Keddie 'Classroom Knowledge' in M.F.D. Young (ed.), *Knowledge & Control*, Collier-Macmillan, London, 1971.

12 P. Willis, *op. cit.*, p. 58 (my emphasis).

13 This point is made by J. Hoetker & W. P. Ahlbrand, 'The persistence of the recitation', *American Educational Research Journal*, Vol. 6.

14 A. Hargreaves, 'Strategies, decisions & control: an analysis of interaction in a middle school classroom' in J. Eggleston (ed.), *Teacher Decision-Making in the Classroom*, Routledge & Kegan Paul, London, 1978. The term 'negotiative' should not imply that the pupil participates in this

process on equal terms with the teacher. Participate he does, however, and no matter how predictable the outcome of his interactions with his teacher might be, the recognition of his involvement in the process is essential to the development of a fuller model of coping strategies.

15 I. Westbury, 'Conventional classrooms, open classrooms and the technology of teaching', *Journal of Curriculum Studies*, Vol. 5, 1973.

16 Sharp & Green, *op. cit.*

17 Ibid pp. 22–23. The phrase 'irrespective of how they define it' is perhaps a little blunt and overlooks the point that even if 'the situation' proves irresistably oppressive, it still generates defining responses on the part of teachers and other actors.

18 The ironic similarity between one particular variant of Marxism and Parsonian functionalism has been noted in M. Erben and D. Gleeson 'Education as reproduction: a critical examination of some aspects of the work of Louis Althusser' in M. Young & G. Whitty, *Society, State & Schooling*, Falmer Press, Brighton, 1977. Bernard Wakefield has also drawn attention to that very same affinity between the two approaches, though in a more appreciative manner, in his 'Polytechnics, professionals and the production of intellectuals', *Higher Education Review*, Autumn 1977.

19 See P. Woods, 'The myth of subject choice', *British Journal of Sociology*, 1976.

20 Nichols & Beynon *op. cit.* make this observation in their comments upon 'worker participation' in the chemical factory they studied.

21 For a discussion of the ideology and practice of 'guided choice' at the routine levels of classroom decision-making see A. Hargreaves, 'Progressivism and pupil autonomy', *Sociological Review*, August 1977.

22 The block timetable approach entails the inclusion of a large proportion of 'open periods' on the school timetable when assignments (which pupils are given or which they select from a narrow range of alternatives) can be worked upon. The choice which pupils exercise in this system is in the pacing of their work and over the order in which assignments are completed.

23 See A. Hargreaves & D. Warwick, 'Attitudes to middle schools', *Education 3–13*, April 1978, for an expansion of this argument.

24 This is not to suggest that educational reform *ever* took the form of a radical wholesale reconstruction of pre-existing arrangements at any time before large-scale State intervention commenced.

25 Supportive evidence for this assertion is available in early documents produced by the West Riding when middle schools were first planned.

26 Matters have improved somewhat since fieldwork was completed. Separate specialist facilities for craft and science are now available and the prospect of a new school opening at Millbeck is now somewhat closer.

27 These points were also raised by Mr. Butcher in other contexts such as parents' meetings, governors' meetings, etc.

28 At times when teacher unemployment is rising and the opportunities for job mobility decrease, one would expect this effect to increase.

29 See various Schools' Council Working Papers, especially numbers 22, 42 and 55 for examples of such ideology. Their ideological content is analysed in A. Hargreaves, 'The ideology of the middle school', mimeo, Department of Sociology, University of Leeds, 1977 (copies available from the author at his present address).

30 'Misplaced' refers to a disparity between teachers' orientation and their placement within a particular kind of school.

31 See Westbury, *op. cit.*

32 The preference for 'indirect' teaching is clearly expressed by N. Flanders in his *Analysing Teacher Behaviour*, Addison-Wesley, New York, 1970.

33 The limitations of the Flanderian definitions of 'direct' and 'indirect' teaching have been discussed in S. Delamont, *Interaction in the Classroom*, Methuen, London, 1976.

34 A point made and substantiated through analysis of interaction in M. Hammersley, 'The organisation of pupil participation', *Sociological Review*, August, 1974.

35 There is a difference between ideologies *in* education and ideologies *about* education. This distinction has been neatly drawn in D. Finn, N. Grant & R. Johnson, 'Social Democracy, education and the crisis' in Working Papers in *Cultural Studies No. 10*. Centre for Contemporary Cultural Studies, University of Birmingham, 1977.

36 Discussion of this point with reference to the United States is made in Bowles & Gintis *op. cit.* An introductory text which offers some helpful summaries (along with some rather loosely constructed critiques) of such theories, is T. Whiteside, *The Sociology of Educational Innovation*, Methuen, London, 1978 (especially Chapter 2).

37 Any bias therefore is neither necessarily intentional nor manipulative. That 'bias' is more usually the product of an unquestioned set of value assumptions is most cogently argued by S. Hall in 'The determinations of news photographs', in S. Cohen & J. Young, *The Manufacture of News*, Constable, London, 1973.

38 Such groups include teachers at Moorhead and, at least for an initial period, students on teaching practice at Riverdale.

39 B. Bernstein, 'Class and pedagogies: visible and invisible', in *Class, Codes and Control*, Vol. 3, Routledge & Kegan Paul, London, 1975.

40 Sharp & Green *op. cit.*

41 A. Hargreaves, 'Strategies, decisions & control', *op. cit.*

42 Though this begs the important question of how far one can have an untheorised observation.

43 A policy recommended by W. A. L. Blyth & R. Derricott in their *The Social Significance of Middle Schools*, Batsford, London, 1977. The remainder of their book is a very useful introduction to the history and organisation of English middle schools.

44 A Gramsci, *Selections from the Prison Notebooks* (translated by O. Hoare & G. N. Smith), Lawrence & Wishart, London, 1971, p. 32. (footnote).

45 Such statements *are* occasional though, and this is not the usual way in which pupils explicitly talk about school life at Riverdale.

46 Stated in interview.

47 D. Storey, *Saville*, Jonathan Cape, London, 1976.

48 P. W. Jackson, *Life in Classrooms*, Holt, Rinehart & Winston, New York, 1968.

1.2

Open classrooms: variability in implementation†

Leila Sussmann

. . . In the case of a far more complex innovation, like open education, teachers implement it in widely differing ways. Walberg and Thomas developed an observational scale which enabled unbriefed observers to distinguish validly between classrooms intended to be open and classrooms not so intended, in Britain and the United States.[1] Nonetheless, the open classrooms we observed differed widely among themselves. We observed five classrooms in the OCT* program at Southside for two and a half weeks each. The rooms we saw included one which we judged as quite highly structured and one which seemed to us very unstructured. The other three fell somewhere between. A trainer of open-classroom teachers who read our field notes,** independently identified these two classrooms as the extremes on a continuum of structure, and also said that they exemplified the two most common ways that open education is being implemented in the United States. For this reason, we shall describe these two classrooms in some detail.

A structured open classroom

Natalie Roseman's first-grade class had twenty-two children, twelve boys and ten girls. Two of the pupils were black, five were Hispanic, and the rest were native-born white. Most of the white children came from upper middle-class homes; the minority children were considerably poorer. There was some correlation between ethnicity and academic skills (though not necessarily ability); none of the highly verbal and

---

† Source: *Tales out of School* (1977), Temple University Press, Philadelphia, pp. 132–53.

* Editors' footnote: OCT stands for Open Classroom teaching.

** This was Professor Diane Levin of Lesley College. I draw heavily on her seminar paper in this chapter.

quantitatively sophisticated pupils in the classroom was a minority child. On the other hand, no child in the room was on such a low level of skill as we saw very often at the Johnson School.[2]

Two student teachers were doing their practice-teaching with Miss Roseman, and one or the other of them was present nearly all the time. In addition, there was a volunteer mother, who also happened to be a teacher-in-training, who came in four mornings a week. This meant there was nearly always an adult-to-child ratio in this room of one-to-eleven, and sometimes of one-to-seven. Furthermore, the helping adults had training in teaching skills. Miss Roseman felt she needed every bit of this assistance. She repeatedly said, 'You need a lot of adults around to run this kind of program.' On this point she was at variance with Professor Wylie, who thought that one teacher plus an aide was about right for an open classroom with twenty-five children. More adults than that, he felt, tended to undermine the children's independence. Even this recommended ratio of about one-to-twelve is higher than one finds in conventional classrooms. The open classroom teachers at Southside nearly all agreed with Miss Roseman rather than Professor Wylie. They claimed that 'slow children' and children with a short attention span could not work independently and required constant adult supervision.

The environment: space and materials

Natalie's classroom was attractive, cheerful, and very tidy. All the materials had a 'right place' to be stored and the children knew these places. In an open classroom, children must be taught to put materials away carefully, in good shape, ready to be taken out and used by the next child who wants them. The importance of this basic organizational principle can hardly be exaggerated. Part of the theory is that 'materials teach' without the teacher. But if children are to use materials freely, they must be able to find them promptly and the materials must be in condition for use. If children don't put materials back where they belong, and if they don't care for materials to see that they don't get broken and that parts don't get lost, the classroom becomes disorganized; children waste much time searching for misplaced things and lost parts. Miss Roseman spent a considerable part of numerous class meetings discussing with the children the need to be careful with materials. She emphasized that all the materials in the room belonged to all of them, so that everyone was responsible for their good condition.

Children's work was on display in the room, but perhaps to lesser extent than in other open classrooms in the school. The teacher's work was relatively more conspicuous in this room: Natalie's chart of the Cuisenaire rods, their colors and letter labels; her chart of the concepts 'shorter and taller,' 'littler and bigger.' But there were also children's paintings, their dictated stories, their rhyming books, and their dancing pumpkins for Halloween.

Basically, the materials were arranged around the four sides of the room, while the center space contained several tables and chairs where children worked. Along the wall to the right of the door was a blackboard and a peg board. The peg board had round tags with the names of the children and stickers with the names of the room 'areas.' The children were supposed to hang their name tags under the areas they were at. Next came a small stove, pots, and other cooking utensils. The children cooked about once a week. Next to that was the 'listening area,' equipped with a recordplayer and earphones, a library of records, and books which went with them. These were stories which children could listen to and look at at the same time.

On the left-hand wall were the children's and teacher's clothing closets and the children's storage cubbies. The door of one closet had a chart of the children's reading groups. There were six groups: one had six children in it, one had five, one had four, one had three, and two had two.

In front of the closets was the 'math area.' It was a table with a lot of materials: geo boards, tape measures, counting books, small- and medium-sized blocks of different shapes, colored cubes, a peg board on which you could put from one to ten rings on a peg, a chart of simple geometric shapes with their names, a number line, Cuisenaire rods with a box of task cards, and some dittoed sheets with tasks to do.

On the window side of the room was the 'art area.' It consisted of a long work table covered with attractive oilcloth. In clear plastic boxes on the window sill, each neatly labeled, were ribbon, foam bits, yarn, macaroni, wooden pieces, beans, buttons, clay, fabric, magazines, scissors, crayons, a ruler, colored paper, and flour for making paste. There were also easels. The paints and brushes were in a closet. Next along this wall, separated from art by an unused piano, came the 'language arts area.' It had some very big building blocks in it. It also had a closet jammed with letter, word, and math games of all kinds – some bought, many made by the teacher.

On the right-hand wall, there was a box marked 'Children's Day Books' containing books which the children had made. Several of them were filled with drawings and labels – some crude, some sophisticated. There was also a box marked 'Math Work Books,' one marked 'Story Books,' and one marked 'Coloring Books.' There was a little bookcase which contained part of the class library. In the corner, covered with plants, was the teacher's desk. She hardly ever sat at it. Instead, she used a filing cabinet backed up against the side of the piano where she kept her records and plans. Finally, toward the middle of the room there was a 'science area.' It had two of the inevitable gerbils, some autumn leaves, a pumpkin, a book on rocks and minerals, and a box of cards with 'things to do' written on them. Natalie felt that science activities were the weakest part of her program – and by comparison with other open classrooms we saw, we would agree. She also felt that her room was very poor in materials, but that too is a relative matter. Compared to many classrooms at Johnson it was very rich in materials. Compared to some open classrooms we have seen in wealthy private schools it was less impressive, but hardly describable as 'poor in materials.'

Schedule and content

In theory, the open classroom structures space strongly, as Natalie's room did, but destructures time. Children are not supposed to move from reading to arithmetic by the clock, but to work at an 'activity' as long as it absorbs them. This ideal is seldom fully realized; most open classrooms have some kind of time schedule, albeit a flexible one. Natalie's room ran on quite a regular schedule. The day began with a class meeting to discuss news, the weather, upcoming holidays, or whatever else the children wanted to talk about. The teacher used the meeting to tell the children about any special activities of the day and to give instructions to the reading groups. Then the children broke up into their ability-homogeneous reading groups. The most advanced group worked alone with programed SRA[3] materials. The teachers worked with the slower groups. Occasionally children were assigned to a language game during this period or given individual help. Natalie and a student teacher had decided one day that 'Joseph has broken the phonics code, but he doesn't understand what he's reading'; the next morning Joseph was taken by a student teacher for special help with reading comprehension.

The reading groups were a source of some friction between Natalie and her OCT adviser. The adviser thought there should be more emphasis on 'experiential reading' and less on formal teaching of reading. An example of 'experiential reading' is to have a child dictate to the teacher an account of something he has done; he then learns to read the account which the teacher has printed for him. Natalie had such stories on display in the room. However, she told us that she had made clear when she volunteered for the program three years previously, that she would not give up her reading groups. She was irritated by 'the pressure' from the adviser to modify her methods of teaching reading.

When the children finished their reading assignments, they were free to choose another activity. The great bulk of the 'free activities' in this room, however, were games, books, or records which reinforced basic reading and math skills. There were only a few more 'open-ended' activities – painting, building with blocks, and modelling with clay.

In the late morning there was another class meeting, and this was a time when children who had signed up to do so, 'shared' something with the class. Natalie saw to it that all the children participated. For instance, one morning she called on a boy to read his primer, which he had just completed. He did so a little haltingly. She commended him and suggested that he might like to help someone else to read that book later in the day.

After the meeting, Natalie took the children to the playground for a recess. Then they went to lunch in the school cafeteria which was under the supervision of the principal, the assistant principal, and aides. Natalie ate her lunch in the classroom and worked right through the lunch period. Lunch time was when she recorded the children's progress in reading, made anecdotal notes on what kind of work they needed next, and set up the classroom for the afternoon's activities.

After lunch there was another class meeting. Sometimes Natalie read the children a story, but on several days of the week this was her 'prep' period. Then the school's language arts, music, or library teacher took over the class. These specialty teachers were the OTPs (Other Teaching Professionals) the principal had told us about: tenured teachers who were confined to covering classes during teachers' prep periods 'to minimize the damage they can do.'

We could see what the principal meant. Natalie's well-behaved class, to whom she never raised her voice, fell apart when Mrs. Katz came in to do 'language arts.' Mrs. Katz could not hold the children's attention, and when they began to converse with each other, or to wander off into an activity area, she said harsh things to them in something close to a shriek. The other OTPs were equally ineffective, and equally out of tune with the methods and spirit of the open classroom. They intruded a completely incongruous note into the children's week. The OCT teachers felt guilty about leaving their children with these 'specialists' – but they needed their prep periods.

A frequent early afternoon activity for Natalie's class was phonics – another formally taught program for which they were divided into two groups. Sometimes the class did mathematics in the afternoon. Some engaged in simple counting activities; some worked with Cuisenaire rods, beginning to develop arithmetic concepts; and some worked at various points in programed math workbooks. Natalie took great care to see that she had taught the children the concepts they needed in order to do the problems in the workbooks; she always told the child where to stop and bring the workbook back to her for checking.

When math or phonics was finished, the children had the rest of the afternoon for free activities. Not infrequently, a mother came into the room for an hour during the day to cook with a group of children, to show them how to make hooked rugs, and so on. Almost anything a mother thought she might like to do with the children was accepted with gratitude.

Relationships

The social climate in Natalie's room was warm, relaxed, and cooperative. Children conversed with each other freely and often worked together by choice or by assignment. They gave and received help with their work, and Natalie encouraged this. She treated all the children alike although, like any teacher, she had her private preferences among them. Natalie's biggest complaint was about the upper middle-class children. At a meeting with the OCT advisers she said that she was hearing more than ever from these children that they 'didn't want to do' what she asked them to. She mentioned somewhat defensively that an English headmaster from an open school had said in a talk that there was nothing wrong with telling children what to do when necessary. She said these children were 'spoiled' at home, and she found them a bit tiresome.

Natalie did all she could in class meetings and in working with the children to encourage cooperativeness. She never set a child in competition with another. Yet the children brought their competitiveness from home – and while it was not a prominent feature of their interaction, they did sometimes make remarks like, 'I'm ahead of you in that workbook.'

The children's groupings in this room seemed, during observation, to be quite fluid. We were unable to distinguish any firmly established peer groups. The only line of segregation was between the sexes. Ironically, when children are left to group themselves, there is more sex segregation than in teacher-made groups. The children in this class did not seem to group themselves either by ethnicity or by ability. There was one interesting example of 'peer effect.' Helen Fuentes was a black Puerto Rican girl who barely spoke a word to the teacher during the first month and a half of school. She pretended not to know English, but Natalie could tell that she understood a great deal. Helen had an attractive personality, however, and other children in the room frequently sought her company. Sometime in October she was adopted as a 'special friend' by a white, upper middle-class girl named Betsy, who was an exceptionally able pupil. The two girls visited each other's homes and spent much time together in school. Suddenly, Helen began to speak English with other children, to adults, and even at class meetings. She volunteered for special activities, became more and more extroverted, more successful at her work, and apparently much happier. Natalie attributed Helen Fuentes' rapid progress to her friendship with Betsy, and all that it implied in terms of exposure to an attractive, English-speaking milieu.

Analysis

Natalie Roseman's classroom conformed to open education philosophy in some respects and departed from it in others. If one follows her daily schedule, it immediately becomes apparent that the greatest emphasis was given to academic skills and above all, to reading and mathematics. Social studies and science received hardly any attention. In addition, most of the children's time was spent doing teacher-determined and directed activities. Within the appointed tasks, children sometimes worked independently and in flexible ways, but because there were nearly always two, or even three teaching adults in the classroom, teachers could and did oversee nearly all the children's activity. Pupils had only a small part of the day in which to make their own decisions about what they would do.

We have already pointed out that Natalie insisted on keeping her reading groups. In her interview, she insisted as well on the absolute necessity of didactic teaching:

I think definitely that teaching is necessary. I mean, that's it! I *don't* believe that kids can acquire things out of the air or from materials. If they're learning sounds or words or whatever, when they've finished with that, and with certain instructions, I like to give them a game they can play well that reinforces that kind of skill. But they have to learn it first. I don't think they're going to learn it through the game or doing an activity or something like that. I think doing that is frustrating to the child.

Here Natalie rejected a key portion of open classroom doctrine. From the open educator's point of view, her classroom was also deficient in that there were no continuing projects, based on the pupil's interests, which would have posed new problems and challenged the children to find solutions. Projects of this kind are relied on to stimulate the children's creativity and their analytic capacities. Other open classrooms at Southside did have such projects. One, for instance, took several walks around the school's block with a parent, noting everything they saw, making rubbings of manhole covers, taking snapshots. Then they dictated essays about what they had seen, which the teacher printed, and which became material for learning to read. They were also working on a scale model of the block, which involved some simple arithmetic calculations needed to keep things roughly in their proper size relationships. When nearly all of the class work is organized around such projects, open educators call it 'the integrated day.' Natalie's adviser was urging her to move in this direction, but again Natalie rejected the suggestion. She told us that the adviser was unrealistic about what could be done in a first-grade classroom because she had never been a teacher herself.* To Natalie, the key tasks of the first grade were to learn reading and beginning arithmetic. Projects were trimmings:

Maybe later these kids will be ready for an integrated day. But right now, I don't think they are and there aren't enough people around to handle that. I feel that if some kids are doing a science experiment and some are doing a math experiment, it's fine. We do that too, but I think in the beginning they need the structure of beginning

*The adviser was, in fact, an experienced teacher.

reading. Once they got into routines and were reading better, then I wouldn't care so much if they were doing a science thing all day or working on a construction project for two or three days. That's what happened at the end of my first grade two years ago. At the beginning there was much more of this scheduled work.

Thus Natalie showed that she did not trust a considerable part of what open education asserts as true. She did not believe that pupils would learn basic reading and arithmetic in the natural course of problem-solving on projects. Unlike open educators, she thought it was necessary for the children to learn to read as soon as they could – as a prerequisite to other kinds of work.

On the other hand, there were substantial parts of the doctrine which Natalie accepted and practiced. She did not believe in whole-class teaching. Most of the work was done in small groups, which took account of the children's rate of development; frequently it was individualized to meet some particular child's needs. Natalie kept careful records of what skills the children mastered and gave much thought to what work she should present each child with next. Group meetings were an important part of the daily schedule. Not only did they serve to enhance communication skills, they provided an opportunity for the children to share interests and to develop an increased social awareness. Their collective responsibility for the state of the room which 'belonged to them' was emphasized. In no situation were children invidiously compared with each other. There was actually little competition in the classroom and what little there was clearly came from home. For the most part, the children were mutually friendly and helpful.

Here we see a well-respected teacher (professors of education were eager to have their students do their practice teaching with her), in her third year in the OCT program, with a classroom which was 'open' only to a rather limited degree. Further, she was firmly resistant to the advisers' suggestions that she move toward what they defined as more openness. From their standpoint, the most they could hope for was that she would initiate some 'projects' during the last part of the academic year. It was most unlikely that Natalie would abandon her firm belief that reading and arithmetic had to be taught as subjects in their own right, rather than as instruments for accomplishing the goals of a project – in the face of contrary suggestions from advisers for whom she had little professional respect.

An unstructured open classroom

Abe Winner's second-grade class had twenty-six children, sixteen boys and ten girls. Six were black, six Hispanic, and fourteen white. As in Natalie's room, the white children were from comfortable, upper middle-class homes with college-educated parents, while the minority children came from homes of much lower income and educational background. When Abe rank-ordered his children for us in terms of reading skill, all the white children, save one, ranked above all the minority children. However, as we noted above, skill and ability are not the same thing. Abe pointed out to us several of his minority children who were poor readers but who, he said, were 'exceptionally intelligent' or 'ingenious.'

Abe welcomed the observer into the class as an 'extra hand,' because he had virtually no help. The paraprofessional aide assigned to him didn't do her job. He had not seen her in weeks and she did not appear in the classroom while we were observing. Two volunteer mothers each gave a few hours a week, but one of them spoke little English and could only help in limited ways.

Just as Natalie's room reflected her views, Abe's reflected his. He told us that he 'wouldn't be caught dead' with reading or math groups because having to perform in front of peers was a 'threatening and punishing' experience for a child. He believed that all learning was individual. He also said, 'The teacher is peripheral'; children must learn from materials and activities. 'The few minutes they spend with me individually is more important than a longer time spent in groups where they would pass a great deal of the time in listening passively, just waiting for their turns.'

Abe's room had the reputation of being the noisiest, most disorderly OCT class in the school. Other OCT teachers and the assistant principal, who was on his floor, complained that some of his children ran shouting up and down the corridors and in and out of other classrooms, disturbing everyone. Natalie, who was on the floor below, said, 'There are some OCT rooms I certainly wouldn't send my children to visit. They'd come back to me *flying!*' These two had a mutual disrespect for each other's philosophies and practices.

The environment: space and materials

As one entered Abe's classroom, it gave an immediate impression of messiness. There was trash and litter all over the tables and floor. There was also a lot of movement and noise. Children chased each other excitedly around the furniture. The mess was bright and gay, however. Children's paintings were strung diagonally overhead on a clothesline. There were a lot of animals: guinea pigs, mice, gerbils, hamsters, fish, and a rabbit. There was a workbench with tools and material for woodwork. There was a math table with much the same equipment as in Natalie's room, but, except for the balance scale, it was unused during the period of observation. There was also a science table with coral, some plants, a fossil, and some coal – all neatly labeled and also unused.

The room had two playhouses which were used incessantly. One, a rectangle at least six feet high, had openings for door and windows. Nearby in a closet were dress-up clothes for dramatic play. The other house was on the floor underneath the tables, and children crawled in and out of it. There was a closet filled with books and games. The right-hand side of the room as one entered was carpeted and partly partitioned off by a blanket hanging from a clothesline. This was the area for class meetings. The teacher's desk was there, too, invisible under the clutter. Like Natalie, the teacher never sat at it. At the front of the room, the alphabet and a number line were above the blackboard. A peace flag hung there and a motto: 'I do and I understand.'

The room was not clearly divided into areas for specific activities. Reading could take place anywhere. The left-hand wall had the clothing closets, children's cubbies, and math table. Woodwork was sometimes in the corridor, sometimes in the room. Books and the fish tank were at the back, under the windows. The rest of the animals and the science table were up front. In the center of the room were tables and chairs which the children used for whatever they happened to be doing.

Schedule and content

The day and the week were no more clearly structured than the space. Perhaps the only routine was that the class usually held three meetings: one the first thing in the morning, one after lunch, and one at the end of the day. The early-morning meeting opened with children reciting the day, the month, and the year. This was often followed by a discussion. The day after Halloween, for instance, Abe asked, 'What did you do last night?':

> Robert and Tim said, 'We got money. We stole it. And we got all kinds of candy.' Another one of the boys said, 'I went trick-or-mugging.' Manuel reported almost being mugged while he was 'trick-or-treating.' Frank said some kids pulled a knife on them and asked for their money, and they said 'No' and ran.

Here is some real experience which seemed to demand that the teacher respond to it in some way, but Abe ignored it; he said nothing. On one other occasion, when the children talked with great excitement about violence seen on television and in the neighborhood, he got them to admit that they would not like to be on the receiving end of violence. But they continued to talk about violence done to others in tones of pleasurable thrill, and Abe did not succeed in bringing the two sentiments into relation with one another.

Class meeting was also used for story-telling. After lunch Abe sometimes read from *Charlotte's Web*, which was over the heads of many of the children. They occupied their time making faces at each other and fussing with their hair. Frequently Abe used the class meeting as an occasion to teach:

The children handed him on little sheets of paper guesses as to how much the Halloween pumpkin weighed. He took out the scale and said, 'Now I'm going to set the scale so that when I stand on it I weigh two hundred pounds.' He had several children check to see that he did. Then he took the pumpkin and he stood on the scale with it and said, 'Now I want you to see what the scale says.' The children had trouble reading the weight, but finally said it was 241 pounds. So Abe began to go through the papers to see whose guess had been closest. The prize was a lollipop. But many of the children didn't understand what was going on. They kept shouting, 'Weigh the pumpkin! Weigh the pumpkin!' Finally Abe did and it was forty-one pounds, but I'm sure the point of the exercise did not get through to many of them. Abe didn't elucidate. This was another manifestation of his disbelief in didactic teaching.

After class meeting Abe said to the children, 'Now you may go to your morning activities.' On one morning, no more atypical than any other, the children scattered in all directions. Some were doing wood-work. They sawed up pieces of wood, glued them together into 'abstract' constructions, and painted them. Other children went and got animals to handle and play with. A few children were building with blocks. Several others were playing in the big cardboard house. One pair was playing a game of chess with quite a group of spectators.

Abe approached individual children and worked with each for a few minutes on a math or reading workbook. Occasionally, a child whom he asked to bring a workbook up to him, didn't do it, and Abe didn't seem to notice.

As we worked with children in their workbooks, we found that often they had gone a dozen pages beyond the point where they understood the concepts needed or the task to be done, and they had done the work randomly. For instance, on a page where the instructions were to draw a line connecting objects whose names rhymed, a child had simply connected every object with another at random. We asked Abe about this, since Natalie was very clear about not allowing it to happen – but his view was different. He said he didn't mind if they went ahead on their own for a bit. 'There is always an increment of learning.'

Abe had another belief: that a child's errors should always be ignored, rather than corrected, unless the child was exceptionally able and had a strong ego. Apparently there was no such child in the class, because Abe never corrected errors. He gave only positive feedback concerning work, and he carried this to such an extreme that – as he told me – some of the children didn't believe he was a teacher. (It is not clear what they thought he was.) As an illustration, one morning he asked Robert to play a high note and a low note on the recorder he had brought into school. Robert played a high note and called it low, and vice versa. Abe laughed, but made no comment. On another occasion, we were caught correcting the spelling of a word by one of the 'faster' children, and Abe admonished us never to correct anything a child had done, and never to give help unless asked for it.

The help that Abe gave when he was asked was often inadequate. One morning Claude came to him wanting to know how to solve the problem: '? − 2= 4.' Abe sent him for the abacus and told him that he must find a number such that, when he took two away from it, there were four left. Then he waved Claude away and turned to another child. Claude looked puzzled. We decided to see what would happen if we helped him. 'Take a guess,' we suggested. He guessed ten, took two away, and saw that he had the wrong answer. 'Take another guess.' He guessed five and got the wrong answer again. We plunged in boldly, 'Ten was too big and five was too small. What do you think you should do now?' 'I'll take something in between.' Luckily he chose six and beamed when the answer was right. Then he went on to do some analogous problems using the same strategy.

On another day, we found Nan, one of the brightest children in the class, looking bewildered at a page in her math book which asked her to make up some addition and subtraction equations using the numbers one, four, and five. Nan knew how to add and subtract, and she had seen the problems in equation form earlier in the book. But she was not quite aware of what the '=' sign meant, and she didn't know what an equation was. It took us five minutes to explain it to her, and then she became so absorbed in making up equations that she was reluctant to stop when cleanup time came. Abe did not explain the meaning of the '=' to anyone in the class until two weeks later. Since he insisted on working on a one-to-one basis, and since he had little help in his classroom, there was always a long wait for children to get help from him – just as long and frustrating, we would suspect, as that of children in a group awaiting their 'turns.'

Here is another example of what Abe's children experienced with their workbooks:

> Verna and Claude were each working in a phonics book doing an exercise I had seen Natalie's children do. They were given endings like 'et' and 'ot' and asked to put consonants in front of them to make words. Neither Claude nor Verna had any grasp of the endings. Not only could they not distinguish between 'et' and 'ot,' sometimes they went so far as to confuse them with 'ing.' They did not know what a consonant was. They didn't seem to know the difference between a real word and a nonsense word. In short, they had no phonics skills whatsoever. Within five minutes, they put their workbooks away and went off to sing 'The Yellow Submarine' with some other children.

Abe had assigned those two children to those pages, so he evidently had a misconception of their level of skill. We never saw him teach reading skills. He told us that the only way nonreaders would learn to read was 'experientially.' To that end, he occasionally had us take down two or three sentence 'stories' which children dictated and which they were supposed to be highly motivated to learn to read, since it was their own product. Again, Abe rarely had the time to do this himself with his nonreaders, so they either did almost no work at all on reading, or they floundered aimlessly through their workbooks. It seemed to us that, from the children's viewpoint, their failure to gain any mastery – which they were well aware of – was a 'punishing' experience.

Abe did not teach the children to care for materials and that, too, made for frustration in his room. Pencils and rubber bands vanished. Equipment was broken. Pieces of puzzles got lost. Children were constantly telling Abe that they couldn't find things they needed, and he invariably replied, 'Well then, you'll have to look for it.' Very often the children didn't bother since the room was so littered that finding anything would have been difficult. A good many lost things turned up at cleanup time toward the end of the day.

Abe had the virtues of his faults. He was always ready to take advantage of a learning opportunity which spontaneously presented itself. One day when he was reading the class a story with his back to the animals, the children said, 'Look at the rabbit!' The rabbit had gotten out of its cage and dug up part of a plant and then gone back in to eat. Abe said, 'Let's see what the rabbit is doing.' 'It's eating dirt.' 'No, it's eating the plant.' 'No, it's eating the roots.' They finally agreed it was eating the roots and had a talk about what rabbits eat. They decided to try feeding it various things to find out. Abe did not comment on the fact that someone had left the cage open.

On another day, Abe found that some voting machines had been installed in the basement for Election Day. He got permission to show the children how they worked, and that became the basis for a discussion of what elections were.

One project and one on-going activity occurred in Abe's room while we observed it. A clique of upper middle-class white boys worked for several days building a maze for the gerbils. They designed it themselves, and it was very successful. The same group of boys carried on a chess tournament, which was watched with interest by the children who understood chess. The minority children in the room did not understand chess, nor did they seem to take any interest in the construction project.

Abe was eager to organize a rather ambitious project involving the whole class – he wanted to build a boat. But he said that to carry that out he needed the collaboration of another adult and lots of materials he didn't have. The following year, when we had lunch with him, he told us that his class was actually building a boat – without another teacher's help and with materials he had bought himself.

Relationships

Like Natalie, Abe had a warm, personal relationship with his pupils. He often shouted at them at the top of his very strong voice, but not angrily. He was extraordinarily patient with a paranoid, disruptive child in the room whom many teachers would not have been able to tolerate. On the playground, he engaged in a lot of horseplay with the boys, which they enjoyed very much.

Abe was a political radical who wanted to promote cooperativeness and mutual respect in his class and to abolish competitiveness on political grounds. However, his methods sometimes produced a result he didn't like. Consistent with his lack of structure in other areas, Abe let peer groups, at work or play, form freely. He never took the initiative in grouping children together to perform a task. In his classroom, there was a fairly clear-cut division of peer groups, not only by sex, but by ethnicity and ability as well. The white boys associated mainly with each other and so did the white girls, with the exception of a low-skilled one who was an isolate. Black and Hispanic boys intermingled and so did black and Hispanic girls. They formed several cliques, more or less divided along ability lines, as Abe estimated ability. The lowest-skilled boys spent most of their time fighting and playing games which involved a chase. The girls played house and 'dress-up' and groomed their own and each others' hair. Abe was not happy about the composition of the peer groups – which he recognized – but he attributed it to the children's associations with each other outside of school.

Analysis

Abe subscribed more wholeheartedly to open education philosophy than Natalie did:

> 'It's my belief that the teacher's role in the children's learning is really very minimal. The teacher should observe the children carefully. You learn a lot about them that way. You never spend more than a very few minutes with any one child, but they interact a great deal with one another and with materials, and that's what they do their learning from. They don't learn from the teacher. Anything a child does, which the child feels is a worthwhile activity, you should let him do.'
>
> He pointed out that Julio had been in a traditional classroom for two years and hadn't learned to read 'because he got yelled at every day. My goal for Julio this year is that he should come to like school. He's really a very bright child.'

Here is Julio's account, given at an end-of-day class meeting, of what he had done that day:

'I had a fight with Manuel in the morning and then I had a fight with Luis. Then I went to recess and I had a fight with Roberto. Then I had lunch. Then I came upstairs and I had another fight with Luis, and he hit me in the eye. Then I played house for a while. Then I had a fight with Manuel and that's all.'

Abe laughed and said, 'Mrs. Edmond* would be very angry if she heard you say that was all you did today. Was that *all* you did?' And Julio answered, 'Yes.'

Abe's theory that Julio, though very intelligent, was not 'ready' for any kind of academic learning was a self-fulfilling prophecy, because Abe didn't give him any work. But Julio was only an extreme case. Although Abe subscribed to the belief that there was no distinction between work and play in a child's learning, work and play were sharply dichotomized in his room. The play had little or no cognitive content and the work was confined to his occasional whole-class teaching at class meetings, and to workbooks. Abe adhered rather rigidly to some of the more extreme beliefs often found among free school teachers. Children's errors should never be corrected; they should get only positive feedback concerning their work. The teacher should seldom teach and then only when asked for help. Small group instruction is 'punishing' to the child who must perform in front of his peers. Basic reading and arithmetic skills can best be acquired by the child through experiential processes and through materials.

Abe seemed to have confused the freedom for children he so passionately believed in, with a lack of structure. Children could not find materials because the materials were in disarray. And the children with short attention spans could hardly have been helped by the absence of routine and predictability in the school day. The little learning which took place in Abe's room took place largely by chance.

In justice, we should say that this was only Abe's second year as an open classroom teacher, and he had been assigned his class on such short notice that he had very little time to prepare the environment. When we saw him informally a year later, his account of his class sounded as though he had adopted the 'integrated day' – around building the boat. He was only able to do it, however, by spending a rather large sum of his own money, which he confessed he felt guilty about diverting from his family's needs.

Abe's experiences illustrate the hazards of 'on-the-job' training. Abe did not understand that open classrooms have their own kind of structure. He might have been brought to understand this eventually, with the help of an adviser he respected, but in the meantime, his pupils were paying a price for his inexperience. Some parents who did not think open classroom was going well at Southside pinpointed the on-the-job training of previously unprepared teachers as a problem:

*An assistant principal.

That's one of the things I've been pressing the administration on. Ellen will be leaving shortly. I told them that I would not want to see another on-the-job training. I would want someone who had some previous experience with and practical involvement with OCT, somebody who is already trained to do it.

Finally, we should say that Abe's room was not the most chaotic that could be found in District 7. Natalie assured us that there were some in other schools which were completely out of control. Abe's personal qualities were surely beneficial to his pupils. He was intelligent, warm, and patient. The children loved him and that kept the class in control.

From the standpoint of an open educator, Natalie's classroom was overstructured and Abe's had insufficient structure. Natalie did not have enough 'open-ended' materials in her room. She did not permit the children enough freedom of choice. She did not trust the children to learn to read 'experientially,' but insisted on teaching phonics and comprehension systematically. She refused to adopt the integrated day.

Abe's room on the other hand, didn't have enough structure. Abe took literally those parts of open education philosophy which de-emphasized teaching; he taught very little. Many things were amiss in his room. Neither space nor time was organized so that children could develop stable expectations about their world. His math and science materials were not used because he never suggested to the children how they might begin to use them. The minority children in his class spent their time playing house and dress-up, chasing each other, and fighting. The middle-class children used their readers and workbooks some and played chess. Both groups of children were bored. As one boy said, 'Ain't nothin' to do in this room. We done it all.'

Abe was alone with his twenty-six children most of the time. Given that circumstance, his insistence on one-to-one teaching, when he taught at all, meant he got to each child only a few times a week. Abe believed that nonreaders, of whom he had several, could only learn to read from their own dictated stories. But he had no time to take this dictation, so the nonreaders received no reading instruction. One girl spent 100 percent of her time drawing pictures, undisturbed. A few children made some headway in their books on their own, but others did dozens of pages in their workbooks incorrectly. We did not see how Abe – with his refusal to correct errors – handled this situation, if and when he caught up with it.

Of the two deviations from an ideal open classroom, Abe, who subscribed more closely to open education philosophy, conducted the less desirable classroom. Natalie's children were learning; Abe's were not.

Sources of variability in implementation

These two classrooms illustrate the variability in implementation of open education. One source of these variations is the vagueness of open education philosophy. There are not many clear formulations of it, because its early proponents took the position that all knowledge is idiosyncratic and cannot be communicated. That included knowledge about open education. Others took a position which explicitly promoted variation in practice:

> the 'philosophy' under consideration is one particularly partial to pluralism; it supports flexibility in application and encourages individual interpretation of its tenets. . . . Indeed practitioners are particularly wary of any conceptualization that suggest there is an unchanging or transplantable methodology. . . . In summary it must be asserted that Open Education does *not* operate directly from theory.[4]

The other source of variation is the personalities of the teachers. Natalie's class probably reflected her need to be in control of her room. If this is a basic trait of her character, it might prove impossible for her to allow 'open-ended' learning situations, which would place unpredictable demands on her, to develop. Conversely, Abe, and teachers like him, may find it very hard to be directive and that, too, could be difficult to overcome.

That character traits help determine how teachers play their roles is not a new idea. In one of the first systematic sociological examinations of the school, Willard Waller talked about the link between teachers' personalities and the authority of the teacher's role.[5] Roland Barth made an analogous suggestion about character traits and the role of the open education teacher:

> Open education is attracting many who find the facilitator-of-learning mantle a comfortable cloak under which to hide – a place where they do not have to reveal themselves or be assertive or directive. Many advocates of open education appear not to have resolved their own authority problems and are unwilling to be, if not incapable of being, authorities themselves. Safe under the aegis of the open educator's role, they resist either becoming directive when necessary or probing into their own difficulties with authority; they identify with the children and see themselves as colleagues in the war against the oppressive administration and less-enlightened teachers.[6]

Of course, many organizations which are engaged in changing people, rather than things – such as mental health clinics, prisons, and schools – are subject to nonuniformity in 'treatments' which are supposed to be the same. Nonuniformity occurs because the treatments themselves are usually complex and because both the professional 'treaters' and their subjects, being human, respond differently to the same stimuli.

However, open education is especially vulnerable to nonuniformity in practice. Its philosophy is at once vague and encouraging to individual interpretation. On the important dimension of the teacher's authority, it permits readings which vary from suggesting a fairly teacher-directed room to suggesting one where the teacher has abdicated all directiveness.

An innovation which lacks clear-cut characteristics and a clear-cut rationale eventually lends its name to all manner of practices and loses its identity. Open education is particularly susceptible of being interpreted as 'let the children do what they please.' Abe's classroom came close to that interpretation and so did some rooms in the next school we shall consider. That particular distortion was bound to give open education a bad name – and has.

Innovation in a complex environment

We have recounted in detail the problems faced by two specific innovations which were introduced into Southside. But there are structural reasons why it is difficult to introduce *any* innovation into politico-bureaucratic systems as complex as Walton's school districts. There are many centers of power and authority in the district, and each has some capacity to resist the others. Here are seven examples of such resistance which we have discussed:

1. The first- and second-grade OCT teachers used the OCT advisers to help them get out of the requirement for filling out the district's diagnostic language instrument.
2. The teachers used their rights under the union contract to escape attending individualized reading clinics.
3. The OCT advisers used the implicit threat of expulsion from the program (and probably transfer out of the school) to compel attendance at the meetings they called.
4. The OCT Advisory also used the implicit threat of withdrawal of its services to prevent our entry into another school in the district, after we had obtained permission from all the line authorities as well as the parents' association and Community School Board.
5. The activist parents used their power over personnel to bypass the school administration, and to attack an OCT teacher whose performance they didn't like at an open meeting of teachers, advisers, parents, and administrators.
6. The principal passively resisted the district's Individualized Reading Program. She conformed outwardly at a minimum level, but she did not use sanctions against teachers who openly refused to write individualized curriculum prescriptions.
7. In a nearby school, parents claimed the right to observe and to evaluate teachers up for tenure. The union told the teachers to walk out of the room if a parents' group came to observe them.

With so many centers of influence potentially able to veto policies they don't like, it is far easier to stop an initiative introduced into the system, than it is to start one and keep it going. The district superintendent's attempt to implement a system-wide reading innovation from the top down failed because the principals and teachers were hostile to it and passively resisted it. The district's response to this passive resistance was threats which – given the near unanimity of the negative response – could not possibly be carried out.

OCT was introduced into Southside far more intelligently. The director, Professor Wylie, sought the support of all the major participants. The university-based Advisory gave the teachers access to all its rich resources and provided as well the services of two on-site trainers. Nevertheless, many things went wrong, as we have seen. We were never able to disentangle the contradictory accounts we were given of parental ballots, but – as two of the leading parent activists said – it is hard to believe that all the black and Hispanic parents both voted for OCT and understood what they were voting for. However, these parents largely stayed away from the school and left the field of 'parent power' to the upper middle-class white mothers.

We have detailed the problems which the teachers had with the so-called 'voluntarism' of their participation in OCT and the hostility of the teachers toward the OCT advisers. We saw how a coalition of advisers and parent-activists was formed and used against the teachers. Instead of mutual cooperation among parents, advisers, and school staff, there was conflict between the teachers, on the one hand, and the adviser-parent coalition, on the other. The principal was somewhere in between, but unable to play the traditional role of defending teachers vis-à-vis parents in public because of the power parents had over her. It was also partly because they knew the advisers were close to influential parents that the teachers feared them.

While the OCT teachers at Southside were not precisely 'closely supervised,' they came under the observation of status superiors far more than is typical for elementary school teachers, whose classrooms are usually their castles. The advisers were regularly in the classrooms, and whatever their role was *supposed* to be, they were occasionally judgmental and occasionally pushed hard to get teachers to modify their classroom practices. An example of this was the adviser's attempt to persuade a first-grade teacher to de-emphasize her reading groups and use more 'experiential reading.' The activist parents were also frequently in the classrooms as volunteer helpers. The teachers said they needed and wanted help. But these upper middle-class white mothers were their status superiors, and also had some power in matters of personnel. The frequent presence in their rooms of status superiors, who had some power over their professional careers, made the OCT teachers understandably tense. That was an unintended consequence of OCT implementation procedures.

Given this difficult situation, we must end our account of OCT at

Southside by saying it was remarkable that it was doing so well. Many of the teachers believed strongly in open education philosophy, or parts of it. They used the rich resources of the Advisory at Walton University to keep them supplied with inspiration and new ideas. Of the five classes we observed in grades one, two, and three, all save one were definitely open classrooms, however varied in quality and degree of openness. Due to the genuine commitment of most of the teachers, the innovation had not merely been adopted; it was slowly being implemented.

The facts of this case lead us to infer that the two most important factors in implementing an innovation in elementary school are real commitment from the teachers, and access by them to an adequate support system. For Southside, the on-site advisers did not supply that support system, but the Walton University Advisory did.

Notes

1 Herbert Walberg and Susan Thomas, 'Open Education: An Operational Definition and Validation in Great Britain and the United States,' *American Education Research Journal* 9 (1972): 197–202.
2 Many of the minority children [at Southside] school came from families which were upwardly mobile. It was the principal who first pointed this out to us.
3 Science Research Associates.
4 Charles H. Rathbone, 'Open Education and the Teacher' (Ph. D. diss., Harvard Graduate School of Education, Harvard University, 1970), pp. 58–9.
5 Willard Waller, *The Sociology of Teaching* (New York: John Wiley and Sons, Inc., 1965). This book was first published in 1932.
6 Roland Barth, *Open Education and the American School* (New York: Agathon Press, 1972), pp. 143–4.

1.3

Teaching and learning as the creation of meanings†

Tony Edwards and John Furlong

1 Classroom knowledge and the reciprocity of perspectives

When we engage in some form of social interaction, like a conversation, we assume that the situation we face means the same to us as to the person (or persons) we are talking to. We assume that we both draw on the same body of commonsense knowledge to interpret what the other says and does. Yet, because we are all individuals with different biographies and possibly separate interests, we may well have different perspectives on the situation at hand. But if we are to maintain social interaction, we will either have to gloss over or suspend these differences, or else establish new meanings we both can accept.[1] What the Humanities teachers were doing in the first weeks of the autumn term was explicitly establishing a common sense of classroom organization.[. . .] Their organizational talk subsumed within it, and was dependent for its comprehensibility on, this common relationship knowledge. After the first few weeks a reciprocity of perspectives about classroom organization was assumed too, and as long as that assumption was maintained, explicit references to procedure largely disappeared from the transcripts. That too could become part of the background knowledge participants were assumed to fill in appropriately when they engaged in curriculum talk.

Despite the fact that teachers and pupils assume a reciprocity of perspectives when talking about organizational and disciplinary work, they both assume that filling in the right meanings is a problem when it comes to the material to be learned. In this chapter we will show that teachers assume that pupils will not know what material means until they have been taught – until, for example, they have had a lead

† Source: A. D. Edwards and V. J. Furlong, *The Language of Teaching* (1978), London, Heinemann, pp. 103–12.

lesson, or been told what to look out for in the booklets. Pupils are likely to assume this too, and until they have been taught they suspend anything they already know about the subject matter. They must accept that they are 'ignorant' until they have taken over the teacher's system of meanings.[2]

In any piece of social interaction, it may become apparent that the participants do not have a reciprocity of perspectives. In the course of conversation, they may become aware that each means something different by a key term. If the difference is too obtrusive, it becomes a stumbling-block to the conversation; they must give their attention to it, and either establish a working definition or else change the subject. In talk between equals, neither has the right to insist on *his* definition or the obligation to wait for a ruling. But in most classrooms, academic meanings are the province of the teacher. The pupil will normally suspend any knowledge he has about the subject until he has found out the teacher's frame of reference, and moved (or appeared to move) into it. For the academic curriculum to proceed, a reciprocity of meanings has to be established. But in the unequal relationship between most teachers and pupils, the movement is nearly always in one direction; the pupil has to step into the teacher's system of meanings and leave them relatively undisturbed.[3] Being taught usually means suspending your own interpretations of the subject matter and searching out what the teacher means. Thus the very process of learning demonstrates and maintains the authority relationship, because the pupil is nearly always attempting to move into the teacher's world of meanings. The pupil's suspension of his own interpretation may be so complete that if he cannot understand what the material means to the teacher, then it becomes literally meaningless for himself.

The following extract illustrates this point. A boy was stuck on the question, 'Why do you think the Abraham Moss Centre is called a community centre?', and called the teacher over to help him.

T: Well, Abraham Moss is a community centre, isn't it? Now why do people come here?

P: To work.

T: What else? Not only – I mean, you come to work, yeah, but there are other things as well.

P: Help.

T: To get help, yes. OK. What else?

P: ((Silence.))

T: Name some other parts of the Centre.

P: ((Mumbles.))

T: Pardon?

P: The gym.

Here the pupil is having difficulty answering questions about the very place in which he has spent a large part of his life for some months past. He must have extensive knowledge about the Centre. But in this context, he sets this knowledge aside and tries to search out the particular meanings which the teacher is after. The suspension of his own knowledge is so complete that he gives only monosyllabic replies – which he hopes, perhaps, can be slotted into whatever the teacher has in mind – and eventually falls into silence. As so often when there is something to be learned, teacher and pupil do not assume a reciprocity of perspectives. They do not assume that the material or the question means the same to them, and that the pupil will therefore be able to fill in the 'right' background meanings. The same meaning has to be *achieved*, and in most teaching this involves moving towards whatever the teacher will accept and validate.

It is possible, however, to look at this pupil's difficulty in a different way. Rather than setting aside his existing knowledge, he is perhaps being faced with a new situation. His silence might be because he has never before had to think about *why* people come to the Centre; this has not been a problem for him. This would frequently be the case with more technical subjects, when pupils are confronting new knowledge on matters which are initially meaningless to them. But even when they are on more familiar ground, a persistent boundary between classroom knowledge and everyday knowledge may lead them to search out meanings in line with what the teacher wants rather than to look to themselves and their own past experience, which might throw some light on the topic.[4] As we will argue in more detail later, the novelty of the task confronting them may not be that the content is new, but that it has to be formulated in unusual ways or with unusual explicitness. As in the example already cited, they may also be required to consider as a problem something that they had previously taken for granted. In either case, they will have to work, in order to generate the same framework of meanings as the teacher has.

The ways in which pupils move into the teacher's system of meanings can be illustrated by looking in detail at the following example. A boy had got stuck on the question, 'Work out using the scale how wide the island is to the nearest mile', and had called the teacher over to him for help. The question involved looking at a map reproduced in the booklet, referring to a scale marked out in miles and kilometres, and then measuring the island.

T:	You know what a scale is?
P:	Sir, yeah.
T:	Right. (Points to the scale.) What's that letter there?
P:	One.
T:	That letter?
P:	Two.
T:	Have you measured the distance between them?
P:	Sir, yeah.
T:	And how far is it?
P:	Sir, one centimetre.

T: No. What's the distance between one and two on the scale?
P: Sir, in miles?
T: Yeah.
P: Sir, a mile.
T: No. What's the distance on the ruler?
P: Twenty millimetres.
T: What's that – convert twenty millimetres into centimetres.
P: Ten centimetres.
T: *Two* centimetres. Look, turn that (*the ruler*) round. It's *two* centimetres, right. So one mile equals how far?
P: Er, two centimetres.
T: Can you work out the distance?
P: Yes, sir.
T: What's the scale again?
P: Er, two centimetres to every mile.
T: Right, one mile equals. . . ?
P: Two centimetres.
T: And then you can work it out?
P: Yeah.
T: Get it right. Do it slow and get it right. (Teacher moves off.)

Here we can suggest that while the pupil may have come across the notion of a scale before, he recognizes that he does not know how to work out this particular question. He does not know what it is supposed to mean. At the end of the sequence we assume, as does the teacher, that the pupil has a new perspective on what the question wants. By following the teacher through a series of operations, he has come to see it in a new light; he now understands what is involved, because he apparently sees it in the way the teacher does. In this process of moving to the teacher's meaning, he offers possible answers of his own but is willing to abandon these if they are not confirmed. His first answer to the question about the distance between the two points – 'Sir, one centimetre' – would have been settled on as *the* answer if it had been confirmed. But it is wrong, and he has to try again. To narrow the area of search, the teacher asks a different question which implicitly provides a clue.

T: No. What's the distance between one and two on the scale?
P: Sir, in miles?

The pupil seems to recognize that he is not 'with' the teacher, and so makes suggestions which force the teacher to do more of the work. Further tentative answers are offered, which again are not confirmed.[5] In the end, the teacher has to *tell* him, but he does not tell him the answer. Rather, he leads him to the edge of it. Through the interaction, by suggesting possible meanings and then abandoning these as they are seen to be wrong, the pupil has come to see the question more in the way it was intended in the booklet – he has entered into the teacher's framework of meanings.

What we want to suggest is that this process of moving pupils towards the teacher's meanings, and maintaining them there, is at the heart of most teaching. Even in the more open environment being developed at Abraham Moss, pupils still have to suspend their own meanings and generate new ones in line with those implied by the teacher. This is not to say that some teaching technologies are not more efficient, and more flexible, than others. But essentially the same process is taking place. It involves pupils in producing tentative suggestions which may then be abandoned or locked in in the light of further clues from the teacher.

To present this view so bluntly is to risk diminishing the quality of much of the teaching we observed, and we return in the next chapter to its superiority to traditional teaching even within the framework of knowledge transmission, and to the considerable diversity of methods employed. It also risks making that process look altogether too easy. We therefore turn at this point to consider some of the major problems involved.

2 From difficulties to problems

As experts, teachers have specialist meanings for the material that they teach, and learning involves the pupils' generating the same specialist interpretive frames. By interacting with teachers and with the written content of the curriculum pupils have to learn to interpret different aspects of their environment as physics, maths, music, or in this case humanities.[6] But if pupils are to learn, if they are to take over and use these specialist meanings, they cannot be simply transmitted. Pupils have to build up or generate the same meanings from the evidence provided in the textbook or from what the teacher says. As we saw in the last example, if the pupil finds his proposed interpretation wrong, if it does not fit the facts as defined by the teacher, he abandons it and attempts to generate a new framework.

This process of generating specialist meanings from evidence provided by the teacher is at the heart of most academic learning, but for most of the time it is hidden from view. [. . .]

How much of what teachers say is being understood, or is already understood, by their pupils? How much pupil knowledge is already within the appropriate frame of reference, and how much new knowledge is being taken? In normal class teaching, finding the answers to these questions is a haphazard business. A few pupils answer questions; and this can give the impression that everyone understands. It is not until the teacher looks at the pupils' written work that he discovers how much of his cherished exposition went over the heads of many of his class. To overcome this difficulty, teachers employ a number of evidential procedures to find out if the class is following them. They may ask questions, or simply monitor pupils' looks and glances to see how much attention they are paying. But this is often doubtful evidence. As John Holt suggests, pupils are highly skilled at hiding the fact that they do not understand.

In resource-based learning, the evidential procedures can be more intensive. Largely released from the role of teller, the teacher has far more time for problem-solving. Indeed, this becomes his major function. He deals with a barrage of questions – some procedural, some to do with equipment and resources, and others to do with the substantive content of the lesson. Most of these contacts are initiated by pupils, though in his quieter moments the teacher himself initiates contacts with pupils whom he has not seen for a while or who do not seem to be working well. The demands on his time make it necessary to assume that if there is no pressing evidence of problems, then the children are working satisfactorily and understanding what they are doing. This assumption was put into words in an early lesson with first-year pupils. The group were asked if they had any problems in 'getting on'. Only four children put up their hands. After a pause, the teacher said, 'Now does that mean that everybody else except Peter, Paul, Abdul, and Shirley can carry on? (Pause.) Right.' He was asking them if *not* putting up their hands meant what he took it to mean, and he took their silence as evidence that they could indeed 'carry on'.

This notion of evidence is important in understanding how the teacher diagnoses the problems of pupils who do come up to him. His first task is to find out where the pupil is, what his precise difficulties are. He has to build up some conception of a problem, and this process of formulation, of making a problem from the pupil's less specific difficulty, is an integral part of providing a solution. We have argued that pupils frequently suspend any meanings which classroom topics may have had for them in the past, and search out the way the teacher sees it. The initial statement of the difficulties being encountered may be very non-specific. For example, this pupil was working on a question about the concept of community:

P: Sir, about the people.
T: What about the people?
P: They all work together?
T: Of course, a group of people all living and working together in the same area – so a community is what, then?

The teacher quickly builds up some notion of what problem the pupil has. The pupil's first utterance is highly ambiguous, even to the teacher, and he is asked to expand it. When he does so, the teacher assumes that he now understands what the difficulty is, and he elaborates, 'They all work together?' into 'a group of people living and working in the same area'.[7] This elaboration of the pupil's statement has introduced two new features of a community: that it involves *living* as well as working together, and that it involves people doing these things in the *same area*. So we can assume that the teacher has engaged in a documentary process by fitting the pupil's initial ambiguous utterance into some category of normal difficulties about what communities are. Since he gets no counter-evidence from the pupil that he is wrong in his assumption that this is where the problem lies, he goes on to integrate the pupil's expanded utterance into this new 'telling'. In a sense he has defined and solved his own problem.

In this section, the teacher seems to be acting as a kind of detective. He integrates his evidence of the pupil's difficulty into some form of normal problem, but, of course, as each case is unique he is creating or at least extending his notion of what a normal problem is at the same time. In this lesson the teacher had already established an idea that normal problems related to the concept of community. The course material was directed to developing an understanding of it, and one of the set questions was explicitly concerned with it. In the course of the lesson, a number of other pupils appeared to have similar difficulties. The teacher therefore quickly recognized their problems. In medical parlance, it was the most available diagnosis of trouble because there was a lot of it about.

The context (in this case the study of communities) therefore determined how the teacher heard the pupil's query and how he constructed a problem from it; it provided him with a theme around which to document the pupil's initial rather confused statement. In the early lessons with new pupils, queries were often heard as indicating that they did not understand how work was to be organized. An ambiguous question like 'Sir, what do we do there?' was likely to be heard not as a question about the content of the lesson but as a question about how to use the booklets. On this occasion, the teacher's reply was, 'There, you read through it again and find out what happened when the earth was made.' As pupils became more accustomed to working independently teachers were more likely to assume that they knew about working procedures, and the 'same' question would be heard as an indication of some semantic difficulty.

A more persistently normal problem related to difficulties with reading. For example:

> *T:* How do you find the reading in that one, John?
> *P:* All right.
> *T:* What's the answer to the first question, then?
> *P:* Tristan lies to the south of the equator.
> *T:* Good.

On this occasion the teacher suspended his judgement about whether the boy could cope with the reading until he had heard some evidence. He then took the fact that the boy could answer the question correctly as an indication that, at least for the moment, he could indeed cope. The teacher had established that one sort of normal problem – in general, and for this boy in particular – was difficulty with reading. This was a main criterion for distinguishing between pupils and the level of work that they could cope with.

In suggesting that teachers often seemed to type pupils in terms of their ability to read, we do not want to underestimate the complexity of their understanding.[8] One advantage of the resource-based method of instruction is that teachers have the time to interact with individual children, and there is more opportunity for each to see the other as a person.[9] Nevertheless, reading ability is obviously critical to the successful operation of this method of teaching. In the context of a wide range of more general abilities and a heavy emphasis on pupils working on their own, reading is *the* strategic skill. The teachers were constantly having to monitor how well pupils were coping with the booklets, and reading skills therefore became a central feature in getting to know them and in comparing one with another. As we have seen, they were also the basis for producing several levels of curriculum material. 'Difficulties with reading' was therefore one of the most readily available definitions of a normal problem in these classrooms, for it was one that all the teachers explicitly recognized and talked about and it was central to the success of their teaching.

We do not want to give the impression that these normal or typical problems were hard-and-fast categories into which pupils' difficulties could be slotted. In fact, the contrary is the case. In the first place, teachers had to create an understanding of what normal problems were likely to be and extend and refine their notions in order to incorporate each individual *instance* that they met.[10] Some of these patterns came to be seen as persistent and general, like difficulties with reading, and teachers became quite expert at identifying them.[11] The more often they came across a problem the more concrete the category became, but they would still have actively to interpret each case as an example of their normal problem and perhaps extend their idea of what, for example, a reading difficulty was so that it included this particular case.[12] Other problems, like the child below who often asked silly questions, were more difficult to understand and as the teacher explained he always had a problem himself in deciding what the pupil really meant. He was asked, 'How would you know if Nicholas was asking a *serious* question?'

T: It would depend on how he had been before he asked it. Because I do think that at times you know he wants to waste time and I'm not quite sure what reasons guide him, but he does like to attract a certain sort of attention to himself at times, whereas Stephen doesn't, and I have confidence, if you like, in Stephen's genuine inquiry, while Nicholas *may* be inquiring genuinely, but because of his past history I simply wouldn't know, so I think I'd go very much on what had happened in the lesson so far and perhaps his whole approach to me about it as well.

Stephen's seriousness provided a relatively constant context for interaction with the teacher, whereas encounters with Nicholas depended more on improvization and on *ad hoc* interpretations of his intent. The teacher often had difficulty therefore in understanding what Nicholas' questions meant. He found difficulty in creating a normal problem from what the boy said, and had to look carefully at the whole context of his behaviour to decide whether he was being serious or silly. In understanding, then, what pupils' problems were, the teachers had to look for evidence, using their spoken and written statements to create some form of pattern. Some of these patterns came to be seen as both persistent and general, like difficulties with reading. Some related to particular pupils – those, for example, who were lazy or who often asked silly questions. Some changed over time, with the diminishing difficulties of procedures of work. Other problems were generated by the course material currently in use, and here the teacher would have to use his knowledge of the learning which should be taking place to build up his picture of what the difficulty was. As we will see, this formulation of non-specific difficulties into specific problems is central to the process of solving those problems. . . .

Notes and references

1 Cicourel *et al.* (1974), *Language Use and School Performance*, London, Academic Press. Cicourel notes: 'The basic issue here is that the participants must assume they are oriented to the "same" environment of objects despite cultural differences . . . If participants cannot make this assumption . . . then their interaction will become difficult at best' (p. 303).
2 The idea of a situationally embedded ignorance is not a new one and of course it is not *always* accepted by the pupils. Keddie (1971), 'Classroom Knowledge', in M. F. D. Young (ed.), *Knowledge and Control*, London, Collier-Macmillan, showed how some middle-class children more readily accepted that they were 'ignorant' than working-class children.
3 Cooper (1976), *Bernstein's Codes: A Classroom Study*, University of Sussex Education Area: Occasional Paper No 6, p. 15.
4 Barnes (1976), *From Communication to Curriculum*, Harmondsworth, Penguin Books. Barnes has recently pointed out how little opportunity there is in most classrooms for pupils to relate their own out of school knowledge to the curriculum.
5 There are parallels here with experiments described by Garfinkel (1967), *Studies in Ethnomethodology*, Englewood Cliffs, N. J., Prentice-Hall, where students were put in deliberately unusual situations. Like these pupils, Garfinkel's students would propose tentative interpretations of their situation and abandon them or lock in on them as *the* meaning of what was going on, depending on whether or not they were confirmed by what happened later.
6 For a discussion of teachers' control over what is to count as legitimate

school knowledge, see Whitty and Young (1976), *Explorations in the Politics of School Knowledge*, Driffield, Nafferton Books.

7 Turner (1972), 'Some Formal Properties of Therapy Talk', in Sudnow, *Studies in Interaction*, New York, Free Press. There is a parallel here with Turner's description of group therapy sessions where the lay member is expected to offer a layman's version of his trouble and the expert transforms it into the language of the expertise involved (pp. 385–6).

8 For a sensitive analysis of how teachers type pupils see Hargreaves, Hestor, and Mellor (1976), *Deviance in Classrooms*, London, Routledge & Kegan Paul.

9 Walker and Adelman (1972), *Towards a Sociography of Classrooms*, SSRC report, Centre for Science Education, Chelsea College, make a similar point.

10 Mehan (1974), 'Accomplishing Classroom Lessons', in Cicourel *et al.*, *Language Use and School Performance*, London, Academic Press. Mehan also describes the considerable degree of improvization contained in teachers' normal form definitions.

11 An analogy can be drawn here with Sudnow's (1965) account of a defending lawyer. The lawyer would interrupt his client as soon as he felt he had enough information to 'confirm his sense of the case's typicality'. (Sudnow, 'Normal Crimes', *Social Problems* 12.)

12 Any two instances of reading difficulties are essentially different and seeing them as the same thing demands that we provide *ad hoc* grounds for their similarity. Garfinkel (1967), op. cit., shows that it is by this process of selectively viewing and continually reinterpreting and re-analysing events that we *create* the stable world that we think we inhabit.

Part two
Pupils' perspectives

2.1

Delinquents in schools: a test for the legitimacy of authority†[1]

Carl Werthman

In the recent sociology on juvenile delinquents, the school is character-
ized as the major instrument and arena of villainy. Cloward and Ohlin
suggest that lower-class delinquents suffer from unequal '*access* to
educational facilities',[2] Cohen points to their '*failures* in the classroom',[3]
and Miller and Kvaraceus argue that a '*conflict* of culture' between
school administrators and lower-class students is precipitating delinquent behavior.[4] Although there are many differences between contemporary sociological portraits of the lower-class juvenile delinquent, the
same model of his educational problem is used by all authors. Regardless of whether the delinquent is ambitious and capable,[5] ambitious and
incapable,[6] or unambitious and incapable,[7] the school is sketched as a
monolith of middle-class personnel against which he fares badly.

Yet data collected by observation and interviews over a two-year
period on the educational performances and classroom experiences of
lower-class gang members suggest that pitting middle-class schools
against variations in the motivation and capacity of some lower-class
boys is at best too simple and at worst incorrect as a model of the
problems faced by the delinquents.

First, during middle adolescence when the law requires gang
members to attend school, there seems to be no relationship between
academic performance and 'trouble'. Gangs contain bright boys who
do well, bright boys who do less well, dull boys who pass, dull boys
who fail, and illiterates. To cite a single example, the grades of thirty
'core' members of a Negro gang, the Conquerors, were equally distributed in the sophomore and junior years of high school. Four of the
gang members are illiterate (they cannot read, write, or spell the names

† Source: *Berkeley Journal of Sociology* (1963), vol. 8 (1), pp. 39–60.

of the streets they live on); twelve consistently receive Ds and Fs on their report cards; and fourteen consistently receive Cs or better. Four are on the honor roll. Yet all thirty were suspended at least once a semester during the tenth and eleventh grades, and the average number of suspensions received per semester was above two. There was a general tendency for the illiterate and dull boys to get into more trouble than the better students, but none of them was immune from difficulty. Twenty-two of these thirty regular members spent some time in jail during this period. Differences in access, success, and failure thus did not seem to have a determinate effect on 'trouble' in school – at least among the Conquerors.

Second, difficulties occur only in some classes and not others. Good and bad students alike are consistently able to get through half or more of their classes without friction. It is only in particular classes with particular teachers that incidents leading to suspension flare up. This suggests that schools are not as monolithic as most contemporary sociologists have argued. Moreover, it suggests that something more specific about teachers than being 'middle class' produces problems, just as something more specific than being 'lower class' about gang members produces the response.

The problem

For events in high school classrooms to proceed smoothly, students must grant teachers some measure of authority. Although teachers are in a position to overlook a great deal of extra-curricular student activity in classrooms, they cannot ignore everything. Some modicum of order must be maintained if anything resembling a process of education is to take place. Most teachers thus find themselves in the position of having to act on definitions of improper behavior and hope that students will stop. The authority of teachers is put to a test in this act of communication.

Authority becomes a stable basis for interaction only when those to whom commands are issued voluntarily obey.[8] Students in classrooms, like all parties judging claims to authority made by others, must therefore decide whether treatments received at the hands of teachers are based on grounds that can be considered legitimate.

Most students accept the authority of teachers to pass judgment on practically all behavior that takes place in classrooms. The teacher is seen as a person who can pay legitimate official attention to everything that happens inside the physical confines of a school plant.[9] Since the authority of teachers is accepted at face value, most students can make sense of the specific actions teachers take towards them. Any specific action is interpreted as an instance in which this general rule is being applied.

This is why, for example, most students do not question the grades they receive. They accept the norm that teachers have the authority to grade them. This authority is more or less traditional. A report card signed by the teacher is accepted on much the same basis as are proclamations of war signed by kings. Neither are required by their subjects to give strict accounts of the decisions they make because the prerogative to make them has been granted in advance of the act.

Gang members understand the treatments they receive in no such way. They do not *a priori* accept the authority of any teacher. Final judgment on the conferral of legitimacy is suspended until it is discovered whether or not authority is being exercised on suitable grounds and in a suitable way. The burden of proof lies with the teacher.

Since teachers exercise authority in a variety of ways, becoming a 'delinquent' depends in large measure on whether these various claims are accepted. This is why gang members are frequently 'delinquent' in one class and ordinary students in the adjoining room. This paper analyses accounts of classroom situations in which gang members received unacceptable treatments, refused to recognize the authority of teachers, and were labelled 'delinquent'. These accounts are compared to classroom situations in which the treatments received were considered soundly based, the authority of teachers was accepted, and gang members remained ordinary students.[10]

Gang members make decisions to accept or reject the authority of teachers on the basis of four criteria. First, they evaluate the jurisdictional claims made by teachers. Some teachers not only insist on the physical presence of students but also expect a measure of intellectual and spiritual 'attention' as well. These teachers frequently take issue with behavior such as sleeping on desks, reading comic books, talking to neighbors, passing notes, gazing out of the window, turning around in chairs, chewing gum, and eating peanuts. Gang members do not *a priori* grant teachers the right to punish this behavior although good reasons for ceasing these activities are often accepted.

Second, under no conditions can race, dress, hair styles, and mental capacities receive legitimate official attention. Failures on the part of teachers to accept these rules of irrelevance often contribute to denial of authority.[11]

Third, gang members are extremely sensitive to the style in which authority is exercised. The frequent and consistent use of the imperative is perceived as an insult to the status and autonomy of those to whom this form of address is directed. Teachers who 'request' conformity are more likely to achieve desired results.

Ultimately, however, the decision to accept or reject the authority of teachers is made on the basis of a weightier concern. Teachers who consistently violate conceptions of proper jurisdiction, irrelevance rules, and modes of address will not find gang members particularly co-operative architects of authority. But the grounds on which teachers make their formal and semi-public evaluations of students tell a more important tale. Grades can be based on a number of criteria, not all of which gang members find legitimate. Moreover, the fact that they get a grade tells them nothing about the basis on which the judgment was made. They must discover the general rule used by particular teachers to assign grades with only a single application of the rule to go on.

Gang members thus find themselves in a rather serious bind. They *must* figure out the general basis on which teachers are assigning grades because their future behavior depends on what they discover. They cannot walk away from the claims made by teachers to possess authority.

Hypotheses

Their task, however, is not hopeless. Gang members do know *something* about the basis on which a grade might have been assigned. In fact, given what they know about their situation, they reduce the rules teachers might be using to four.

First, the grades might be given out fairly. Although as a rule gang members have no idea how much knowledge they possess relative to other students, they have a general idea of how 'smart' they are relative to others. They judge the intelligence of the boys and girls they know personally, and they estimate the intelligence of strangers from the contributions they make in class. They thus generate a set of expected frequencies on the basis of the hypothesis that bright boys will do better than dull boys.

(Is there any relationship between getting into trouble in school and getting good grades?) Naw. Take like Charles. He in my classes. He bad outside, and he doing well in school. There ain't no difference. Let's put it like this. Friday, Saturday, Sunday, that's the nights for fucking, drinking, driving, fighting, killing, doing the shit you want to do. There's a lot of guys like Charles in my classes that gets A's on their report cards in school, but when they on the outside, the hell, they bad! They crazy! Dice, drink, shoot people. (How about the ex-President of the Club? How does he do in your classes?) Johnny's smart. Johnny's got a good brain. He doing good. Everytime I see Johnny, he always got his books. He goes to the bathroom – smokes cigarettes and shoots dice like all of us – but you don't see that man cutting no classes. I swear to God, I think he really got a swell mental brain. (How about the rest of the club?) It just that some people lazier than others. Just like Donald. He in my classes. I ain't got no more brains than that man. I may know a little more than he do from the past things, but as far as that class is related and all, I don't know no more than him. The class is just as new to me as it is to him. Now if I can pass that class, he can pass that class. He didn't pass this time. He flunked. He got a F. He got a F in all his classes. I passes those classes with flying colors,

with a C. That's average. I always get average grades. I don't look
for no A's and B's. (Do you think you could get A's if you tried?)
I doubt it. I don't see racking my brains to death to get no A on
no paper. Cause I feel like a A ain't nothing. A C will get you just
as far. I mean truthfully I think the highest grade I could ever get
was a D. (How about Carson?) He's not smart. He dumb. I mean
he goofy. He just ain't got it up here, period. We gonna get kicked
out. (What for?) Fighting, gamblin, cutting classes, nasty attitude.
(How about the guys who don't get in trouble. How do do they
do?) Just like us. Some of them smart, some of them stupid. I mean
there's a couple dudes in my classes that's born to be somebody,
people with straight A's like Johnny, and then there's the real stupid
ones. They just sit there all quiet, get to class on time, never gamble,
smoke or nothing and they flunk. You might say we got smart ones
and they got smart ones just like we got average ones and they got
average ones and we got dumb ones and they got dumb ones.
Everybody born on this earth ain't got the same brains.

Second, their response to the presumed authority of the teacher may
enter into the grade they receive. They are conscious that the grade is
a source of power, and they understand that it may be used as a weapon
against them. When teachers use grades as sanctions in this way, gang
members perceive it as discrimination. On the basis of the behavior
observed in class, gang members divide their fellow students into those
who *a priori* take as legitimate the claims to authority made by teachers
and those who do not. (As a rule, the latter category is filled with
friends.) Expected frequences are thus generated under this condition
also. The distinction between scientists and sell-outs lies at the heart of
what gang members consider the essential difference between their kind
of person and 'squares'.

There's some teachers that treats everybody differently. He always
get wise with the studs that ain't gonna take no shit, and they real
nice to the people that just sit there, the people that kiss ass behind
him. He give the good grades to the ass-kissers and he give us bad
grades cause we ain't gonna suck up to him. (Are there many kids
in class who kiss up to teachers?) Yeah. There's enough. Like this
one girl, she's kiss behind everybody, and the President of the
school! He'll eat you if you ask him to! The bad teachers give the
kiss-asses good grades and make us eat shit. They always looking
for the ones that run errands, shit like that. (What kind of people
are the ass-kissers? Do they wear any special kind of clothes?) Some
of them come looking like a farmer or something. Jeans. Or maybe
they wear a tie or something. They not like us. We come to have a
good time in school as well as sometimes learn something. Some of
those boys don't even enjoy parties and things like that. They allergic
to girls. They just poopbutts.

The third dimension that may affect a grade is the amount of power possessed by particular students. The sources of this power stem from the possibilities of physical assault on teachers and an ability to keep a class in constant turmoil. Delinquents thus hypothesize that teachers may award grades on this basis. The boys define this possibility as 'bribery'.

(Are there any teachers who give you good grades because they are afraid of you?) Yeah. Like Mr F. He say, 'Aw, come on, why don't you go give us a break or something.' And all the lady teachers, I won't let them go with nothing. Like these teachers say, 'You do me a favor and I do you one. You straighten up in class and I'll make your grade better.' Shit like that. If you control that class, you gonna get a good grade. They afraid of you or they want you to stop fucking up the class. I control a lot of those classes. (What do you do when the teacher tries to make a deal with you?) I don't take shit. That way they gotta keep giving me a good grade. They try to con me, but I ain't going for it. Like that stud that kicked me out of class yesterday? He tell me, 'Come on, why don't you be a good guy? I'll give you a good grade if you be quiet. Why don't you go on and give me a break?' I said, 'I sure will, right on your neck!' When you get a good grade, sometimes you know the teacher is afraid of you. That's why he give it to you.

The final alternative is that grades are randomly distributed. This is a distinct possibility in large classes such as gym where teachers cannot possibly interact personally with all participants. Some students become visible of course, either as athletes, delinquents, or 'flunkies'. But it is quite possible for a particular boy to be graded on the basis of the way his name happens to strike the teacher when he sees it printed on the report card.

When I think I deserve a C and I get a D? That's when I'm gonna bitch. I'm really gonna have something to say about it. Cause when I feel like I got a better grade? And get something lower? I feel like that teacher either prejudiced or he just, you know, he just don't give a damn. He just go down, read your name and everybodies' name, and go A, B, C, – A, B, C. He get to a special name. 'Well, I don't like this fellow, I'll give him a C. I don't like him. I'll give him a D.' You know, so on and so on. Shit. That's like they do in gym, seem like to me. Every damn time it seem like my report card came up to be a C. I don't mind a C if I have to get it, but I seen the gym teacher, you know, in the office. They have a whole stack of report cards. Now how a gym teacher gonna look at your name and go straight down the line, just put a grade on? Like he going, A, B, C, – A, B, C, – A, B, C. And he just throw them away! And if he run across a name he know real good? Somebody that, you know, real tight with him? Go out for all the sports? You know, he flunky for him. Work around the gym. Shit like that. You know you gonna give him a B or something. Somebody that deserve a B, he gonna give a C or D. All kinda shit like that.

Thus before grades are handed down, gang members construct four alternative hypotheses or rules about the basis on which teachers evaluate them. Given what they know about the student population being graded, they make predictions about how fellow class members will be marked under three of the four alternative conditions. They know that the grade they receive will be a single case of one of these four classes of rules, but the single grade they receive will not tell them *which* rule the teacher is using. Their problem is to discover it.

Methods

As soon as the grade is handed down, gang members behave like good social scientists. They draw a sample, ask it questions, and compare the results with those predicted under alternative hypotheses. The unit of analysis is a *set* of relevant grades. The one received by a particular student is only a single member. No interpretation of a grade can be made before the others are looked at.

The sample is not selected randomly from the class. The class contains types of students constructed from the knowledge on which the predictions were based. Gang members thus divide the class into four basic sub-groups: bright students who recognize the authority of teachers; duller students who recognize the authority of teachers; bright students withholding judgment about teachers; and dull students withholding judgment about teachers. The latter two types are like himself. They are his friends. If the gang member conducting the inquiry possesses power, this dimension will also be of concern.

As soon as the grades are delivered to the students in class, representatives of all types are sampled. First, gang members typically ask their friends what they received, and then others in the rest of the class are interviewed. Most of the 'poopbutts', 'sissies' or 'squares' will usually show a gang member their report card. Refusals to reveal grades are often dealt with sharply.

(How do you know how the teacher is grading you?) Sometimes you don't man. You don't know whether the stud bribing you with a grade, whether he giving you a bad one cause you don't kiss behind him, or whether he straight. Or maybe he like the gym teachers that give out the grades any which way. (But how do you find out what basis the teacher is using?) Well, you gotta ask around the class. Find out what other kids got. Like when I get my report card? I shoot out and ask my partners what they got. Then I go ask the poopbutts what they got. (Do they always let you look at their report cards?) They can't do nothing but go for it. Like they got to go home

sometime. I mean we shoot them with a left and a right if they don't
come across. I mean this grade shit is important. You gotta know
what's happening. (Why?) Well, shit, how you gonna know what
the teacher like? I mean if he straight or not.

After the grades have been collected, the process of analysing data
begins. Final conclusions can be reached at this point, however, only
if the teacher has previously provided an account of the grounds being
used to grade. Some teachers voluntarily provide these accounts and
others do not. Although there is considerable variation in this behavior
among teachers, the variation is not random. Teachers who believe that
their authority in the classroom should be accepted *a priori* are less
likely to volunteer the basis on which they judge students. In fact they
are less likely to offer explanations of any action they take. Claims to
authority are often demonstrated by not having to account for all
decisions made.

On the other hand, some teachers are careful to make visible at all
times the basis on which they grade. These teachers understand that
they have certain students who will not accept authority in advance of
proof that it is being legitimately exercised.

(What made this teacher fair?) He'd give the class an equal chance
to be graded. Like he'd say, 'How'd you like to be graded on this?
Class average, individual, or what?' And you know, let's say half
the class want to be graded on class average and the other half on
individual. He just take the group out like that, you know, and he
would grade you as such if that's the way you want to be graded.
I mean I felt that the teacher real fair. See, after the first report
card, after he see the grades wasn't too good? He asked us how we
would like him to grade, and what we would like him to do. (The
grades from the first report weren't very good?) No, they weren't
so hot. Cause, you know, he wanted to see how his approach did
and how we would react to it. Anyway, the results wasn't so hot.
Anyway, he gave us a choice. So I felt that was helping them,
helping me, and that he seemed fair.

In addition, teachers who attempt to bribe certain students will also
signal the basis on which they behave in advance of the grade. If a
gang member receives a better grade than the one he expected relative
to other students, he suspects a 'con'. He thus reviews his previous
relationship with the teacher. If the teacher has offered him a good
grade in return for good behavior, he has sufficient grounds to conclude
that the grade he received was based on his power to control the class.

(How do you know when you get a good grade whether you deserved
it or whether the teacher is trying to buy you off?) When they tell
you personally. You know, we was in the class by ourself when they
told me I could get a good grade if I stop being a troublemaker.
Like Mrs C. Like in class she told the whole class, 'If you be quiet

you get a good grade!' You know, everybody get a C or something on their report card. But she told me privately, I guess maybe cause I was such a troublemaker. When I see what everybody else got? And I see that they all fail or get something else? I know I got the grade cause I control the class.

Similarly, if the teacher has recently left him alone in class regardless of what he has done, he concludes that the teacher is afraid of him. In this case also he thinks that the teacher is trying to buy control.

(How do you know when you get a good grade because the teacher is afraid of you?) After you ask around the class, you know, you see everybody that shoulda done bad done bad and shit like that. And you got a good grade? Well, sometimes that teacher just leave you alone. I mean you be talking and everything and they won't say nothing. Then you know he afraid of you and he afraid you'll fire on him [slug him] if you get a bad grade.

If teachers provide the rules used to grade students in advance of the grading period, regardless of whether they are using fair criteria, bribing, or discriminating, gang members do not need to request information in order to find out what is going on. As soon as they receive their grade and compare it to others, they 'know what's happening'.

But if gang members need more information to discover the rule being used and it has not been provided in advance of the marking period, they will go to the teacher and ask for an account of the grade they received. This event typically takes place a day or two after report cards have been handed out.

If a gang member is given a grade he thinks he deserves relative to others, he suspects that the grades have been awarded fairly. But his suspicions are based only on the perceived relationship between grades and mental capacity. He can only confirm his suspicions by checking with the teacher. Moreover, if the gang member suspects that the grade is fair, his request to have the grade explained is uniformly polite.

The teacher's response to a request is crucial information to the gang member. If he receives an account of his grade and the account is at all reasonable, he concludes that the teacher is grading fairly. The very fact that the teacher provides a reason at all predisposes him to conclude that the criteria being used to pass and fail students are on the 'up and up'.

After we got our compositions back I went up to him you know. I asked him about my composition. I got a D over F and I ask him what I did wrong. He told me that he could tell by the way I write that I could do better than what I did. And he explained it to me, and he showed me what I need to improve. And he showed me, if I correct my paper, I would get a D, a straight D instead of that F. O.K. And I got the D for half the work. But anyway he showed me how I could get a regular D and pass his class. I mean I feel like that teacher was helping me. I mean he was showing me a way I could pass the class and how he was grading everybody. I mean the way he explained everything to me, I knew he was straight, that he was grading fairly.

Similarly, if a gang member receives a lower grade than expected, he suspects that teachers are using grades as a weapon to award those who accept their authority and punish those who reject it. Again, he can come to no final conclusions about the rule being used to give grades until he checks with the teacher.

If the gang member feels there is a possibility he is being discriminated against, he *demands* an account of the grade. He typically asks, 'What the *hell* did I get this for?' Moreover, since each gang member is in a slightly different position with respect to mental capacity and power, they all approach the teacher alone instead of in groups, even though they compare notes carefully after the encounter has passed.

See, me and that man, we always be fighting. Maybe because of my attitude. See, a lot of teachers grade you on your attitude toward them and not your work. And like sometimes you be talking, you know, and he say, 'Why don't you hush! Shut up! I told you once or twice already not to be saying that in class!' Everybody else be talking.

He say, 'Trying to get smart with me?'

'No, I say, 'I ain't trying to get smart with you.'

He say, 'What are you trying to do? Start an argument?'

And you know, I get tired of copping pleas.

'Hell yeah I'm trying to start an argument!'

So he say, 'If you keep fooling around I'm going to lower your grade.'

On the report card, the dude give me a D. I told that son of a bitch today, I know damn well my work better than a D! Cause all my tests have been C's, you know, and everybody else getting a C. I'm hip to shit like that, man.

Then he gonna tell me, 'Well, I grade on the notes and the homework more than I do the tests.'

I say, 'Well, what kind of a teacher are you? What bull shit you got on your mind?' I cussing at him all the time. That man don't move me! He bore me! He get on my damn nerves!

He look up at me. 'You trying to start a fight?'

I say, 'I'm gonna start the biggest fight you ever seen! I want my grade changed!'

And he say, 'Why don't you go sit down?'

'No man, I ain't gonna sit down till you straighten my grade out! You show me my grade in the book and I show you. I know I got a C!'

And he just say, 'Go on and sit down before I call the boys' dean to come up here and get you.'

I say to myself, 'I can't get suspended no more. If I gets suspended again, I fucked. I never will pass.' So I went and sit down. That nasty ass motherfucker just don't like bloods.

If a gang member receives a bad grade and finds the teacher frightened and apologetic, he concludes that grades have been awarded randomly. The gang member reasons that if the teacher is frightened during the encounter and grades had not been given randomly, he probably would have received a better one.

Like my gym teacher today. That fucking freak! F? Aw hell no! Nobody get no F in gym. And I stripped every day! My gym suit wasn't clean every Monday. That's just three points minus. All right. Six weeks times three is eighteen. Right? Eighteen points minus out of a hundred. How the hell you gonna get a F? And I stripped every day. All right then. So I went in there and told Mr C. I say, 'Now look here, the man gave me a F! I stripped every day. My gym suit wasn't clean every Monday. I took a shower after class every day. Now why I get a F?'
He looked in the book. 'Oh, I guess he made a mistake. I'm not sure cause I wasn't with you all during the six weeks so I give you a D.'
So I say, 'Look, man, I don't think a D's fair either. I think I ought to get a B or C just like everyone else.'
'Well, I'll give you a D and you'll get a better grade next time.'
All the time I was talking to him he had his head in a book, and when he looked up it seemed like you could see in his eyes that he was almost scared. You know. Didn't want to say too much. It seem like almost everything you say, he agrees with you and make you look like a ass. 'Yeah. Yeah. That's right, that's right.' Stuff like that. And you know that some of the things you be saying you know is wrong. You'd be expecting him to say, 'No, that's wrong.' You know. And he'd be agreeing with everything you say. He just say, 'Well, do things right next time and I'll go on and give you a better grade than you deserve, not a worse one!' That gym man! They don't know what they give you. They just hand them out as they come up.
I finally say, 'O.K. Fuck it!' You know. I didn't want no F so I took the D. And I say, 'Well look here, man, I hope to hell I don't have your stupid ass for a gym teacher next term!'

If he is dealing with a teacher who believes it is not necessary and in fact demeaning to explain decisions to students, the gang member may receive no answer at all. His search is then frustrated, and he has been directly insulted. This frustration and anger is typically reflected in loud and obscene outbursts directed at the teacher. This is a 'classic' scene in the folklore of a delinquent gang. After blowing up at the teacher and storming from the classroom, he comes to the conclusion that he is being discriminated against, regardless of whether or not this is in fact true.

(How did Tyrone get kicked out of school?) Putting down the teachers. He didn't feel that he was given adequate grades for a term paper or work that he had passed in. He went up and told the teacher to get fucked. She went up to the Dean of Boys, and he tell Tyrone that he'd have to let him go. (Were you in his class?) Yeah. (Did you see him tell off the teacher?) Yeah. I was standing right behind him. (What happened?) Well, see we get these papers back and Tyrone, he start asking everybody what they got. So he go up to this one stud, Art, and he say, 'You see Mrs G., that bitch, she gave me a F. What's the story?'

Art say, 'She gave me a passing grade.'

Tyrone say, 'Shit. You don't do a damn thing. How come you pass and I don't?'

Art say, 'I don't know, man. Maybe she don't like you.'

So Tyrone goes up to her. He said, 'What the hell's going on here? Why I get that F? I felt the answer to this question was right! I think it's right!'

She said, 'Well, no, it isn't. I'm sorry.'

He say, 'Why ain't it right?'

She say, 'I corrected it the way I saw fit.'

He say, 'Well shit! Why ain't it right?'

She say, 'Uh, would you stop using so much profound [*sic*] language. I'll have to tell the Dean.'

He say, 'Tell the fucking Dean! He ain't nobody! Aw fuck you!'

She told the Dean, and the Dean kicked him out.

It is important to point out that not all gang members are able to learn something about the rules teachers use to grade by using this procedure. The illiterates or relatively dull students who expect Fs even under the fair condition, and the bright gang members who expect As and Bs, are in a further bind. The F students cannot distinguish between the fair case and the case of discrimination, and the A student cannot distinguish between the fair case and the case of being 'bribed'. Unlike the F student, however, the A student will be particularly sensitive to discrimination. Gang members who fall in these two categories use other grounds to decide whether or not to co-operate with teachers. The procedure being discussed here thus works best for average students, those who can learn something by receiving As and Fs. Most boys, including gang members, however, fall into this category – at least while they are attending school.

Conclusions

Once gang members have either requested or demanded accounts from teachers, they have all the materials needed to come to a conclusion.

The accounts that teachers give or fail to give furnish warranted grounds for understanding one aspect of what goes on in the classroom. The gang member has discovered the class or rule being used to grade and thus can understand the single grade he received. Once having discovered the rule, however, he then faces the question of what to do about it. It is in the decisions he makes about his future course of action that we discover the essence of the delinquent.

If he concludes that he is being either discriminated against, bribed, or treated randomly, he does not modify his behavior. Even though he becomes aware that 'kissing ass' will get him a better grade, he does not avail himself of the technique. He is prevented by his sense of morality. The tactic is considered illegitimate. After all, he reasons, 'If I go for that shit I might as well stick to the streets and pull some big-time action!'

> (So you know your attitude toward the teacher gets you bad grades sometimes?) Yeah, sometimes it does. (Why don't you change your attitude?) I wouldn't go kiss up to them motherfucking teachers for nothing! Shit! They prejudiced or they gonna hit you over the head with that fucking grade so you gonna kiss up to them? Well no! We supposed to be graded on what we know. Right? Ain't that supposed to be how it is? Damn teachers are something. I tell you they ain't got shit but a racket going, man. Motherfuckers get down there and kiss them God damn principals' asses, the bosses' asses. That's the last motherfucking thing I do! I wouldn't go kiss that damn horse's ass for nothing! I wouldn't do shit for that man. If I go running over there, I'm gonna feel funny. Cause I'm always getting in trouble. What if I go running over there and ask him, 'Look man, why don't you help me out in gym. Tell this man to kinda lighten up on me cause he kinda fucking my grades around. I ain't for all this shit. I know I'm doing right.' You know. Shit like that. He gonna say, 'Lee, you always want favors, but you never want to do nothing in return. You're always messing up in class.' And this and that and the other shit. I'd rather be raped, man. If I go for that shit I might as well stick to the streets and pull some big time action! Shit! If I gonna be corrupt? If I gonna get me a racket going like that, shit, I ain't gonna waste my time sucking up to no teachers! I gonna pull some big time shit.

Practical applications

How do gang members act in classroom once they decide that a teacher's claims to authority are illegitimate?

While gang members remain in school, either before graduating or before being kicked out, they do not comply with the grounds teachers use to treat them. This fact explains much of their delinquency in the classroom. If they feel that a teacher is discriminating against them because his claims to authority are not being granted, they are careful to avoid all behavior that implicitly or explicitly recognizes this authority. Raising a hand in class, for example, is a gesture used by students to present themselves as candidates for speaking. Implicit in the gesture is an understanding that the student may not be called on. The gesture implies further that the teacher has the authority to grant speaking privileges in class. If a student raises his hand, he thus implicitly makes the authority of the teacher legitimate. This is why gang members refuse to raise their hands in some classes and prefer interjecting comments without being recognized. This behavior would no doubt be treated by some theorists as a rude and unruly by-product of 'lower-class culture'. Lower-class or not, the behavior has its reasons.

I'm not the quiet type in that class [California history]. Like when we're having a discussion or something? I don't go for all that raising your hand. Cause everybody else on the other side of the room might – while the teacher asking you a question? – well the one that just went by, people probably still discussing it. And you might want to get in on that. And you just come on out and say something, and he tell you to get out of class. Well that shit ain't no good, man. So you know that kinda get on my nerves. But I don't mind getting kicked out of class. That ain't no big thing. I feel like – that class I got now? – if I try hard I can pass. My citizenship may not be worth a damn, but I can pass the class. (Do you always forget to raise your hand?) Hell no! I raise my hand in Civics and some of the other classes. That's interesting. But California history ain't shit. It's easy. It's simple. It's just that teacher. He a punk! He just ain't used to us. He just don't understand bloods [Negroes]. I don't raise my hand for that freak! I just tell the dude what's on my mind.

The time and circumstances that surround entering and leaving class also have implications for the implicit acceptance or rejection of authority. If a student consistently comes to class on time, he implicitly gives teachers grounds to assume that he accepts both their authority and the legitimacy of school rules. This is why gang members frequently make it a point to arrive five minutes late to class. It is no accident that gang members are suspended most frequently for tardiness. Not only is tardiness an affront to the authority of teachers but it also flaunts the claims to authority made by the school system as a whole.

We came in late to class today because he threatened us. He see us between fifth and sixth period when he was supposed to be going to one class and coming from another. We was on our way to his class. I was standing by my locker. My locker right next to his class. So he come up to me and say, 'Lee, you tell Wilson that if you two come late to class I'm gonna get you both kicked out of school.'

So I went and told Billy, and we made it our business to be late. We walked in about five minutes late. Knocked on the door. He opened the door. Just went in and sat down. I looked him in the eye. Would have put a ring around it if he'd said too much. The door comes in through the back. We made a little bit of noise sitting down to make sure he see us. We giggled and laughed a little bit to make sure he noticed we were there. We try to remind him that he suppose to kick us out. It was almost to the end of the period before he kicked us out.

Gang members also have the choice of leaving class before the bell is rung, when the bell is ringing, or when the class is formally dismissed by the teacher. When they occasionally leave class before the bell is rung, they flaunt the authority of both the teacher and the school.

(What do you do when you discover that the teacher has been grading you unfairly?) Lots of times we just get up and walk out. Like you say, 'Oh man, I'm tired of this class.' You just jump up and walk out and shut the door. (What do the teachers do?) Mostly they just look at us and then resume with the rest of the class and don't say nothing. (Why don't they report you?) I guess they be glad for us to be out of their class.

More frequently, however, they wait until the bell rings to leave class instead of waiting for a sign of dismissal from the teacher. This act implicitly accepts the authority of the school while explicitly rejecting the authority of the teacher. When this happens teachers who feel they have authority to protect often take action.

After class, as soon as the bell rang, everybody jumped up. The teacher said, 'Everybody sit back down! You're not leaving right now!' So Alice jumped up. She starts walking out. He say, 'Alice, go sit down!'
    Alice say, 'Who the hell you talking to! I'm tired of school. I'm going home!'
    She walked to the door. He grabbed her. She looked at him. 'I'm gonna count to three, and if you don't get your hands off me . . . No, I ain't even gonna count! Take your hands off me!'
    He took his hands off. He say, 'We're going to the office this minute!'
    She say, 'You going to the office by yourself unless you get somebody else to go down there with you!'
    And so she walked away. So she was down talking to some other girls, and he say, 'Alice, would you please come!'
    She say, 'No! And stop bugging me! Now get out of here!'
    I didn't see all of the argument. I just went off and left. When I passed him I said, 'Man, you ain't nothing!'
    He looked at me. Then he say, 'One of these days you gonna get yours.'

In addition, gang members are careful never to use forms of address that suggest deference. 'Yes Sir' and 'No Sir' are thus self-consciously stricken from the vocabulary.

And you know like in some classes the teacher tell you you don't say 'Yes' and 'No'. It's 'Yes Sir' and 'No Sir'. They would have to whip my ass to make me say that. I don't go for it. Shit. They don't call me Mr Lee! Teacher once tried to tell me to say, 'Yes M'am'. I say, 'All right, you call me Mr Lee.' I don't like it. I feel if I did, I'd probably feel funny saying 'Yes Sir' and 'No Sir' to somebody. (How would you feel?) I'd feel like I was a little old punk or something.

But of all the techniques used by gang members to communicate rejection of authority, by far the most subtle and most annoying to teachers is demeanor. Both white and Negro gang members have developed a uniform and highly stylized complex of body movements that communicate a casual and disdainful aloofness to anyone making normative claims on their behavior. The complex is referred to by gang members as 'looking cool', and it is part of a repertoire of stances that include 'looking bad' and 'looking tore down'. The essential ingredients of 'looking cool' are a walking pace that is a little too slow for the occasion, a straight back, shoulders slightly stooped, hands in pockets, and eyes that carefully avert any party to the interaction. There are also clothing aides which enhance the effect such as boot or shoe taps and a hat if the scene takes place indoors.

This stance can trigger an incident if a teacher reacts to it, but it is the teacher who must make the first overt move. The beauty of the posture resides in its being both concrete and diffuse. Teachers do not miss it, but they have a great deal of difficulty finding anything specific to attack. Even the mightiest of educators feels embarrassed telling high school students to 'stand up straight'. As the following episode suggests, teachers typically find some other issue on which to vent their disapproval.

The first day I came to school I was late to class so this teacher got smart with me. He didn't know me by name. See a lot of people have to go by the office and see what class they in or something. Like there was a lot of new people there. So you know I was fooling around cause I know nothing gonna happen to you if you late. Cause all you tell them, you tell them you got the program mixed or something.

When I came into the class you know I heard a lot of hollering and stuff. Mr H. was in the class too. He's a teacher, see. I guess he had a student teacher or something, you know, because he was getting his papers and stuff. So Mr H. went out. Well this new teacher probably wonder if he gonna be able to get along with me or something. Cause when I came in the class, you know, everybody just got quiet. Cause the class was kinda loud. When I walked in the class got quiet all of a sudden. Like they thought the Principal was coming in or something.

So I walk into class and everybody look up. That's natural, you know, when somebody walk into class. People gonna look up at you. They gonna see who it is coming in or something. So I stopped. You know, like this. Looked around. See if there was any new faces. Then a girl named Diane, she say, 'Hey Ray!' You know, when I walk into class they start calling me and stuff. They start hollering at me.

I just smile and walk on. You know. I had my hands in my pocket or something cause I didn't have no books and I just walk into class with my hands in my pockets a lot of times. I mean I have to walk where I can relax. I'm not going to walk with my back straight. I mean you know I relax. (What were you wearing?) About what I got on now. I had a pair of black slacks and a shirt on but they weren't real high boots. They came up to about here.

Then I looked over at the teacher. I see we had a new teacher. He was standing in front of the desks working on some papers and doing something. He looked at me. I mean you enter by the front of the classroom so when you walk into the classroom he's standing right there. You gotta walk in front of him to get to the seats. So then I went to sit down. Soon as I passed his desk he say, 'Just go sit down.' Just like that. So I stop. I turn around and look at him, then I went and sat down. (What kind of look did you give him?) You might say I gave him a hard look. I thought you know he might say something else. Cause that same day he came he got to hollering at people and stuff. I don't like people to holler at me. He was short, you know, about medium build. He might be able to do a little bit. So I say to myself, 'I better sit down and meditate a little bit.'

So I went and sat down. I sat in the last row in the last seat. Then he say, 'Come sit up closer.' So I scoot up another chair or two. Then he tell me to come sit up in the front. So I sat up there. Then you know a lot of people was talking. A lot of people begin telling me that he be getting smart all day. You know Studdy? He a big square but he pretty nice. He told me how the teacher was. And Angela start telling me about how he try to get smart with her. He say, 'This is where you don't pick out no boy friend. You come and get your education.' I mean just cause you talk to a boy, that don't mean you be scheming on them or nothing. It just that you want to be friends with people.

Then he say something like, 'You two shut up or I'll throw you out on your ear.' So he told me he'd throw me out.

So I say, 'The best thing you can do is ask me to leave and don't tell me. You'll get your damn ass kicked off if you keep messing!'

Then he told me to move over on the other side. See I was talking to everybody so he told me to move away from everybody. And so I moved to the other side. He told me to move three times! I had to move three times! And then he got to arguing at somebody else. I think at somebody else that came in the class. You know, a new person. So while he was talking to them, I left out. I snuck out of class.

So I walked out the class. Went out in the yard and started playing basketball. We were supposed to turn in the basketball out there so I took the ball through the hall on the way back in. I was gonna go back out there and play some more. See I had the ball and I passed by his class and I looked in. I seen him with his back turned and I didn't like him. That's when I hit him. I hit him with the ball. Got him! I didn't miss. Threw it hard too. Real hard!

It is easier for teachers to attack the demeanor of students directly if the encounter is formal and disciplinary. If a gang member is 'sent' to someone for punishment, the teacher or principal he appears before often makes demeanor an issue. In the following incident, a gang member is suspended for ten days ostensibly because he faced the music with his hands in his pockets and the touch of a smile on his face.

Miss W., she sent me to Mr M. cause I cussed at her. When I came to class he was talking to some gray boys [white boys] and he called me in. He talked at me like he gonna knock me out. Talked about fifteen minutes. He wasn't coming on nice. He got right down to the point. 'I think you know what you're in here for. I think you know what you did fourth period concerning Miss W.'

I say, 'Yeah, I know what I done.'

And so he just sat down and went on and talked. He told me to sit down. I was already sat down. I had my hands in my pockets. He told me to take my hands out of my pockets. (Why?) I guess he wanted my attention. I was looking down at the floor and he told me to look at him. I look at him and look down at the floor again. He didn't say nothing then. And I walked out the woodshop and I just smiled. And he say, 'Come on back here! I want to talk to you again.' So I went back there. 'What was that smile for? That little smile you gave.'

I say, 'Ain't nobody can tell me if I can smile.' He said, 'You smiling as if you gave me a bad time. You didn't. I gave you a bad time!'

So he told me to go on down to the Principal. He told me the Principal was gonna suspend me for ten days. (Did he?) Yup.

Yet when gang members are convinced that the educational enterprise and its ground rules are being legitimately pursued, that a teacher is really interested in teaching them something, and that efforts to learn will be rewarded, they consistently show up on time, leave when the class is dismissed, raise their hands before speaking, and stay silent and awake.

I mean I feel like that teacher was helping me. I mean he was showing me a way I could pass his class. And then all the time he was telling me, you know, he was leaving me with confidence that I could do better if I wanted to. Like I mean he'd be up in front of the class you know, and he'd give the class an equal chance to be graded. I mean I felt that the teacher was real fair. Cause some of the people that were slow, he would help. I mean he wouldn't take off time just for that few little people but he would help you. He'd give you confidence. Tell you can do better. That man used to have a desk full of people. Everyday after class you know there be somebody up there talking to him. Everybody passed his class too. He let you know that you wasn't in there for nothing.

Notes

1 This paper is part of a larger research project done with Irving Piliavin on delinquent street gangs in San Francisco. The project was initiated by the Survey Research Center at the University of California on a grant from the Ford Foundation and was later moved to the Center For the Study of Law and Society where funds were made available from the Delinquency Studies Program sponsored by the Department of Health, Education, and Welfare under Public Law 87–274.
2 Richard A. Cloward and Lloyd E. Ohlin, *Delinquency and Opportunity* (Routledge & Kegan Paul 1961), 102.
3 Albert K. Cohen, *Delinquent Boys: The Culture of the Gang* (Routledge & Kegan Paul 1956), 115.
4 Walter B. Miller and William C. Kvaraceus, *Delinquent Behavior: Culture and the Individual* (National Educational Association of the United States 1959), 144. See also Walter Miller, 'Lower-class culture as a generating milieu of gang delinquency', *Journal of Social Issues* (1958), vol. 14 for a more explicit statement of this position.
5 Cloward and Ohlin, op. cit.
6 Cohen, op. cit.
7 Miller, op. cit.
8 Chester I. Barnard, *The Functions of the Executive* (Cambridge, Mass.: Harvard University Press 1938), 163.
9 This assumption is widely shared by both sociologists and gang members. Hopefully we will some day put it to a test.
10 This model of events is based on the assumption that regardless of how students are behaving in class, they can only misbehave if a rule about proper conduct is invoked by teachers. It is in this sense that 'social groups create deviance by making the rules whose infraction constitutes deviance, and by applying those rules to particular people'. See Howard S. Becker, *Outsiders* (Collier-Macmillan 1963), 9.
11 For a general discussion of the problems created by contingent or purposive infraction of irrelevance rules see Ervin Goffman, *Encounters* (Indianapolis: Bobbs-Merrill 1961), 17–85.

2.2

The class significance of school counter-culture†[1]

Paul Willis

> This new type of school . . . is destined not merely to perpetuate
> social differences but to crystallize them in Chinese complexities.
> (Antonio Gramsci on 'democratic' educational reforms in Italy
> during the early twenties[2])

The existence of anti-school cultures in schools with a working-class
catchment area has been widely commented upon.[3] The raising of the
school-leaving age has further dramatized and exposed this culture,
often in the form of a 'new' crisis: disruption in the classroom. Teachers'
unions are calling more and more vehemently for tougher action against
'violence' in the classroom, and for special provision for the 'unruly'
minority. The 'reluctant fifth', difficult 'RSLA classes' and young,
'always in tears' (usually female) teachers, have become part of
staffroom folklore.

The welter of comment and response, has, however, served to
conceal certain crucial features of this culture: the profound significance
it has for processes of job selection, and its relation to the wider
working-class culture. In what follows I want to draw attention to these
omissions. Concretely I want to make two suggestions. (1) Counter-
school culture is part of the wider working-class culture of a region and
ultimately of the nation, and, in particular, runs parallel to what we
might call shop-floor culture. (2) The located anti-school culture
provides powerful informal criteria and binding experiential processes
which lead working-class lads to make the 'voluntary' choice to enter
the factory, and so to help to reproduce both the existing class structure
of employment and the 'culture of the shop floor' as a segment of the
overarching working-class culture. My argument is, then, that the stage

† Source: M. Hammersley and P. Woods (1976) (eds), *The Process of Schooling*,
London, Routledge & Kegan Paul, pp. 188–200.

of affiliation with the counter-school group carries much more significance than is usually acknowledged. I therefore go on to examine, in the latter part of this chapter, when, how and why this process occurs. I will conclude with some comments on the meaning and status of this general class culture, of which the school and factory variants are part.

Studies of the transition from school to work, which might have made the connection between the school social system and the world of work, have simply been content to register a failure of the agencies and their rational policies – derived basically from middle-class preconceptions. The matrix of inappropriate middle-class logic – self-development, self-knowledge, matching of lifestyle/career profile – overlying the located, informal cultural processes in the institutional practice of the Youth Employment Service and the relentlessly descriptive set of the main writings on the 'transition',[4] have effectively obscured the essential connectedness of working-class experience for the young male proceeding from school to work. Studies of the school[5] have been absorbed by the cultural divisions in the school itself, and have, implicitly at any rate, isolated the school from its surrounding networks. Consequently they have failed to address the central question of the determinacy of counter-school culture – is it the institution or the class context, or what mixture of both, which leads to the formation of this culture? In general the omission of the context in which the school operates would seem to imply that the institution be given primacy in the determination of the social landscape of the school.

My own research suggests that there is a direct relationship between the main features of working-class culture, as it is expressed in shop-floor culture, and school counter-culture. Both share broadly the same determinants: the common impulse is to develop strategies for dealing with boredom, blocked opportunities, alienation and lack of control. Of course the particular organization of each located culture has its own history and specificity, and worked-up institutional forms. The institution of the school, for instance, determines a particular uneven pattern of extension and suppression of common working-class themes. In one way a more protected environment than the shop floor, and without the hard logic and discipline of material production, the school is nevertheless a more directly face-to-face repressive agency in other ways. This encourages an emphasis on certain obvious forms of resistance specific to the school. In one sense this is simply a question of inverting the given rules – hence the terrain of school counter-culture: smoking, proscribed dress, truancy, cheek in class, vandalism and theft.

At any rate, the main cultural and organizational aspects of shop-floor culture (at least in the Midlands industrial conurbation where I did my research), and for the moment ignoring the range of historically and occupationally specific variants, bear a striking similarity to the main features of school counter-culture. I concentrate here mainly on shop-floor culture. [. . .]

The really central point about the working-class culture of the shop floor is that, despite harsh conditions and external direction, people do look for meaning and impose frameworks. They exercise their abilities and seek enjoyment in activity, even where most controlled by others. They do, paradoxically, thread through the dead experience of work a living culture which is far from a simple reflex of defeat. This is the same fundamental taking hold of an alienating situation as one finds in counter-school culture and its attempt to weave a tapestry of interest and diversion through the dry institutional text. These cultures are not simply foam paddings, rubber layers between human and unpleasantness. They are appropriations in their own right, exercises of skill, motions, activities applied towards particular ends.

More specifically, the central, locating theme of shop-floor culture – a form of masculine chauvinism arising from the raw experience of production – is reflected in the independence and toughness found in school counter-cultures. Here is a foundry-man talking at home about his work. In an inarticulate way, but for that perhaps all the more convincingly, he attests that elemental, essentially masculine, self-esteem in the doing of a hard job well – and to be known for it.

> I work in a foundry . . . you know drop forging . . . do you know anything about it . . . no . . . well you have the factory know the factory down in Bethnall Street with the noise . . . you can hear it in the street . . . I work there on the big hammer . . . it's a six-tonner, I've worked there 24 years now. It's bloody noisy, but I've got used to it now . . . and its hot . . . . . . I don't get bored . . . there's always new lines coming and you have to work out the best way of doing it . . . You have to keep going . . . , and it's heavy work, the managers couldn't do it, there's not many strong enough to keep lifting the metal . . . I earn 80, 90 pounds a week, and that's not bad is it? . . . it ain't easy like . . . you can definitely say that I earn every penny of it . . . you have to keep it up you know. And the managing director, I'd say 'hello' to him you know, and the progress manager . . . . they'll come around and I'll go . . . 'all right' (thumbs up) . . . and they know you, you know . . . . a group standing there watching you . . . . working . . . I like that . . . . there's something there . . . watching *you* like . . . working . . . like that . . you have to keep going to get enough out.

Here is Joey, this man's son, in his last year at school, and right at the heart of the counter-culture:

> That's it, we've developed certain ways of talking, certain ways of acting and we developed disregards for Pakis, Jamaicans and all different . . ., for all the scrubs and the fucking ear-oles and all that (. .) There's no chivalry or nothing, none of this cobblers you know, it's just . . if you'm gonna fight, it's savage fighting anyway, so you

might as well go all the way and win it completely by having someone else help ya or by winning the dirtiest methods you can think of like poking his eyes out or biting his ear and things like this.

There's a clear continuity of attitudes here, and we must not think that this distinctive complex of chauvinism, toughness and machismo is anachronistic or bound to die away as the pattern of industrial work changes. Rough, unpleasant, demanding jobs *do* still exist in considerable numbers. A whole range of jobs – from building work, to furnace work to deep sea fishing – still involve a primitive confrontation with exacting physical tasks. The basic attitudes and values developed in such jobs are still very important in general working-class culture, and particularly the culture of the shop floor; this importance is vastly out of proportion to the number of people involved in such heavy work. Even in so-called light industries, or in highly mechanized factories where the awkwardness of the physical task has long since been reduced, the metaphoric figures of strength, masculinity and reputation still move beneath the more varied and richer, visible forms of workplace culture. Despite, even, the increasing numbers of women employed, the most fundamental ethos of the factory is profoundly masculine.

The other main, and this time emergent, theme of shop-floor culture – at least in the manufacturing industries of the Midlands – is the massive attempt to gain a form of control of the work process. 'Systematic soldiering' and 'gold bricking' have been observed from the particular perspective of management from F. W. Taylor[6] onwards, but there is evidence now of a much more concerted – though still informal – attempt to gain control. It does happen, now, sometimes, that the men themselves actually run production. Again this is effectively mirrored for us by working-class kids' attempts, with the resources of their counter-culture, to take control of classes, insert their own unofficial timetables, and control their own routines and life spaces.

Joey:	(. .) of a Monday afternoon, we'd have nothing right? Nothing hardly relating to school work, Tuesday afternoon we have swimming and they stick you in a classroom for the rest of the afternoon. Wednesday afternoon you have games and there's only Thursday and Friday afternoon that you work, if you call that work. The last lesson Friday afternoon we used to go and doss, half of us wagged out o'lessons and the other half go into the classroom, sit down and just go to sleep, and the rest of us could join a class where all our mates are.
Will:	(. .) What we been doing, playing cards in this room 'cos we can lock the door.
PW:	Which room's this now?

Will:	Resources Centre, where we're making the frames (*a new stage for the deputy head*), s'posed to be.
PW:	Oh! You're still making the frames?
Will:	We should have had it finished, we just lie there on top of the frame, playing cards, or trying to get to sleep.
PW:	What's the last time you've done some writing?
Will:	When we done some writing?
Fuzz:	Oh ah, last time was in careers, 'cos I writ 'yes' on a piece of paper, that broke me heart.
PW:	Why did it break your heart?
Fuzz:	I mean to write, 'cos I was going to try and go through the term without writing anything. 'Cos since we've cum back, I ain't dun nothing. (*It was half-way through term.*)

Put this against the following account from the father of a boy who was in the same friendship group as the boys talking above. He is a factory hand on a track producing car engines, talking at his home.

Actually the foreman, the gaffer, don't run the place, the men run the place. See, I mean you get one of the chaps says, 'Allright, you'm on so and so today.' You can't argue with him. The gaffer don't give you the job, the men on the track give you the job, they swop each other about, tek it in turns. Ah, but I mean the job's done. If the gaffer had gid you the job you would . . . They tried to do it, one morning, gid a chap a job you know, but he'd been on it, you know, I think he'd been on all week, and they just downed tools. (. . . .) There's four hard jobs on the track and there's dozens that's, . . you know, a child of five could do it, quite honestly, but everybody has their turn. That's organized by the men.

Of course there is the obvious difference that the school informal organization is devoted to doing nothing, while in the factory culture, at least, 'the job's done'. But the degree of opposition to official authority *in each case* should not be minimized, and production managers in such shops were quite as worried as deputy heads about 'what things were coming to'. Furthermore, both these attempts at control rest on the basic and distinctive unit of the informal group. This is the fundamental unit of resistance in both cultures, which locates and makes possible all its other elements. It is the zone where 'creative' attempts to develop and extend an informal culture are made, and where strategies for wresting control of symbolic and real space from official authority are generated and disseminated. It is the massive presence of this informal organization which most decisively marks off shop-floor culture from middle-class cultures of work, and the 'lads'' school culture from that of the 'ear-'oles' (the name used by the 'lads' of my research to designate those who conformed to the school's official culture).

The solidarity, and sense of being 'in the group', is the basis for the final major characteristic of shop-floor culture that I want to describe here. This is the distinctive form of language, and the highly developed humour of the shop floor. Up to half the verbal exchanges are not serious or about work activities. They are jokes, or 'piss-takes', or 'kiddings' or 'wind-ups'. There is a real skill in being able to use this language with fluency: to identify the points where you are being 'kidded' and to have appropriate response in order to avoid further baiting.

This badinage is necessarily difficult to record on tape or represent, but the highly distinctive ambience it gives to shop-floor exchanges is widely recognized by those involved, and to some extent re-created in their accounts of it. This is a foundry-worker talking at home about the atmosphere in his shop:

> Oh, there's all sorts, millions of them (*jokes*). 'Want to hear what he said about you', and he never said a thing, you know. Course you know the language, at the work like. 'What you been saying, about me'; 'I said nothing', 'Oh you're a bloody liar', and all this.

Associated with this concrete and expressive verbal humour is a developed physical humour; essentially the practical joke. These jokes are vigorous, sharp, sometimes cruel, and often hinge on prime tenets of the culture such as disruption of production or subversion of the bosses' authority and status. Here is the same man:

> They er'm play jokes on you, blokes knocking the clamps off the boxes, they put paste on the bottom of his hammer you know soft little thing, puts his hammer down, picks it up, gets a handful of paste, you know, all this. So he comes up and gets a syringe and throws it in the big bucket of paste, and it's about that deep, and it goes right to the bottom, you have to put your hand in and get it out (. . . .) This is a filthy trick, but they do it. (. .) They asked, the gaffers asked – to make the tea. Well it's fifteen years he's been there and they say 'go and make the teas'. He gus up the toilet, he wets in the tea pot, then makes the tea. I mean, you know, this is the truth this is you know. He says, you know, 'I'll piss in it if I mek it, if they've asked me to mek it.' (. . . .) so he goes up, wees in the pot, then he puts in the tea bag, then he puts the hot water in. (. . . .) – was bad the next morning, one of the gaffers, 'My stomach isn't half upset this morning.' He told them after and they called him for everything, 'you ain't makin' our tea no more,' he says.
> 'I know I ain't not now.'

This atmosphere of rough humour and horseplay is instantly recognizable among the 'lads' in working-class schools, and obviously missing from the more hesitant 'polite' exchanges amongst the 'ear-'oles'. The ethnography of school cultures is full of similar – virtually interchangeable – incidents. There is the same felt desire to brighten grey prospects with a 'larf'. Certainly for the group of 'lads' who were the focus of my 'main' case study, reliance on the group, verbal humour and physical trickery, was the continuous stuff of their informal relations.

Joey:	You know you have to come to school today, if you're feeling bad, your mate'll soon cheer yer up like, 'cos you couldn't go without ten minutes in this school, without having a laugh at something or other.
PW:	Are your mates a really big important thing at school now?
– Yeah	
– Yeah	
– Yeah	
Joey:	They're about the best thing actually.
Spanksey:	You like to come to school, just to skive, 'cos you get bored at home. You'd rather come here and sit in the Youth Wing or summat.
Joey:	(. .) You'm always looking out on somebody (*when skiving*) and you've always got something to talk about . . . something.
PW:	So what stops you being bored?
Joey:	Talking, we could talk for ever, when we get together, it's talk, talk, talk.

There is no space to pursue the point any further, but in more detailed ways, from theft, vandalism and sabotage to girlie books under the tool-bench or desk, it is apparent that shop-floor culture and school oppositional culture have a great deal in common.

The parallelism of these cultures suggests, of course, that they should both be thought of as aspects of the larger working-class culture, though a fuller account would obviously further differentiate regional, occupational and institutional variations. The fundamental point here is to stress that anti-school culture should be seen in the context of this larger pattern, rather than in simple institutional terms. This wider connection has important and unexamined implications for the school's management of the 'disruptive' minority. Put at its most obvious, strategies conceived at the institutional level will not overcome problems arising from a profound class-cultural level. In fact the concerned teacher may be effectively boxed in, since the undoubted level of institutional determinacy – which I am not denying – may well block those strategies which do take into account the wider working-class culture. I mean that the teacher who tries to use working-class themes or styles may be rejected because he's a teacher: 'there's nothing worse than a teacher trying to be too friendly', and that a teacher who innovates organizationally – destreaming, mixed ability groupings, etc. – can never prevent the emergence of oppositional working-class themes *in one form or another*. It is the peculiarly intractable nature of this double determinacy which makes this form of working-class culture present itself as a 'crisis'. It shows up in high relief some of the unintended consequences and contradictions inherent in the state's ever-expanding attempts to make inroads into located working-class culture.

I do not wish, here, to go into the complex questions concerning what makes working-class culture – in all its variety and sectionalism – what it is. Nor – having, I hope, established the similarity between shop-floor and anti-school culture – do I want to claim any simple causation between them. My aims are more limited; my immediate text is that of job choice among working-class lads. What I want to argue about the parallelism I have described is that it accomplishes – in practice – a continuity between the two cultures, between work and school, in terms of the experiential passage of the working-class individual and his group. Processes within the school culture generate unofficial and deeply influential criteria which guide kids to similar, though expanded, situations: i.e. the shop floor. These unofficial criteria make a much more compelling case for particular job choices than does any amount of formal guidance.

Before looking at these located criteria, though, let us look at the manner in which the counter-school culture blocks, or reinterprets, the formal information concerning work with which it is saturated. All official communications about careers and work are importantly filtered through the group. By and large what might be termed as the *denoted*[7] messages from teachers and careers officers are most heavily filtered. This is the manifest content of particular communications concerning either the practical details of specific jobs or general principles about the best form of approach to work. Unless an individual has already decided to do a certain specific job, information about it is simply not taken in. It is certainly not true that new information is fed into a rational grid system which matches job profile with ability profile, or lifestyle with job/ambition profile. If things are remembered, they are picked up by some highly selective living principle of the counter-cultural school group. The following discussion is on careers films:

Perc:	I wonder why there's never kids like us in films, see what their attitude is to it? What they'm like and what we'm like.
PW:	Well, what sort of kids are they in the films?
Fuzz:	All ear-'oles.
Perc:	All goody-goodies.
Will:	No, you can tell they've been told what to say. They'm probably at some acting school or summat y'know and the opportunity to do this job – film careers for other kids – and you gotta say this, 'Wait for your cue', 'Wait till he's finished his lines.'

Information that is given to the kids concerning what might be thought of as an ideology of getting a job, and of getting on in a job, is either blocked, interpreted into unrecognizable forms or simply inverted. The following conversation is from a discussion on careers sessions:

Spanksey: After a bit you tek no notice of him, he sez the same thing over and over again, you know what I mean?

Joey: We're always too busy fucking picking your nose, or flicking paper, we just don't listen to him.

PW: How about the speaker who came from the College of Education?

Fred: They try to put you off work . . . Joey, he says to him, 'Do you want to be a painter and decorator, painting a wall, you can get any silly cunt to paint a wall', or 'Do you want to do the decorative pieces, sign writing.'

Spanksey: Got to be someone in society who slops on a wall . . . I wanted to get up and say to him, 'There's got to be some silly cunt who slops on a wall.'

In terms of actual 'job choice', it is the 'lads'' culture and not the official careers material which provides the most located and deeply influential guides for the future. For the individual's affiliation with the nonconformist group carries with it a whole range of changes in his attitudes and perspectives and these changes also supply over time a more or less consistent view of what sorts of people he wants to end up working with, and what sort of situation is going to allow the fullest expression for his developing cultural skills. The located 'lads'' culture supplies a set of 'unofficial' criteria by which to judge not individual jobs or the intrinsic joys of particular kinds of work – indeed it is already assumed that all work is more or less hard and unrewarding – but generally *what kind* of working situation is going to be most relevant to the individual. It will have to be work where he can be open about his desires, his sexual feelings, his liking for 'booze' and his aim to 'skive off' as much as is reasonably possible. It will have to be a place where people can be trusted and will not 'creep off' to tell the boss about 'foreigners' or 'nicking stuff' – precisely where there were the fewest 'ear-'oles'. Indeed it would have to be work where there was a boss, a 'them and us', which always carried with it the danger of treacherous intermediaries. The experience of the division 'ear-'ole'/ 'lads' in school is one of the most basic preparations for the still ubiquitous feeling in the working class proper that there is a 'them' and an 'us'. The 'us' is felt to be relatively weaker in power terms, but also somehow more approachable, social, and, in the end, more human. One of the really crucial things about the 'us' which the 'lads' wanted to be part of was that they were in work where the self could be separated from the work task, and value given to people for things other than their work performance – the celebration of those independent qualities which precisely the 'ear-'oles' did not have. Generally, the future work situation would have to be one where people were not 'cissies' and could handle themselves, where 'pen-pushing' is looked down on in favour of really 'doing things'. It would have to be a situation where you could speak up for yourself, and where you would not be expected to be subservient. The particular job would have to pay good money fairly quickly and offer the possibility of 'fiddles' and 'perks' to support already acquired smoking and drinking habits. Work would have to be a place, most basically, where people were 'all right' and with whom a general culture identity could be shared. It is this human face of work, much more than its intrinsic or technical nature, which confronts the individual as the crucial dimension of his future. In the end it is recognized that it is specifically the cultural diversion that makes any job bearable. Talking about the imminent prospect of work:

Will: I'm just dreading the first day like. Y'know, who to pal up with, an er'm, who's the ear-'oles, who'll tell the gaffer.

Joey: (. .) you can always mek it enjoyable. It's only you what makes a job unpleasant, . . I mean if you're cleaning sewers out, you can have your moments like. Not every job's enjoyable, I should think. Nobody's got a job they like unless they're a comedian or something, but er'm . . , no job's enjoyable 'cos of the fact that you've got to get up of a morning and go out when you could stop in bed. I think every job's got, has a degree of unpleasantness, but it's up to you to mek, . . to push that unpleasantness aside and mek it as good and as pleasant as possible.

The typical division in school between the 'lads' and the 'ear-'oles' also has a profound influence on thoughts about work. It is also a division between different kinds of future, different kinds of gratification and different kinds of job that are relevant to these things. These differences, moreover, are not random or unconnected. On the one hand they arise systematically from intra-*school* group oppositions and, on the other, they relate to quite distinct job groupings in the *post-school* situation. The 'ear-'oles'/'boys' division becomes the skilled/unskilled and white-collar/blue-collar division. The 'lads' themselves could transpose the divisions of the internal cultural landscape of the school on to the future, and on to the world of work outside, with considerable clarity. Talking about 'ear-'oles':

Joey: I think they're (*the 'ear-'oles'*) the ones that have got the proper view of life, they're the ones that abide by the rules. They're the civil servant types, they'll have 'ouses and everything before us (. . .) They'll

	be the toffs, I'll say they'll be the civil servants, toffs, and we'll be the brickies and things like that.
Spanksey:	I think that we . . , more or less, we're the ones that do the hard grafting but not them, they'll be the office workers. (. . .) I ain't got no ambitions, I doe wanna have, . . I just want to have a nice wage, that 'ud just see me through.

Not only does the 'lads'' culture and its opposition to conformism provide criteria for the kind of job which is relevant to them, it also possesses internal mechanisms – the 'kidding', the 'piss-take', the 'larf' – to enforce a certain view of appropriate work. In a discussion on what jobs they wanted:

Eddie:	I wanna be a jeweller.
PW:	A what?
	/ Laughter /
Eddie:	A jeweller.
PW:	I dunno, what's the joke. What's funny about a jeweller.
	/ Laughter /
	– he's a cunt.
	– he's a piss-taker.
	– 'im, he, he'd nick half of the jewels he would.
Spike:	He wants to be a diamond-setter in six months.
Derek:	He'd put one in a ring and six in his pocket.
PW:	Do you know anything about jewellery?
Eddie:	No.
	/ Laughter /

Altogether, in relation to the basic cultural groundshift which is occurring, and the development of a comprehensive alternative view of what is expected from life, *particular* job choice does not matter too much to the 'lads'. Indeed we may see that, with respect to the criteria this located culture throws up, most manual and semi-skilled jobs *are* the same and it would be a waste of time to use the provided middle-class grids across them to find material differences. Considered, therefore, in just one quantum of time – the last months of school – individual job choice does indeed seem random and unenlightened by any rational techniques or end/means schemes. It is, however, confusing and mystifying to pose the entry of working-class youth into work as a matter of *particular* job *choice* – this is, in essence, a very middle-class construct. The criteria we have looked at, the opposition to other more conformist views of work, and the solidarity of the group process, all transpose the question of job choice on to another plane: these lads are not choosing careers or particular jobs, they are committing themselves to a future of generalized labour. Even if it's not explicitly verbalized, from the way many of the kids actually get jobs and their calm expectation that their jobs will change a lot, they do not basically make much differentiation between jobs – *it's all labour*. In a discussion on the jobs they had arranged for when they left:

Perc:	I was with my mate, John's brother, I went with 'im to er, . . he wanted a job. Well, John's sister's boyfriend got a job at this place, and he sez to Allan, he sez, 'Go down there and they might give you a job there', and he went down, and they sez, 'You're too old for training', 'cos he's twenty now, he sez to Allan, he sez, 'Who's that out there', and he sez, 'One of me mates', he sez, 'does he wanna job', and he sez, 'I dunno.' He sez er'm, 'Ask him.' He comes out, I went back in and he told me about it and he sez, 'Come back before you leave if you want it.'
——:	What you doing?
Perc:	Carpentry, joining. And a month ago I went back and, well, not a month ago, a few weeks ago and I seen him.
PW:	Well, that was a complete accident really. I mean had you been thinking of joinery?
Perc:	Well, you've only got to go and see me woodwork, I've had it, I ain't done woodwork for years.

In a discussion of their future:

Eddie:	I don't think any of us'll have one job and then stick to it, none of us. We'll swop around.
Spike:	It just shows in your part-time jobs don't it, don't stick to a part-time job.

Shop-floor culture has, as we have seen, an objective dimension which gives it a certain strength and power. Now this quality chimes – unexpectedly for some – with the criteria for acceptable work already thrown up by the counter-school culture. The young adult, therefore, impelled towards the shop floor, shares much more than he knows with his own future. When the lad reaches the factory there is no shock, only recognition. He is likely to have had experience anyway of work through part-time jobs, and he is immediately familiar with many of the shop-floor practices: defeating boredom, time-wasting, heavy and physical humour, petty theft, 'fiddling', 'handling yourself'.

There is a further, perhaps less obvious, way in which the working-class boy who is from the 'lads' is drawn in to the factory and confirmed in his choice. This is in the likely response of his new employer to what he understands of the 'lads'' culture already generated at school. The reverse side of the 'them' and 'us' attitude of the 'lads' is an acceptance by them of prior authority relations. Although directly and apparently geared to make some cultural interest and capital out of an unpleasant situation, it also accomplishes a recognition of, and an accommodation to, the facts of power and hierarchy. In the moment of the establishment of a cultural opposition is the yielding of a hope for direct, or quasi-political, challenge. The 'them' and 'us' philosophy is simultaneously a rescue and confirmation of the direct, the human and the social, and a giving up – at any conscious level – of claims to control the under-workings of these things: the real power relationships. This fact is of central importance in understanding the peculiar density and richness, as well as the limitedness and frequent short-sightedness, of counter-school and shop-floor culture.

Now, curiously enough, those conformist lads who enter the factory unaided by cultural supports, diversions and typical, habituated patterns of interpretation can be identified by those in authority as more threat-ening and less willing to accept the established *status quo*. For these lads still believe, as it were, the rubric of equality, advance through merit and individualism which the school, in its anodyne way, has more or less unproblematically passed on to them. Thus, although there is no surface opposition, no insolent style to enrage the conventional onlooker, there is also no secret pact, made in the reflex moment of an oppositional style, to accept a timeless authority structure: a timeless 'us' and 'them'. Consequently, these kids are more likely to *expect real* satisfaction from their work; to expect the possibility of advance through hard work; to expect authority relations, in the end, to reflect only differences in competence. All these expectations, coupled frequently with a real unhappiness in the individual unrelieved by a social diversion, make the conformist lad very irksome and 'hard to deal with'. In manual and semi-skilled jobs, then, those in authority often actively prefer the 'lads' type to the 'ear-'ole' type. Underneath the 'roughness' of the 'lads' is a realistic assessment of their position, an ability to get on with others to make the day *and production* pass, and a lack of 'pushiness' about their job and their future in it. Finally, the 'lads' are more likeable because they have 'something to say for themselves', and will 'stand up for themselves', but only in a restricted mode which falls short of one of the 'us' wanting to join the 'them'. It is precisely this parlous ground upon which the conformist often unwit-tingly and unhappily stands. For one of the 'lads', not only is the shop floor more familiar than he might expect, but he is also welcomed and accepted by his new superiors in such a way that seems to allow for the expression of his own personality where the school had been pre-cisely trying to block it – this is an initial confirming response which further marks up the 'transition' from school as a liberation.

What is surprising in this general process of induction into the factory is the voluntary – almost celebratory – nature of the 'lads'' choice. The recognition of themselves in a future of industrial work is not a question of defeat, coercion or resignation. Nor is it simply the result of a managed, machiavellian process of social control. It is a question, at any rate in part and at least at this age, of an affiliation which is seen as joyous, creative and attractive. This fact is of enormous importance to us in understanding the true complexity of the reproduction of our social order: there is an element of 'self-damnation' in the acceptance of subordinate roles.

It is the partly autonomous functioning of the processes we have been considering which surprisingly accomplishes the most difficult task of state schooling: to 'direct' a proportion of kids to the unrewarding and basic tasks of industrial production. The word 'direct' is carefully chosen here since it need not have connotations of coercion, but it does make the unequivocality of the destination clear.

Pierre Bourdieu[8] argues that it is the exclusive 'cultural capital' – among other things, skill in the symbolic manipulation of language and figures – of the dominant groups in society which ensures the success of their offspring and so the reproduction of their class privilege. This is because educational advancement is controlled through the 'fair' meritocratic testing of precisely these skills which 'cultural capital' provides. We can make a bleak inversion of this hypothesis and suggest that it is the partly 'autonomous' counter-cultures of the working class at the site of the school which 'behind the back' of official policy ensure the continuity of its own underprivilege through the process we have just been considering. This process achieves the reproduction of under-privilege much more systematically than could any *directed* state policy. Of course state policy *says* it is doing the opposite. In this case, then, 'autonomous' working-class processes achieve the 'voluntary' reproduc-tion of their own conditions *in spite of* state policy. We cannot unravel this complex knot here, save to observe that the widespread *belief* in the egalitarianism of state policy – not least among teachers themselves – may be an essential prerequisite for the continual functioning of those *actual* processes which are working to the opposite effect.[9]

We have looked at aspects of the process whereby some typical working-class kids come to regard their future in the factory as natural, inevitable, and even freely chosen. We have seen the pivotal importance of the 'lads'' counter-school culture in this process. Analytically, there-fore, the most basic parameter in terms of so-called 'job choice' is affiliation or non-affiliation with this group, rather than the more or less random (correctly recorded in the major studies) influences – official and other – operating during the specific period of the actual passage from school to work. From my own work it is perfectly clear that this affiliation with the counter-school group can happen at any time from the second year onwards. I want to term this important process of affiliation *differentiation*: the separation of self from a pre-given system.[10]

Even where there had been some form of social division in the junior school – and there is plenty of evidence in 'ragging of teacher's pets' that there was, – in the first years of the secondary school everyone, it seems, is an 'ear-'ole'. Even the few of those who come to the school with a developed delinquent eye for the social landscape behave in a conformist way because of the lack of any visible support group. On 'coming out' as a 'lad':

> *Spike:* In the first year . . . I could spot the 'ear-'oles'. I knew who the fucking high boys was, just looking at 'em walking around the playground – first day I was there (. . .) I was just, was just quiet for the first two weeks, I just kept meself to meself like, not knowing anybody, it took me two years to get in with a few mates. But, er . . . after that, the third years was a right fucking year, fights, having to go to teachers a lot.

Still, whether the process is resumed or starts from afresh in later years, what can we understand of its elements and nature? Basically I suggest that we should understand *differentiation* not as some quality or change within the individual but as a *change in the relationship* – at a greater or lesser speed – between staff and pupils. The founding relationship between teacher and pupil in our society, and one which can endure for the entire pupil career of some individuals, is of superior/inferior established in the axis of institutionally-defined qualities – knowledge, development, effort, probity – and on the destruction, suppression or suspension of 'private' or 'other' axes of knowledge and control. This is something of an ideal type, and has been hardened here for the sake of clarity. Certainly some reformists might argue that there is more now allowed under the school roof than a conventional model of this type. Be that as it may, in terms of how schools are *actually* run in working-class areas, and certainly the ones I saw, this axial definition gives us the most useful paradigm for understanding actual behaviour. In a very obvious sense, despite much vaunted curriculum reform, teachers control what is taught in classes – most certainly in the early school years. This model, and especially what it tells us about the attitude to privacy, becomes most valuable, however, when we come to look at face-to-face relationships – and remember that the school is the agency of face-to-face control *par excellence*. The stern look of the inquiring teacher; the relentless pursuit of 'the truth' set up as a value even above good behaviour; the common weapon of ridicule; the accepted arrangements for tears after a caning; the stereotypical deputy head, body poised, head lowered, finger jabbing the culprit; the unexpected head bearing down on a group in the corridor: 'Where's your tie, think you own this place?' are all tactics for exposing and destroying, or freezing the private. What successful conventional teaching cannot tolerate is private reservation. And in the early forms in virtually any school it's plain to see that most kids are reciprocating in this relationship. The eager first-form hands reaching and snapping to answer first are all seeking approval from an acknowledged superior in a very particular institutional form. And in the *individual* competition for approval, the possibility of private reservations becoming *shared* to form any oppositional definition of the situation is decisively controlled. The teacher is given formal control of his pupils by the state, but unless he can exert his social control through an *educational* paradigm, his position would become merely that of the prison guard.

For the members of the 'lads'' culture, of course, that is exactly how the teachers are seen and, for the teacher, the change in relationship this implies makes his situation increasingly untenable and one of survival rather than of education. *Differentiation* is where the teacher's superiority is denied because the mode in which that superiority is expressed is delegitimated – there are *other* ways of valuing oneself. This valuation comes from those 'private' areas, *now shared* and made visible, which were held in check before. These resources are mobilized to penetrate the nature of the teacher's previous authority and to develop forms of resistance. The following is a classic statement – albeit exaggerated – of an attempt by a teacher to act against the 'private' or 'independent' area of the pupil's life, and of a resistance born of an essential belief that the teacher's authority is arbitrary, and predicated on an illegitimate suppression of other meanings and activities. In a discussion on teachers:

Joey: (. .) the way we're subject to their every whim like. They want something doing and we have to sort of do it, 'cos, er, . . er, we're just, 'cos, er . . , we're under them like. We were with a woman teacher in here, and 'cos we all wear rings and one or two of them bangles, like he's got one on, and out of the blue, like, for no special reason, she says, 'Take all that off.'

PW: Really?

Joey: Yeah, we says, 'One won't come off', she says, 'Take yours off as well.' I said, 'You'll have to chop my finger off first.'

PW: Why did she want you to take your rings off?

Joey: Just a sort of show like. Teachers do this, like, all of a sudden they'll make you do your ties up and things like this. You're subject to their every whim like. If they want something done, if you don't think it's right, and you object against it, you're down to Simmondsey (*the head*), or you get the cane, you get some extra work tonight.

And of course once this pupil analysis develops it soon moves off from a defensive resistance to an offensive one.

Joey: It's a sort of a challenge, coming to school thinking, 'How can I outwit the teachers today?', like. The teachers 're the establishment, they've done things to you, you don't like what they've done, how can you get back?

During this period of *differentiation* and after, one really decisive way of blocking the teacher's attempts to penetrate that which is private and informal is to be 'ignorant': to be uninterested in what the teacher has to offer. In a system where knowledge and the educational paradigm are used as a form of social control, 'ignorance' can be used in the same way as a barrier to control. The traditional notions of the causality of counter-school culture in low (measured) intelligence would, perhaps, be better reversed.

If the conventional paradigm of the teaching relationship is expressed powerfully in face-to-face situations, so is the differentiated resistance of the 'lads'. There is a particular overall style which communicates quite clearly to any teacher that 'this guy is not going to be pushed about'. It's a surly, disdainful look; a way of standing in the corridor as an obstruction though it could never be proved; a foot-dragging walk; an over-friendly hello; an attention on ties, fingers, shoes, books, anything rather than the inquiring eyes of the teacher which might penetrate too far.

For those involved the process of becoming a 'lad' is seen as a definite step towards maturity; it's 'coming out of your shell' or 'losing your timidity'. Diligence, deference, respect – these become things which can be read in quite another way.

PW: Evans (*the careers master*) said you were all being very rude, (. .) you didn't have the politeness to listen to the speaker (*during a careers session*). He said why didn't you realize that you were just making the world very rude for when you grow up and God help you when you have kids 'cos they're going to be worse. What did you think of that?

Joey: They wouldn't. They'll be outspoken. They wouldn't be submissive fucking twits. They'll be outspoken, upstanding sort of people.

Spanksey: If any of my kids are like this, here, I'll be pleased.

That area which I have called 'private' or the 'independent', which the teaching relationship attempts to suppress and which *differentiation* liberates, is, of course, the input to the school social system which derives most clearly from the outside. Fairly obviously, in a working-class area it derives from the working-class culture of the neighbourhood. In the accounts of the boys in the crucial period of affiliation with the 'lads', the external (to the school) content of their experience is evident. Often physically outside of the school, these incidents also draw on codes of conformism to delinquent or oppositional values which are not those of the school.

Spike: I'll tell you how it first started. It was Joey, Bill, Fred and Farmer (*all from his year at school*), they come round for me and I was . . never been out with them

and I was fucking shittin meself. I was scared I was.
I was only twelve or thirteen. Joey picked a crate of
bottles up, threw a bottle to each of us, and said,
'throw 'em' and we fucking threw 'em and Joey threw
the crate and it led from there to throwing bricks
into train windows, dropping fucking big boulders on
to trains, running from the screws, smoking. The
reason I say this smoking was to be big. I thought
'Oh, fucking hell, I'm thirteen, here I am, y'know,
great, fucking smoking.'

Bill: We all got together and started knocking about and
realized that we got to go up a bit like, you know,
we started to grow up a bit, bit more sensible things
you know . . , the third-years was the main, the
main year for us, when all the Crombies, and all the
Skinheads all started really, and we used to knock
about together up the (*name of a football ground*).

It will readily be seen that there is a huge reservoir of located cultural
meanings and possibilities for experience on the streets open to the
'lads' which is fundamentally working class. This is the basic material
which fuels the growing 'private' and 'independent' sector of school
experience. Understanding something of how these working-class
materials are taken up in the school, and into relationships with
teachers, it can be seen that counter-school culture is a particular,
worked-up, form of working-class culture taking on specific appearances
at the institutional level. We have, in the school counter-culture, a
classic case of the circle of entanglements which can occur between
state institutions and a situated class.

The very typical bottle-smashing incident described above cannot
reasonably be thought of as a *determining* instance of allegiance to
counter-school culture. Rather it should be thought of as a *crystalliza-
tion* of a basic shift in attitudes and loyalties. The boys, themselves,
very rarely identify for us any deep causes for the changes they describe
so vividly. Apparently, for them, it really is a question of *accidental*
causality – sitting by so-and-so in class, meeting 'the lads' at night by
chance or being 'called for' unexpectedly. Of course what these
accounts do testify to is the importance of the group, and the sense in
which, for particular individuals, the group always seems to have been
in existence. It is very clearly the strength and presence of the group
which allows the 'private' and previously reserved areas within the
individual to be expressed and become public.

Attempts to uncover the basic determinants of school counter-culture
are fraught with difficulties. It is here that we skirt the deep waters of
the determinacy of basic class cultures. Certainly we should be wary of
simplified causal explanations. We can, however, suggest some of the
possible factors which first break the individual from the mould of the

conventional teacher/pupil paradigm – and once opposition is born it is amplified through group processes and staff reaction, and ultimately becomes self-justifying.

Though it is only rarely verbalized, and though it is finally expressed only at the level of action and cultural involvement, we can discern at the heart of the 'lads'' culture a fundamental assessment of the real conditions facing them. At some basic level they weigh up and compare the likely outcomes of the possibilities facing them. Now since many of the boys involved enjoy a considerable native intelligence, we cannot assume that the outcome of taking the 'conformist road' is reckoned to be academic failure and obloquy. There is, therefore, at some level, an estimation of how even the *successful* outcome of the 'conformist road' – CSE, perhaps GCE passes and an office job – measures up to the results of taking the 'non-conformist road' – independence, social collectivity, celebration of direct experience. In one way these are, of course, the obvious and immediate pay-offs, the 'instant' as against 'deferred' gratifications. It *seems to be* these interests, as such, which win the day. In a discussion on 'ear-'oles':

Joey: (. . .) We wanna live for now, wanna live while we're young, want money to go out with, wanna go with women now, wanna have cars now, and er'm think about five, ten, fifteen years' time when it comes, but other people, say people like the 'ear-'oles', they'm getting their exams, they'm working, having no social life, having no fun, and they're waiting for fifteen years' time when they're people, when they've got married and things like that. I think that's the difference. We are thinking about now, and having a larf now, and they're thinking about the future and the time that'll be best for 'em.

However, I want to argue that this is not the thick-headed animal choice for the nearest bale of hay but the result of a collective and individual cultural process of some maturity which takes a sensible wager on the meaning and pay-offs of *several* possibilities over time.[11] The possibility of reaching up to the highest strata of employment through the school system as it confronts them in the working-class area seems to be so remote as to be meaningless.[12] The route of *relative* success – an office job – through conformism is more possible. Such an achievement, however, is viewed in a very ambivalent light. The 'real world', they felt in their bones, was not quite like the school account of it. The institution might give you a few CSEs but what did that matter if you were an 'ear-'ole'. 'Immediate gratification' might be the basis for the development of highly necessary *long-term* skills. It does not pay to be too 'timid' in the strange, modern, industrial metropolis. In a discussion of 'ear-'oles':

Spike: Well, they've got no push, I tell yer. Jones, Percival, or . . ., they've got nothing inside 'em to get up there, (. .) If they've got nothing inside 'em – no spunk to give 'em the push – they've gotta have somebody behind 'em to push 'em all the time, and that's no good. You can't survive like that.

In a specifically *cultural* mode, then, I am suggesting that the 'lads' make some basic assessment of their situation: most obviously of where their *immediate* interests lie, but also of the distinction between 'how things really work' and how the state institution of the school says they work;[13] of how actually to survive in the society which *they know*. Their own analysis is, in many ways, superior to that given to them by their teachers, and it clearly exerts a determining pressure upon the extent of allegiance to the 'lads'.

Another more obvious determining factor on this allegiance is the influence of parents. Involved in some form of shop-floor culture themselves, it is hardly surprising that their attitudes help to influence the behaviour of their offspring. Certainly for the 'lads' there is a widespread sense that their behaviour, in particular their opposition to the school and scorn of the weak and conformist, fits into a larger pattern, is expected of them in some way, and is part of an alternative pattern of being supported and protected by their parents against more official views; much in the way that they collectively supported their own alternative culture against the pressure of the school. In a discussion on 'ear-'oles':

Spanksey: (. .) you know, he ain't a mastermind (*his dad*) you know. He was a ruffian when he was younger you know, he's a larf you know. I couldn't. I don't think he'd like to see me, his kids, you know, me or our Barry or me little sister, 'ear-'oles, you know what I mean.

Will: Yeah, and with me, our old man, he was brainy like, but soon as he left school, started to work at the brewery, used to get the booze down him like you know I dare say, that influenced me.

Spanksey: What's that school on the way to the football Petty Coat Lane, something like that, that was a real rough school that was, in our dad's time, you know what I mean, and he's rough.

At the institutional level, it's also possible to suggest a possibility for how the *process* described above is initiated. In what might be called an act of 'cultural prolepsis', staff often put kids into a double-bind situation which can be broken only by fulfilling the *worst* expectations of the teacher. Often the teacher upsets his own conventional teaching paradigm by assuming *too early* that particular groups or individuals reject his superiority and the standards by which it is maintained – and who can grudge him this cultural assumption, faced with what has happened massively in the past? This means, however, that the pupil is presented with a goal which he is simultaneously told he can never reach. This is a very characteristic attitude of teachers towards kids on the edge of, or heading towards, or even actually in, counter-school culture: to make exhortations for behaviour of which it is denied the recipient is capable. In a discussion on recent urges by the staff:

Derek: (. .) They say you'm adults and that and yet, some things they, they'll say you're adults and then they'll say you'm responsible and all this, and then the next thing they'll turn around and say er, 'Walk down the corridor quietly in a line' and they'll treat us like children.

Since, apparently, it's impossible to be good, why not, at least, enjoy the devil's tunes.

The preceding has over-neatly divided the two categories of conformist and non-conformist. Any living school year is a complex mixture of individuals somewhere between these two points. Furthermore, it is also true that staff do not necessarily rate *very* conformist behaviour highly. Their own institutional axis of approved values registers a certain kind of obedience as 'girlishness', so that they often see a watered-down 'lads'' influence in a positive light. Certainly, there is a very important zone between the 'ear-'oles' and the 'lads' not dealt with in this paper, where the staff are able to control a certain independence, with its roots in the 'lads'' culture by the exercise of curriculum areas and practices which include elements of both the conventional teaching paradigm and the oppositional culture. Sport is the obvious example here, and the following extract comes from a boy who is precisely on this middle ground.

If it was true I wouldn't mind admitting I was an ear-'ole, but I think I come somewhere in between . . I suppose in the first year I was a bit of an ear-'ole, you know, and, like more, I've got on with the sports teachers, because I enjoy me sport and I've progressed, because I don't mind having a joke. I don't take it too serious but sometimes I crack a joke about the teachers, you know to their face sort of thing, and they see the funny side of it all. They don't seem to have relationship like that with the ear-'oles. They teach 'em, nice, good lads. They seem to treat me as somebody to talk to like.

I have been stressing the 'cultural level' and the way in which 'semi-autonomous' processes at this level have profoundly important material outcomes. In order to do this I have necessarily emphasized the 'creative', independent and even joyous aspects of working-class culture as it is, anyway, for the 'lads' during the 'transition' – they may well have different views a few years *into* work. Certainly we need to posit the attractiveness of this culture to avoid simple determinist and economist views of what makes kids go to the factory, and to establish properly the level of the 'voluntarism' by which these lads go to a future that most would account an impoverished one. However, we should be careful not to lionize or romanticize our concept of working-class culture. School counter-culture and shop-floor culture are fundamentally limited and stop well short of providing any fully worked-out future which is an alternative to the one they oppose. Indeed, in certain fundamental respects, we are presented with the contradiction that they actually – in the end – *do the work of bringing about the future that others have mapped for them*. The basic shortcoming of these cultures is that they have failed to convert *symbolic* power into *real* power. The real power thus still creates the most basic channels along which symbolic meanings run so that the symbolic power is used, in the end, to close the circle the *actual* power has opened up, and so finally to *reinforce* the real power relationships. The insistence of a human meaning which must justify its situation, but which does not have the *material* force to change its situation, can simply operate all too easily to legitimate, *experientially*, a situation which is fundamentally alien to it. To put it more concretely, the school counter-culture, for all its independence, accomplishes the induction of manpower 'voluntarily' into the productive process, and its mate, shop-floor culture, encourages an accommodation to, rather than a rejection of, the *fundamental* social relations there.

Something in the spirit of betrayal implicit in this kind of powerful and intensive, but formally limited, cultural organization is often caught in the semi-mythical, apocryphal, cultural folk wisdom of the shop floor. The following is an explanation of why young lads want to go on the shop floor given to me by a middle-aged worker in an engineering factory,

I was thirteen, like, an impressionable age. I s'pose, and this is something I've never forgotten. I was with my old man and we were at the zoo, and we saw a crowd up on the 'ill like, people were clapping, and all crowding around a gorilla's cage. We pushed to the front, like, Dad was more curious than me, like, he got right to the front, and there was this gorilla clapping and stamping, and lookin' around like, havin' a good time. All the people were clapping, egging him on like. Then he suddenly come to the front of the cage and spat a mouthful of water, comin' forward, clapping like, then spitting the water out all over 'em.

My old man stood back really shocked like . . . then he went back in the crowd and waited for some other silly buggers to push forward. I didn't realize then, like, I was only a kid, what it meant like . . ., but I do now. We don't all grow up at once, see, that's life, we don't grow up at the same time, and when you've learnt it's too late. It's the same with these kids comin' in the factory, every time, they think it's great. 'Oh, what's this, I wanna be there', y'know what I mean. You'll never change it, it's the same with everything, comin' to work, getting married, anything – you name it.

There is a fairly clear theory here about what makes kids want to start work, as well as a long-suffering, half-amused, typical working-class fatalism. There is also the ironic dynamic of the morality play. What is most noticeable, however, is a naturalized sense of timelessness: 'life's like that'. It's nobody's fault, nobody's failure, that makes the gorilla spit, or shop-floor life kill with monotony, or the wife nag to an early grave. It's simply the grim reality that humans have *always* faced. The same principle of the treacherous appearance disguising – and leading to an entrapment in – the real situation below is common to many aspects of working-class culture, and particularly in people's attitudes to the main transitions of life: birth, death, marriage, retirement, religious conversion. Even sometimes, it seems, death will turn out not to have been worth the trouble, though of course, the compelling unity of the drama means that the full ritual of the funeral cortege, plus cars bigger than ever were ridden in during life, must be gone through. We may suggest, however, that this final powerlessness before nature might be less of a universal law, and more a product of a specific, historic and continuing failure of working-class culture to achieve a basic modification of the conditions which brought it into being. For all its symbolic resistance, the moving spirit of working-class culture till the present has been accommodation to a pre-given reality, rather than an active attempt to change it.

The reasons for this basic limitation stretch right back to the history of the world's first industrial proletariat and we cannot go into them now, but two contemporary factors might be mentioned specifically in relation to shop-floor culture. The trade union is the institutional extension of the culture of the workplace, the form in which culture and its meanings might have become more visible and the vehicle through which really concrete attempts have been made to transform *symbolic* into *real* control.

Trade unions, however, can be seen in their modern function merely as a mediation between shop-floor culture and the dominant managerial culture. Unionism negotiates the space between them and, in this negotiation, gives up much that is really central to the shop floor for what is often simply an accommodation in managerial interests. The nature of unionism and its organization is not, however, evenly textured. While the union bosses adopt a form of managerial culture and join the main industrial establishment,[14] the shop stewards and local organizers are still very much of the local culture. While trying to achieve union and organizational aims, they use specifically cultural forms of communication – spectacle, buffs, drama, jokes, sabotage, to mobilize the man.[15] The union structure, then, is a complex and varied institution which strikes different degrees of appeasement at its various levels. The power of shop-floor culture determines at least the *form* of union activity at plant level, but the higher administrative level has completely lost that detailed binding-in with the lived culture of the work-place which was the original guarantee of true representativeness. To put it another way, the unions have lost touch with, even betrayed, the real roots of working-class radicalism – the culture of the shop floor.

From the side of capital, one of the most important controls on the power of shop-floor culture to challenge its own conditions is the practice of management science and human relations. Under the banner of a 'neutral' humanization of the work process, it has been one of the most formidable techniques of social control ever developed. Essentially, human relations rest on a simple and obvious discovery: informal groups exist. This is precisely, of course, the area covered by the culture of the shop floor. Hard on the discovery of this territory came techniques for colonizing it. Techniques of 'employee-centred supervision', 'consultation', 'open door relations' can neutralize oppositional shop-floor culture on its own grounds by claiming the informal group for management ideology. This can unbend its springs of action. The sense of control given to the workers by these techniques is usually illusory – the basic structures of power remain – and yet the located, rich, potentially dominating culture of resistance is being destroyed.

Whatever the final balance-sheet drawn of strengths and weaknesses in shop-floor and working-class cultures,[16] the point of this article has been to stress the continuity of school culture with the wider class culture, and to draw attention to the deep-moving processes of regeneration among this class – some of the most important of which occur at the site of the school. These processes should not be mistaken, in the sociology of education, for mere institutional flux or localized disturbance. What is *not supposed* to go on in school may have more significance for us than what is *supposed* to go on in school.

Key

( )	background information
(inaudible)	part of sentence inaudible
/ /	description relating to collective activity
. . . .	long pause
. . .	pause
. .	short pause
. . ,	phrase incompleted
, . .	phrase completed, then pause
(. .)	phrase edited out
(. . .)	sentence edited out
(. . . .)	passage edited out

–	speaker interrupting or at same time as another speaker
- - -	transcription from a different discussion follows
—	speaker or name not identified

Notes

1 This article is based on the findings of a project at the Centre for Contemporary Cultural Studies between April 1973 and June 1975, financed by the SSRC, on the 'transition from school to work' of white working-class average to low ability boys in a Midlands industrial conurbation. It used intensive case-study methods and participant observation based on a number of schools and factories in this region. The 'main' case study was of a friendship group of twelve boys as they proceeded through their last four terms in a single-sex secondary modern school (it was twinned with a girls' school of the same name). The school was adapting itself organizationally – mixed ability groupings, timetable blocking, destreaming, etc. – in preparation for an expected redesignation as a comprehensive school which finally occurred only after the case study group had left. All of the parents of the lads were interviewed in depth, and a period of participant observation was spent with each of the lads at some point in the first six months of their respective work situations. The full results of this work will be available in *Learning to Labour: How Working-class Kids get Working-class Jobs*, from Saxon House, 1977.

2 A. Gramsci, *Selections from the Prison Notebooks of Antonio Gramsci*, ed. and trans. Q. Hoare and G. Nowell Smith, Lawrence & Wishart, 1971, p. 40.

3 D. H. Hargreaves, *Social Relations in a Secondary School*, Routledge & Kegan Paul, 1967; M. D. Shipman, *Sociology of the School*, Longman, 1968; Ronald A. King, *School Organization and Pupil Involvement*, Routledge & Kegan Paul, 1973; Michael F. D. Young, *Knowledge and Control: New Directions in the Sociology of Education*, Collier-Macmillan, 1971; Colin Lacey, *Hightown Grammar*, Manchester University Press, 1970.

4 See for instance M. P. Carter, *Into Work*, Penguin, 1969, Kenneth Roberts, *From School to Work: Study of the Youth Employment Service*, David & Charles, 1972.

5 For instance the admirable and pioneering D. H. Hargreaves, op. cit.

6 *Scientific Management*, Greenwood Press, 1972; first published 1947.

7 For a fuller explanation of this concept and its relation to the 'connoted', see Roland Barthes, *Mythologies*, Cape, 1972; Paladin, 1973; Barthes, *Elements of Semiology*, Cape, 1967. Basically the difference between *denoted* and *connoted* refers to the difference between the direct and intended message of a particular communication, and the indirect, often unintended, messages which are communicated at the same time through such processes as association, generalized suggestion and use of available cultural stereotypes. I consider the important 'connoted' level of careers information elsewhere, see *Learning to Labour*.

8 Pierre Bourdieu and Jean-Claude Passeron, *La Réproduction; éléments pour une théorie du système d'enseignement*, Editions de Minuit, 1971.

9 *Learning to Labour* deals more fully with these questions.

10 I argue elsewhere that this is a fundamental principle of working-class

culture in general: 'Human Experience and Material Production: the Culture of the Shop Floor', University of Birmingham, Centre for Contemporary Cultural Studies (duplicated).

11 A mathematician could tabulate these possibilities in the form of a non-zero-sum-game and come up with very similar results.

12 And surely figures for university entrance amongst the working class proper support them in this.

13 This bears an interesting relationship to the Marxist distinction between the 'state' and 'civil society', as does the 'lads'' *cultural* concept of generalized labour to the notion of general labour power, and as does the folk wisdom notion of false appearances (described later) bear a relationship to the Marxist notions of real relations/phenomenal forms. I develop the meaning of these 'coincidences' for a notion of advanced proletarian 'consciousness' in *Learning to Labour*.

14 Tony Lane, *The Union Makes us Strong: the British Working Class, its Politics and Trade Unionism*, Arrow Books, 1974.

15 H. Beynon, *Working for Ford*, Allen Lane, 1973.

16 These questions are taken up more fully in *Learning to Labour*.

2.3

Qualified criticism, critical qualifications†

Mary Fuller

Deviant pupils will always merit the attention of the sociologist of education since, on the basis of a relativistic conception of deviance, they can be interpreted as 'cultural critics' or 'political dissenters'.

. . . it is held that deviant pupils' opposition is a rational response grounded in their partial demystification of the social systems of which they are members.

(Hargreaves 1979)

I want in this paper to examine young people's criticisms of and dissent from the social systems in which they operate. [. . .]

I shall look at the linkages between young people's criticisms of 'society' and their stance as pupils within school, focusing especially on the extent to which a pupil's dissident position in relation to school is associated with a critical view of the other social systems of which s/he is a member. I do this because there is a strong sense in the literature that deviant pupils are cultural critics not only of education/schooling but also that this criticism extends to some if not all other aspects of their lives. The obverse of this, though not usually explicitly stated, is that those pupils who are not deviant are conformers in school and, by extension, within the other social systems of which they are members.

. . . My research involved males and females and included pupils of white British, Afro-Caribbean and Indo-Pakistani parentage, which enables me to discuss acquiescence and opposition as these are manifested by pupils who are differentially located in the same social systems. By coming at this discussion from two different angles I hope to show that a more complex analysis is required of the relationship between in-school behaviour and pupils' critical attitudes to their lives

† Source: L. Barton and S. Walker (eds) (1983), *Race, Class and Education*, Croom Helm, London, pp. 166–90.

outside school. I shall look first at the incidence of deviant and other pupils at the school which I call Torville, trying to relate their dissidence concerning school to their attitudes to life outside school, taking their critical awareness of two forms of domination (sexism and racism) as the focus for establishing their degree of acquiescence or opposition to the social system generally. Then, taking those people who are resisting sexual and racial domination, I shall look at the extent to which they demonstrate the kinds of behavioural and attitudinal orientation which is recognised as criticism of school culture.

I shall be re-examining some research which I completed in 1978 which came up with some information about whose interpretations I have remained unsatisfied. The problem was how to reconcile others' writing about girls' conformity and acquiescence (actually in most cases an impression left by their failure to be mentioned in the literature concerning school deviants rather than an established fact) with my own observations of young women at Torville school being actively critical and contemptuous of much that was going on around them in and outside school. Indeed, in regard to many aspects of their current and likely future lives some of the fifth-year girls were markedly *more* critical and politically sophisticated than most of the boys. Yet in terms of overt 'symptoms' within the school the girls' opposition to what was actually, and what in the future they thought was likely to be, happening to them, did not come across as obviously oppositional or troublesome in the terms that others describe 'troublesome' male pupils.

The school was a large, mixed multi-racial comprehensive in the London borough of Brent. For the Autumn and Spring terms in 1975/76 I observed the school lives of a group of fifth-year pupils. Wherever possible I also participated in that life. My role was as a non-teaching adult, a kind of 'honorary pupil' who attended lessons, socialised with pupils outside the classroom (within school hours) and who in the second term more obviously engaged in research in that I administered questionnaires and more formally and systematically interviewed pupils using a tape recorder.

[. . .] I kept a running record of information about pupils which I used to build up a reputational profile of each pupil. There was a fair degree of overlap concerning any particular pupil's reputation among the teachers who taught him/her and a more than expected consensus between pupils and teachers concerning the reputation of each particular pupil. Most pupils also, when asked in interview how they were seen by staff, had a pretty accurate understanding of their status in teachers' minds. . . . I also recorded teachers' comments about every pupil from the pupils' most recent school report, a source of information which was relatively free from biases introduced by my own skills and weaknesses as an observer. [. . .] Using only the reports I was able to devise an independent typology of pupils, according to the total number of positive and negative comments each received on their report. (Full details of this in Fuller 1978.) [. . .] This provided independent confirmation of the typology based on hearsay and pupils' observed behaviour in the classroom. Pupils could be described as one of the following: good, bad, conspicuous and unobtrusive. In some measure all except the first category were troublesome to teachers. [. . .]

Bad pupils included all those who were overtly antagonistic but this category was not made up exclusively of such pupils. A pupil could be seen as bad in terms of having undesirable 'personality' characteristics and not solely on the basis of simple behavioural resistance. Good pupils were those who worked hard and effectively, who 'contributed to the school' but who did not draw their positive attitude to school to the teacher's attention. Unobtrusive pupils included the few recent arrivals, but also some whose lack of connection with teachers and school routines meant that they were hardly known to the teachers. They were a puzzle to the teachers but not a 'problem' in the sense of being troublesome enough to greatly exercise teachers' attention. The conspicuous were, in terms of effort and achievement, similar to the good pupils but in addition, unlike the good, they came in for a disproportionately large number of negative comments as well. Well-known to the teachers, they were also a puzzle, being a mixture of 'bad' and teacher-approved behaviour and attitudes. What lay behind this mixture was the view 'I can get something (vocationally worthwhile) from school even though school work is itself boring.'

Table 6.1 distinguishes male and female pupils in each of the categories.

	Good	Bad	Unobtrusive	Conspicuous
Girls	19	13	7	5
Boys	26	31	15	6

Rather more boys than girls are defined as bad pupils, a finding which in itself is unsurprising given what others have written about pupil resistance. Of considerably more interest is the relatively high proportion of girls seen as bad pupils by the teachers at Torville, and the fact that the difference between the sexes is not statistically significant. This categorisation of pupils does not isolate the overtly antagonistic but includes them with other pupils who are defined by teachers as educationally problematic because of certain disapproved of characteristics. Nevertheless all 'bad' pupils deviate from Torville teachers' concept of acceptable attitudes and behaviour, a concept which, as already mentioned, was shared by many of the pupils (including the 'bad' ones).

At Torville school there seems to be no support for the view that girls are massively more approved by teachers, nor that being troublesome in educationally relevant ways is the prerogative of boys. It is also important to note that there were no significant differences between the female and male pupils in terms of why they were viewed as bad – the types of attitudinal and behavioural characteristics of which teachers disapproved were more or less equally evident in their reports about both girls and boys.

[. . .] A much higher proportion of good pupils aspired to taking a large number of public exams ('O' level and/or 'CSE') and a much larger proportion of bad pupils had low aspirations in this respect. Others have noted a close association between teachers' perceptions of a pupil and that pupil's attainment at school. Although a relationship of this kind could be established in the Torville study, it broke down when specific groups of pupils were analysed. Of relevance to the present paper is the fact that Afro-Caribbean girls' high levels of attainment bore no relationship to the way teachers saw them. It was when I started to try to make sense of these findings that I became aware of some of the limitations and conceptual confusions surrounding conformity and deviance in school settings.

Wilkinson (1975) has suggested that black youth in America 'must still contend with social issues that never confront white youth'. Black youth in Britain – female and male – experience relations of racial domination and exclusion, a 'social issue' never far from the surface of their discussions with me when I was carrying out the research already mentioned. Women, whether black or white, experience relations of sexual domination and exclusion and this, too, was central to their thinking about their lives inside and outside school.

One of the major themes emerging from interviews with fifth-form girls at Torville school was that of control. For girls of all ethnic groups there were three inter-related aspects of their discussions. Firstly, their being controlled by others in and out of school; secondly, their wish for control for themselves at some time in the future; and lastly (and perhaps paradoxically), their need to exercise forms of self-control and suppression of resentment now in order to achieve self-determination later. In all these respects girls, whether white, Afro-Caribbean or South Asian, consciously compared themselves with boys of their own age and ethnic group as a means of examining their experiences and reflecting on their schooling. Most of them had brothers, all had friends with brothers, some had boyfriends and all were attending a co-educational school. In short, they were all speaking from direct experience of sexual differences in social relations.

The girls almost without exception described their lives as 'restricted' and lacking in 'freedom', a state of affairs for which parents were held mainly responsible. For some there was the knowledge or hope that as they grew older their parents would reduce the areas of control, though none felt that the simple passing of time would bring them the degree of freedom their brothers or male peers could expect. Thus they saw young women older than themselves enjoying more freedom of movement than they themselves had, but even so being still subject to more parental attempts at control than male peers. For many more, and this applied especially to ethnic minority girls, even small gains would have to be struggled for. This is not to suggest that black parents are more repressive than white parents, but to recognise that they saw that as women of colour their prospects of obtaining some degree of independence through work outside the home as being considerably restricted.

To wrest small gains meant adopting various strategies – some self-denying – such as 'biting back' their criticisms and resentments or acquiring characteristics of, for example, deceit or 'toughness' about which they were somewhat ambivalent. Interestingly, when completing the Bem Sex Role Inventory (Bem 1974) both Indo-Pakistani and Afro-Caribbean girls endorsed the following characteristics as applying to them: self-reliant, defends own beliefs, independent, athletic, has a strong personality, analytical, self-sufficient and ambitious. These are all, according to Bem's trials, supposedly masculine traits and were certainly less frequently endorsed by white girls at Torville.

Schooling and education provided an alternative and less under-mining possibility in their search for greater freedom and control. Concentration on education as a way out was something which all the black girls whom I interviewed stressed, though as will be seen and as they pointed out this strategy had its drawbacks. In particular the vocational aspects of schooling and further education were attractive in that their achievements in these areas were thought to lead to better prospects of a 'good' job. Being aware of both sexual and racial discrim-ination, the girls did not assume that good educational performance was the sufficient requirement for obtaining such jobs, but they did believe it was a necessary one.

It is for these reasons that I describe qualifications as 'critical' for these girls. And it is partly because of the critical importance of qualifi-cations in their current thinking about the future that the girls them-selves qualify and temper their criticisms of both their school experience and their treatment by parents. [. . .] The following accounts depend on the girls' own words and on their ways of representing the dilemmas they face and of thinking their way through them. It is not possible to say whether these girls are representative of the young, female black population in Britain, because there are so few accounts of young women's lives in school and among those that exist there is hardly a mention of young black women.

Afro-Caribbean girls

Parents were judged more or less 'strict' or 'old-fashioned' according to whether they placed numerous or relatively few restrictions on their daughter's life out of school. By this yardstick the parents of all but one girl were described as strict. This showed itself particularly in a double standard in which boys were positively encouraged to be out of the house and were allowed considerable freedom of movement, while girls were given little option but to remain within the home. According to Michelle, West Indian parents are:

More protective over girls, they reckon that the boys from the time they hit 13, they should be out, mucking around playing football. If they do anything 'boys will be boys', but girls (are) supposed to stay at home and sit there. [. . .] . . . My mum keeps going on at my brother, when he was younger she kept going on at him, wondering what he was doing in the house. She expects him to be out, but if I ask to go out, good grief, hits the roof. She wants to know where I want to go, why, and I must be back at a certain time, who am I going with, and I must leave a phone number, all that sort of stuff.

Within the home girls are kept busy: as one girl succinctly put it, the choice is 'housework or homework'. Christa says of one of her friends:

. . . her mum told us that Marcia likes work, she's always got a maths book, always got some reading, some book with her. . . . She does that excuse to get away from the housework.

Considerable arguments take place between girls and their mothers and brothers at the differential expectations concerning domestic tasks. Boys are apparently expected to help very little around the house:

The work that my brother does, that mum sets him in the house, it's just the bins. (Christa)

I have to tidy up behind him (brother), so I suppose he thinks I'm like a maid or a slave. (Joan)

They are resentful, vociferous in their dislike of such 'favouritism', but also take pride in their domestic skills; especially as they believe it indicates greater competence than their brothers have and as they appreciate the degree of overwork to which their mothers are subject.

Despite having considerable criticisms of the sexual division of labour within their own families, all the girls expressed great fondness for their mothers. Mothers were the ones who talked to and encouraged them, to whom they could talk and who, much more than fathers, interpreted the world outside the family. Talking about friends who have both parents living with them, Christa observes:

. . . their mother is always first, their mother is more like their . . . . It's like they haven't got a father at all, their mother is just there.

[. . .] Several other girls talked about their fathers as not so much uninterested in them as being the parent who basically laid down the rules, but was not around to ensure that they were complied with. That task was left to mothers. Once some of the girls had realised this they had decided to stop rebelling directly, bide their time and then enlist their mother's support in sidestepping their father's attempts at controlling them. In this they had sometimes been successful, but the resulting better relation with their mothers was accompanied by ambivalence at their deceit and an increased sense that it was not possible to achieve what they wanted by rational argument with their fathers.

. . . I've settled down, because you see before, my friends have a lot more freedom, they can go out and all that kind of thing, whereas I wasn't allowed to at that time, and I used to moan about it and kick up a big fuss. But then I went quiet and just left it and I think well maybe they feel she's grown up a bit now . . . (Beverley)

. . . I would say that women are more understanding, they can reason out things with you. There's only a few men that can do that. Men, they lose their temper . . . Men are more stronger than women . . . Women are more advanced, but men are more physical. . . . she's better at talking and explaining than my dad. He stutters – well he doesn't explain himself properly. . . . I mainly just talk to my mum. (Monica)

The inability of males to engage in rational arguments and their resort to physical forms of control was an important part of the girls' discussions about relationships with boys of their own generation. Although none of them looked to marriage as bringing greater autonomy (as many white girls did), and indeed only two looked forward to marrying, most supposed they would marry in the distant future. When that time came they would want their husbands to be black. Janice speaks for a number of others in describing marriage as follows:

Well you're tied to one person, that can be boring, you can get tired of it. You're restricted in what you can do, what you can't do, then the kids come in. . . . That's what you get married for, really, just that it will be legal for the kids.

Even where they were not allowed or did not themselves yet want boyfriends, the girls nevertheless considered black boys an important source of friendship. Boys were claimed to resort frequently to 'beating' girls in order to establish their dominance over them and to retain their reputation with male peers.

[. . .] You know most coloured boys tend to knock their girls about. . . . They've got this vicious streak in them, so I warn them 'If you think you can knock me about, you've got another thought coming, because I'll knock you back then I'll walk off'. (Janice)

. . . well most West Indian boys . . . definitely aren't going to let a woman dominate them or tell them what to do. They firmly believe that they're the boss and she has to do everything they tell them. I think West Indian men are more aggressive because there's this thing that as soon as a woman gets out of place they hit her for it . . . . (Beverley)

Consequently the girls felt they needed to acquire some skills to back up a reputation for not being a 'softy' and to become at least partly inured to boys' violence – actual or threatened. In so doing a number were described by the black boys at Torville as girls who 'like to try to bully about'. In addition girls were often divided from each other by competition for boys, sometimes engaging in physical but more often in verbal attacks on each other. As Marcia, in her own words 'a well-known softy', explains:

> If someone did come up against me I'd try my very best to beat them and show them that I can actually fight. Because that would be a real achievement for me because I try to be tough because people really trample on you if you're not. I'm soft in nature.

Looking to boys for friendship had other hazards – many of the girls felt they had to keep their school and job ambitions to themselves for fear that if they were discovered they would be subject to undermining ridicule from their male peers.

> I find that most boys do have ambitions but they're influenced by their friends so they never get put into practice anyway . . . I think the girls are more ambitious but if they want to do something they don't feel embarrassed about it except when boys, when they hear you're doing 'O' levels, they won't come out with it and say you're a snob but they treat you a bit differently and you can feel it . . . (Joan)

Marcia describes the pressures from boys in the following way:

> I've always got my head in a book. I don't think they like it because they are always commenting on it and they say 'You won't get anywhere', and sometimes I think that they don't want me to learn or something like that, you know, but I spoke to my mum about it, and she said I shouldn't listen and I should keep working hard.

The experience or expectation of ridicule from boys is not confined to Afro-Caribbean girls. Shaw (1980) argues that it is a fact of life for girls to be the butt of boys' abuse and scorn in school, especially the nearer they come to challenging male dominance. Shaw, and Coleman (1961), point out that the result of this is that girls either withdraw from the competition or adopt various dissembling strategies. These black girls most certainly did not withdraw and it is to their attitudes and behaviour in school that I now turn.

[. . .] They had an instrumental orientation to education, believing that it could offer them something useful (paper qualifications) in their longer terms efforts to obtain a measure of control over their lives. So long as it was providing those opportunities they were prepared to conform minimally within the classroom and maximally in terms of doing the work that was set. But beyond a certain point they felt constrained by boys' disapproval for showing enthusiasm for school. School itself was 'trivial', 'boring', a place in which it was vital to introduce an element of 'liveliness', partly for its own sake, partly to mask their ambitions.

> . . . I talk to me friends in the corridor and if they talk about
> something interesting I'm not going to rush off to my lesson, am I?
> I want to hear what they say first before I go, so that makes me late
> sometimes. . . . Miss G., well sometimes I go late to her lessons,
> but when I go to the classroom if she's not there so I go out again.
> I try to get back in again before she comes . . . Just go and talk to
> your friends – if their teacher hasn't come in as well, you go in and
> talk to them and then you keep an eye on the door to see if your
> teacher's coming and when you see her coming down the corridor
> you just rush in quick. You know that she sees you but you still
> rush in. (Michelle)

They were frequently in conflict with teachers as a result of this 'bad'
behaviour and because they would insist on teachers 'doing their job
properly' even though they might subsequently appear to ignore the
teaching. The girls hoped to obtain 'good' jobs (within the restrictions
of traditional women's work) and talked of the need to be ambitious if
they were to avoid unemployment or dead-end jobs. Janice was aiming
to become a Personal Secretary because it paid well and because it is
the kind of job where 'most of the work depends on you, you know
you're relied on to use your initiative'. The value they placed on educational qualifications as a necessary preparation for work was clearly
related to their knowledge of high unemployment levels nationally and
locally and to their certainty that they would face discrimination in the
job market. As part of their attempts to sidestep discrimination all the
girls remained in full-time education for at least one year beyond the
statutory school leaving age. Those who, at about age seventeen, had
taken up work all mentioned that they were continuing their studies on
a part-time basis. By the time I had completed the study the girls had
obtained a mean of 7.6 passes at 'O' level or CSE and generally with
creditable grades.

Their commitment to achievement through the job market can be
seen in the following extracts:

> I want a proper job first and some kind of skill so that if I do get
> married and have children I can go back to it: don't want just
> relying on him for money, cause I've got to look after myself, there
> must be something I can do. (Michelle)

> I should go out to work because, really, if I don't start learning to
> get on with it, I maybe will just have to leave home, get married
> and depend on the husband and I don't want that at all . . . Maybe
> I'll be a housewife or something like that, but I always picture
> myself working. (Monica)

I would suggest that the girls' cherished hopes of greater control over
their future lives and their consequent emphasis on acquiring qualifications and a 'good' job are not some form of individualistic self-improv-
ement. Rather, they are necessary strategies for survival where the

poor employment prospects and low wages which black males can command make it essential even in intact families for women to contribute financially to the family income. Whether to seek employment is not a real issue for most black women, but how to maximise their wage is. The young women at Torville are aiming to have some choice about the type of work they obtain and the conditions in which they carry out such work. Unless their efforts to circumvent racial and sexual exclusion in employment are successful they are likely to find themselves in unskilled and semi-skilled jobs and being paid at even lower rates of pay than their male counterparts.

Some already have experience of attempts to exclude them from the job market:

> When I first went for the job I was very crafty when I wrote the letter I put that I was a student and they thought I was coming from university and I did it in perfectly good English so they wouldn't think it was a foreign person. And then when I went and they actually saw I was coloured I think they were a bit shocked, so they kept stalling and said 'Come back tomorrow' . . . . Every time they said come back I'd go back and I'd go back. My dad was backing me all the way and in the end I got through. (Christa)

It is perhaps not surprising that, taken up with their resistance to sexual and racial exclusion, the girls much admire perseverance, stamina, resourcefulness and a thick skin. In the circumstances it should not be too surprising that few of them have a clear idea what specifically they will make of their 'freedom'.

> My grandmother . . she's another one who had things tough so she's always going on at me to succeed . . . I know what I want out of life, I know where I'm heading. I think all I really want to do is just succeed. I don't know what I'll do when I do succeed though! (Beverley)

Asian girls

I shall use the term Asian in referring to these girls who were of Indo-Pakistani parentage. One girl was British born, three had been born in the Indian subcontinent, and seven had been born in East Africa and so were, at the time of the study, relatively recent arrivals in Britain.

Their reflections on their current and future lives were framed much more in terms of sexual than racial politics. This is not to suggest that they were unaware of social relations of racial domination – indeed some had been subject to racial attacks on their way to and from school. But as far as they were concerned these would (and did) impinge on them less than relations of sexual dominance and political forces within their own group. So, for example, when talking about employment they were exercised about whether they would be allowed or discouraged from working by their future husband or mother-in-law: racial exclusion in the job market was, at that stage in their lives, a concern of secondary importance.

Marriage would be a fact of life, as Nirmala among several others stressed: 'In our culture, we have to get married, we can't stay at home.' As young women of fifteen or sixteen, they were approaching (if they had not already passed) the age when their own mothers had married. From my interviews marriage emerged as the central fact which organised their thinking about their present lives at home and their opportunities at school. Their present strategies at home and in terms of education could be best understood as attempts to manoeuvre for themselves some choice within some definite and basically accepted constraints. Girls might be critical of the most traditional aspects of arranged marriages, and sometimes discussed a particular marriage which did not seem to be working well:

> I saw some marriages that were arranged and they were disasters, for the girls especially, she had to suffer. . . . On the surface many marriages look nice and they try to look happy. (Sadhana)

Whether to marry was not at issue – the girls knew that they would and that their husband would be chosen for them by parents. As a principle, and despite some worries about it in practice, the arranged marriage system was something they supported:

> If I like a boy I wouldn't want to get serious with him, but if it can't be helped . . . but even in the end I would marry the person my father said. I wouldn't want to hurt my parents. (Ila)

Uppermost in their minds was how to obtain a measure of control about when and whom they would marry. They wanted to marry at a later age than their mothers (the early twenties was the commonest preference) and hoped for a boy who was not 'traditional', by which was meant a boy from the subcontinent. These could be matters for negotiation depending on whether the girls perceive their parent as 'modern' or 'advanced' (that is, willing to consult and take into account the girl's opinions about particular prospective husbands) and partly on their ability to persuade parents to 'trust' them. Beyond this their futures were much more uncertain – a future husband and/or mother-in-law, both of whom would have considerable say in what she could do, might turn out to be sufficiently 'old-fashioned' as to want to prevent her working outside the home.

> . . . honestly, if you ask any Indian girl at the present 'If you get married what would worry you the first thing?', the husband would be modern type but the mother-in-law they are sort of old fashioned, they prefer it happens as in old fashioned times, you see . . . . I wouldn't like to get married yet, especially in our Indian marriages.

> If you get mother-in-law, all they want from us is to cook food and
> not to go to work . . . (Amita)

Being a 'traditional' wife was not a cherished dream and to avoid the
situation outlined by Amita they believed having a 'decent' job would
help in negotiating a less traditional role. Consequently they were
aiming for jobs which could not be dismissed as unrespectable. . . .

Girls could strengthen their bargaining position with parents now and
in the near future and, they hoped, with in-laws in the more distant
future by successfully pursuing certain aspects of education which will
be discussed later. 'Trust' was a more complex issue. It was certainly
one of the main areas for complaint about parents' differential treatment of girls and boys in the family. Girls talked as though they were
assumed to be inherently untrustworthy or at the very least so weak-
willed as to be readily led astray.

> My mum treats my younger brother really well than she treats me.
> It's not really fair, so I have to argue. I say 'It's just because he's
> a son and we're daughters that you don't let us go out' and all that.
> So they say 'If you were a boy we would let you go out, but you're
> a girl and boys do sorts of things to you these days'. She says 'I
> know it wouldn't be your fault if you went out with a boy . . . but
> boys give you such a lot of energy, and they heat you up in such a
> way that you're bound to get up to something with them and things
> are bound to go wrong'. . . . boys have more freedom, they have
> more respect than girls do. (Meena)

Since their parents' belief in them as untrustworthy did not appear to
be based on specific incidents of bad behaviour, the girls found it
puzzling to know how this reputation could be refuted, other than by
the most stern self-control. The girls complained bitterly of a double
standard which granted boys some latitude, but blamed girls for
bringing dishonour on the family when they attempted to behave in
similar ways. According to the girls family honour rested more heavily
on their shoulders, but boys could afford some lapses. Everything a girl
did, especially in public, had direct bearing on her future marriageability, and within her own family on her bargaining position about
marriage.

> . . . if I were to run away with a boy, and the time comes up for
> my little sister to get married people would say her sister was one
> of those flirts so she might be one . . . they say it runs in the family,
> so my sister wouldn't find a nice bloke to get married . . . So that's
> how the family reputation gets ruined . . . boys get girls to marry
> easily, but girls have to suffer because it's girls that can get pregnant
> when they go round with boys . . . (Meena)

There was much criticism of the unfair sexual division of labour within
the family and of the greater freedom of movement which brothers

enjoyed. However, the girls tempered their criticisms at home because they believed such sentiments might be interpreted as a wish on their part to be more 'westernized' and so bring down further restrictions on them.

But their criticisms are not only qualified by these considerations. The girls believed that their parents were sometimes prevented from being as 'modern' as they would choose: firstly, by the fear of gossip with its potential for ruining a family's reputation; and secondly, because England is less 'decent' than the subcontinent and East Africa and so their children must be protected more here.

While some girls described their parents as 'modern' in the sense already described, they took it for granted that parents and children had somewhat distant relationships with each other. So none looked to parents as people in whom they confided or with whom they would consider discussing 'personal' matters. Support of this kind was sought from sisters, cousins and friends of about their own age and was offered to those younger than themselves.

> . . . I've got a little sister, so I would have to look after her . . . and explain to her and generally look after when she gets into trouble. Things she can't tell my parents she will have to tell me, won't she, because there are certain things you can't tell your parents. (Ila)

With homework and housework commitments and with some restrictions on visiting friends, opportunities for conversations about the matters they could not raise with parents tended to be limited. This was one of the values of school – parents could not disapprove of them attending [. . .] and it was a place which afforded frequent opportunities for discussions in mixed or girls-only groups. It is perhaps not surprising that in these circumstances the girls were less critical of school than Afro-Caribbean girls nor that they engaged in fewer openly confrontational incidents with teachers or other pupils. The majority were seen as 'good' pupils, but they were by no means docile conformists. For example, they could be highly critical of teachers who, as they saw it, failed to keep classes in order, did not explain work adequately, or who expected too little of pupils.

> . . . sometimes I have a tiff with Mr. Jameson [. . .] And sometimes I'm horrible and say things like 'I'm a failure again, how did you become a teacher?' and things like that. It hurts him sometimes. (Sadhana)

> . . . they are quite good teachers really, but some they can't control the class and some are really nasty . . . Mr. Grieves, for instance, I can't stand him, he doesn't encourage you. If you make a mistake he won't say 'You've made a mistake here, I will tell you how to correct it and you must concentrate on that now', he'll take your paper, rub it all out, do it for you and then start hollering at you.

I don't like that, but some teachers are weak in controlling the
class . . . . (Zargoona)

Both Zargoona and Sadhana were seen as good pupils.

The girls also placed high value on what the school could offer in
other ways. They had an instrumental orientation to education for
reasons which were somewhat different from the Afro-Caribbean girls'.
While they were certainly hoping to obtain academic qualifications and
consciously doing so as a means to finding 'respectable' work, they had
other reasons for putting so much effort into their school work. They
believed that parents would want to arrange their marriage soon after
the girl had completed her formal education. All the while she was
being reasonably successful she could hope to persuade her parents to
let her stay into the sixth form and maybe beyond, thereby buying
herself some time and putting off the time of a marriage till nearer the
age she would prefer. It was not just a question of being successful,
but also of pursuing prestigious courses of work at school. Eight of the
eleven girls were taking science courses (i.e. physics and chemistry)
and intended to continue these studies beyond the fifth year. This
was a much higher proportion than other girls and was similar to the
proportion of Asian boys taking science courses. Knowledgeable about
science-based careers, the girls believed such careers enjoyed high
prestige among parents here and in the subcontinent.

[. . .] I haven't got much choice because in the medicine world
there are about three or four degrees which are counted as very
high. Medicine is out because I'm not capable of that. Dentistry
perhaps I could if I work really hard, but pharmacy is in between
very good and a bit lower than average, degree-wise. There's
biochemistry, and I'm not really interested in that. I've got quite
an interest in optics . . . (Sadhana)

By pursuing prestigious subjects the girls thought their parents might
be disinclined to interrupt academic careers with premature pressures
to take up a domestic one.

By the time I had completed my study the girls had achieved a mean
of 6 passes at 'O' level/CSE – a rather low number for the fifth year as
a whole, but with average grades higher than any other group at the
school. All those about whom I have information remained at school
beyond the statutory school-leaving age and were committed to some
form of higher or further education.

Those who have researched the school lives of young people have been
mainly working in the interpretive tradition in which the researcher is
aiming to 'make problems' rather than 'take problems'. That is, the
task is to make the everyday exotic and to take nothing for granted in
the ordinary worlds being studied.

There is now quite a history among British researchers of work of this type in schools and among those studying deviant youth cultures. Although this has produced some interesting achievements those achievements have their limitations. The limitations are of two kinds – technical and conceptual – and both have implications for what we know about the experiences of girls and young women inside and outside educational institutions. The first concerns a failure to rigorously suspend common-sense understandings throughout the research process. Previous researchers' emphasis on the male is my starting point, because it indicates some important ways in which they have [. . .] taken the everyday world for granted. Most of those researchers have been male. They have not made sexism problematic – their own or that within the institutions or cultures they write about. And many continue not to do so. Documenting the existence and effects of sexual divisions has in the main been left to those who are most sensitised to it through their own experience – the women who are beginning to research and write in this field and the women whom they study. Another way in which this research can be seen to be based on taking rather than making problems is that its focus is interestingly consistent with teachers' perspectives, though that has not been what researchers have set out to do, nor the way in which their research is written up. In defining the male experience as most interesting, important and worthy of explanation and description researchers (maybe unwittingly) are working within teachers' definitions. That is, they take as their problem that which is 'a problem' for teachers – boys' behaviour. Drawing on Douglas's work, Blackstone (1976) summarises teachers' views as follows:

> Teachers find boys difficult and unresponsive, and are much more likely to categorize them as lazy or poor workers, lacking in concentration or both. By contrast teachers expect girls to be more docile, attentive, diligent and less adventurous. (Blackstone 1976, pp. 210–11)

[. . .] Researchers [. . .] have given the lion's share of their attention to one specific group – the visible, troublesome male pupil.

This brings me to the second (conceptual) limitation of such studies, which has important sociological consequences and has been usefully summarised by Hargreaves (1979). Hargreaves discerns three emphases in the study of deviance in educational (mainly school) settings: a focus on deviance as an expression of values and behaviour originating outside school; an emphasis on the process by which deviant labels are produced in educational institutions; and thirdly, deviance as 'cultural criticism' in which there is a concern with the rationality of pupil deviance and on the experience of school deviants. He argues that researchers need to be more sophisticated in their conceptualisation of deviance and conformity. This would entail recognising that the deviant pupils on whom researchers have so far spent so much time are considerably less sociologically interesting than other pupils. The overtly antagonistic, resisting pupil ('the opposition' he calls them) are the normal deviants – 'those who mark the boundaries of our moral rules' (p. 22) and whose activities serve to both underline and underpin the status quo. (Willis' (1977) 'lads' being a case in point.)

Researchers have been slow to see the sociological significance of other kinds of pupil, who in not being defined as deviant are relegated to the realms of the sociologically uninteresting and unremarkable. To use Hargreaves's terms, the 'committed' raise important issues about how and why people come to wholeheartedly accept the prevailing and dominant norms, values, and forms of conduct; they deserve more than to be dismissed as conformist (a categorisation which is not, in any case, explanatory). Those who are 'indifferent' or 'instrumental' are *more* deviant, more threatening to social order and consequently of greater interest for the researcher than the oppositional pupil whose existence and stance is thoroughly predictable. Instrumentalists are not committed to school norms but 'know' (I would say 'believe') that school can offer them a great deal; the indifferent are also uncommitted, being bored, but offering no active resistance to schooling. Although they may be numerically more typical than the oppositional pupils, they are (sociologically) abnormal because they exhibit egoism and anomie which is inimical to social solidarity. Their deviance is therefore more undermining than that of the overtly antagonistic.

It is not part of Hargreaves's project to look at the implications of his argument for the study of girls and young women, [. . .] but for those who feel justification is required for researching women, it may be useful to remember that Durkheim suggested that the social/sexual division of labour has something to do with solidarity in organic societies; and there are those who believe that schools may have a hand in the reproduction of the division of labour. Hargreaves, then, is concerned with the sociological sterility of concentrating on oppositional pupils. Others (see Acker (1981) for example) have drawn more political conclusions from research in this tradition, pointing out that the effect of concentrating on 'deviance' as popularly understood, is that we have numerous accounts of boys in educational settings but know virtually nothing about girls. Another way of putting this is to say that until very recently research in this tradition reflects the kind of marginalising or ignoring of women which is common for many women (teachers as well as pupils) in educational institutions.

I am not suggesting that researchers should be trying to set the record straight by looking for girls who are deviant in the sense of being overtly antagonistic and challenging of school. [. . .] Nor am I suggesting that there is no interest in further studies of such boys defined in this way as deviant. Where studies of this kind are still undertaken it behoves the writers to be more explicit about the limitations of such an enterprise – firstly to disclose that their definition of deviance is a commonsense one and secondly that studies based on one gendered group cannot be passed off as studies of 'pupils', 'kids' etc. [. . .]

Another thing which seems important to me is that current definitions of deviance have the effect of presenting girls as uncritical. It may well be true that girls make up an insignificant proportion of those pupils who are overtly antagonistic – a fact (if it is one) which is in itself interesting and worthy of some analysis. Ignoring girls in discussions of deviance at a school leaves an impression that their acquiescence (supposed or actual) is unproblematic – a sign of their non-criticism of schooling.

Anyone who bothers to listen knows that this is not the case and knows equally that the girls' criticism cannot be readily accommodated into a definition of deviance or resistance that relies on the flashy, visible and physically confrontational. It should be possible to start from a position of understanding sexism and knowing that it is unlikely to be absent either from one's own thinking or in the educational settings to be studied. We can be confident that there are few if any manifestations of human behaviour which are restricted to one or other sex, only manifestations which show themselves differently because females and males are encouraged to differentiate their behaviour in certain systematic ways. Put another way, it seems likely that both female and male pupils are deviant, both in the popular sense and in terms of Hargreaves's 'instrumental' and 'indifferent' typology, but that there will be systematic differences in the proportion of girls and boys who are oppositional, in the proportion who are 'instrumental' and so on. Just because girls do not, typically, confront, does not mean they do not have their criticisms of schooling. What it suggests to me is that the form their criticism takes (and their resistance) is integrally related to and shaped by their having been successfully engendered as feminine. Their forms of critical/resisting behaviour will be more feminine than masculine. [. . .] Similarly, because boys (most of them) will also have been successfully engendered, being masculine, their typical form of resisting behaviour will reflect this. Their resistance will show itself in more visible ways and in forms more consistent with traditional defini-tions of masculinity.

[. . .] I would suggest that in concentrating on pupils other than the opposition we can get away from seeing pupils' cultural criticism as residing solely or even mainly in overt resistance to schooling. It may be that girls are too busy resisting other aspects of their life for resistance to schooling to have a high priority for them.

Acknowledgments

I should like to record my thanks to the teachers and pupils at 'Torville' school. My especial thanks to the young women whose accounts appear in this chapter, and to Ann Caro, Frances Hudson and Myna Trustram.

References

Acker, S. (1981) No Woman's Land: British Sociology of Education, 1960 to 1972. *Sociological Review*, 29, 77–104.

Bem, S. (1974) The Measurement of Psychological Androgyny. *Journal of Consulting and Clinical Psychology*, 42, 155–162.

Blackstone, T. (1976) The Education of Girls Today. In J. Mitchell and A. Oakley (eds.) *The Rights and Wrongs of Women*, Penguin, Harmondsworth.

Coleman, J. (1961) *The Adolescent Society*, Free Press, New York.

Fuller, M. (1978) Dimensions of Gender in a School, unpublished Ph.D. thesis, University of Bristol.

Fuller, M. (1980) Black Girls in a London Comprehensive. In R. Deem (ed.) *Schooling for Women's Work*, Routledge & Kegan Paul, London.

Fuller, M. (1982) Young, Female and Black: The World of Difference. In B. Troyna and E. Cashmore (eds.) *Black Kids*, Allen & Unwin, London.

Hargreaves, D. (1979) Durkheim, Deviance and Education. In L. Barton and R. Meighan (eds) *Schools, Pupils and Deviance*, Nafferton, Driffield.

Shaw, J. (1980) Education and the Individual: Schooling for Girls, or Mixed Schooling – a Mixed Blessing? In R. Deem (ed.) *Schooling for Women's Work*, Routledge & Kegan Paul, London.

Wilkinson, D. (1975) Black Youth. In R. Havighurst and P. Dreyer (eds.) *Youth*, University of Chicago Press, Chicago.

Willis, P. (1977) *Learning to Labour*, Saxon House, Farnborough.

2.4

A working-class girl in a grammar school†

Irene Payne

Our education system positions the future generations according to both their class and gender. Within capitalism there is a limited amount of social mobility, but overall the education system perpetuates existing social relations, based on class and gender divisions. Males have to take on the behaviour appropriate to their future role in production. Females have to take on the behaviour appropriate to their future role in reproduction as well as in production. Paul Willis (1977) documents the ways in which working-class boys take on culture and values, directly related to their future role as waged workers. He shows how their 'rebellion' against school has its roots in a realistic understanding of their own situation within capitalism. Angela McRobbie and Jenny Garber (1975) have conducted a smaller survey to show how a group of girls are positioned within both sexist and class ideology. Working-class girls need to learn their future position as low paid wage earners in the work force. However, there is a further dimension to the structuring of their material/social relationships. Girls must internalise their position in relation to men, through which process they will become domestic workers and child bearers and rearers. They must learn to give this labour freely, based on a notion of individual love.

My own experience of schooling, at a single sex girls' grammar school, is located within this context. I was one of a minority of working-class girls who went to grammar school. My experience was therefore not typical of that of most of my working-class contemporaries who went through secondary education in the 1960s. However, the way in which I negotiated my experience gives some limited indications of the class and sexist ideology within which it took place. I want to attempt to

† Source: D. Spender and E. Sarah (1980) (eds), *Learning to Lose; Sexism and Education*, London, The Women's Press, pp. 12–19.

describe the difficulties which I experienced, as an indication of a more general picture. This can only be a very tentative offering.

The first problem after passing the eleven-plus exam was a material one because attendance at grammar school depended on money. School uniform and specified equipment made heavy demands on my parents' income. I can remember that many items had to be obtained on credit and that there was a definite sense of 'making a sacrifice' so that I could have an education. My family was probably what could be termed 'respectable' working class, that is, a particular segment who, for a complex of reasons, had taken on a certain set of beliefs about education. Their faith in education would not have been shared by many of the parents of my contemporaries. The material sacrifice necessary for a grammar school education would certainly not have been made by all working-class families. Thus any notion of equal opportunity, based on ability, is much too simple because of the complex forces at work which determine how people view the world. Working-class people have their decisions shaped by material reality. If education really did offer us all the same chances, how would the social relations of exploiter and exploited be reproduced? Attitudes to education are part of a whole structure of relationships to society, which have their roots in real material divisions.

There is a further element to this 'decision' about education, based on sex. I can remember the reaction to my own 'success' in obtaining a place at grammar school. Many relations and neighbours said that education wasn't really important for girls, as they only got married and had children. My brother's success was seen as much more crucial than mine. However, my own parents, and particularly my mother, never questioned the fact that I should be educated. It would probably be interesting to research more fully the experiences leading to this position, adopted by only a minority of working-class people. I can only speculate, on the basis of my knowledge of my mother's own educational experiences. She was regarded as able but couldn't take up any opportunity because of her family's material position and the patriarchal attitudes of her father. My mother certainly did not have a confident attitude towards education, but accepted the advice of some 'experts' who counselled sending me to grammar school. This passivity is, I think, a significant element in being 'respectable' working class. It goes hand in hand with a desire to conform. There was no element of understanding the educational system, let alone of actively using it, rather you took what the experts offered and just 'did your best' with it. My mother's relationship to schooling was very different from that of her middle-class counterparts. This inexperience and passivity had implications for the way I subsequently experienced education.

The major point I want to make, however, is that my education took place via a particular class/sexist ideology, which I experienced as a series of pressures in different directions. I want to examine the contradictions for a working-class girl being educated within a society which, by and large, didn't educate this particular segment of society. I want to examine the value system of my school in relation to the value system of my working-class neighbourhood. These school values are not always explicit but can be found in the total set of practices in the institution. It is useful to look at what I learned, both implicitly and explicitly, within this school.

The first clear set of values was characterised by the school uniform. The class roots of school uniform are fairly clear because their origins are in the public schools. Institutional colours, mottoes and crests were all part of a total image derived from the ruling class. The uniform represented a sobriety and discipline whose power extended beyond the school. I can remember that prefects had the responsibility of ensuring that girls wore their berets on the bus journeys on public transport to and from school. The power of the ideology showed itself in the fact that they meticulously performed their function and reported girls seen without their berets. The uniform was part of a process of destroying individual and class identity, in order that pupils would submit unquestioningly to school authority and what that represented. School control extended even to such hidden recesses as underwear and was enforced with a vengeance, by regular inspections. Punishable offences included wearing the wrong coloured knickers or socks. These practices were part of the process of enforcing a particular set of bourgeois values, based on ideas of respectability, smartness and appearances.

However, I think there was a further dimension to this, in terms of gender. The uniform couldn't have been better designed to disguise any hints of adolescent sexuality. I suppose the shirt and tie, the 'sensible' shoes, thick socks and navy blue knickers were part of a more 'masculinised' image. It was as though femininity had to be symbolically sacrificed to the pursuit of knowledge. Modesty was implicit as there were regulations about the length of skirts and the covering of your arms. Jewellery, make-up and nylon stockings were taboo. Ideas about dress were based on notions of 'nice' girls and 'not so nice' girls, with both class and sexual connotations. We were, after all, to be turned into middle-class young ladies.

I wore the uniform without too much suffering at school but it was the greatest source of embarrassment to me beyond the school gates. I can remember being terrified that someone from my neighbourhood might see me wearing it. I was worried that I might be regarded as a 'college pud' or a snob by my peers. If they saw anyone in school uniform they would usually jeer and hurl abuse. But it had sexual as well as class connotations. As I got older, I was particularly concerned that potential boyfriends didn't see me in this 'unfeminine' garb. The first thing I always did when I got home from school was dash to my bedroom to change out of my uniform. However, my rebellion against school uniform was never very strong as I wanted to do well at school and wearing uniform was part of the process of earning approval.

It is interesting, in the light of what Angela McRobbie and Jenny Garber's study reveals, that the rebellion against school uniform did take on a very 'feminine' form. Within the grammar school, there were groups of working-class girls as well as disaffected middle-class girls who were alienated from school and just wanted to leave as soon as possible. Their rebellion manifested itself in the usual things like smoking or being rude to teachers. However, it was also structured along 'feminine' lines, in opposition to the 'masculinity' of school rules about appearance. I can remember bouffant hairstyles, fish-net stockings, make-up and 'sticky out' underskirts being the hallmarks of rebellious girls. All of these stressed femininity and the girls involved were also noted for being 'experienced' with boys. The rebellion's ultimate culmination was in getting pregnant, which meant that a denial of sexual activity was no longer possible. Such matters were always carefully hushed up and the girl concerned quickly removed.

The school even had an 'official' attitude to boyfriends. I can remember the headmistress insisting that her girls didn't have time for boyfriends. This was another way of denying our sexuality. Social life was disapproved of and we were inundated with homework which made it difficult to do much else in your own time. I suppose we were being prevented from growing up so that we would conform to the demands of the school. Saturday jobs were totally disapproved of which shows the middle-class ideology of the school. I needed to work as my parents found it a struggle to keep me. These jobs also provided one of the few opportunities to participate in the adult world and gain some experience of work. Our horizons, however, were supposed to be narrowed down to working for school. All these practices were part of what it was to be a 'young lady'.

Another manifestation of these implicit values was in the whole area of language. Again, there were two dimensions to this. In terms of class I had to learn to 'speak properly', that is, like middle-class people, and in terms of gender I had to learn to speak politely, that is, talking like a lady. This meant learning to speak both 'correctly' and 'nicely' and the pressure to conform can be quite inhibiting for a working-class girl. In our first two years of school we had speech training which was designed to teach us the correct way to pronounce words. I can remember thinking how 'posh' the teacher's voice was and she successfully instilled in us a belief in the importance of our pronunciation and diction. We were to avoid sounding 'common' at all costs. But as girls we had to consider more than these factors: we had to try to be refined at all times and therefore such things as loudness of voice were discouraged as raucous and unfeminine. There was a total image to be borne in mind and to which we all aspired: we worked very hard to present ourselves as 'educated young ladies'. Any form of ostentatious verbal behaviour (shouting, arguing, challenging) was considered inappropriate and was often considered a punishable offence. One teacher gave us the following lines from King Lear to write out because we had been noisy: 'Her voice was ever soft, Gentle and low – an excellent thing in woman' (*King Lear*, Act 5, Sc.3, Line 272).

Implicitly and explicitly we were inculcated with our role in the 'art of conversation' which encouraged us not only to be correct (as no doubt working-class boys would be encouraged in the grammar school) but also polite and deferential (an attribute not necessarily encouraged among boys). My grammar school education reveals a class and a gender ideology at work on my language.

I managed to conform and meet the linguistic requirements of the school, but they could only be used within the school. I had to abandon them when I left the school gates and had to change my language for home. Such 'bilingualism' is not without its disadvantages and can work to make one feel inadequate and unconfident in all language use. Mistakes at school could be an offence, but so too could mistakes at home. I was in constant terror of being exposed as a 'freak'. My way of dealing with this threat was to over-react. In my home environment I made a concerted effort to appear as 'one of the girls' and to do this I felt obliged to be louder than anyone else, to swear more, just to prove I wasn't different and hadn't been corrupted by the grammar school.

It was like leading a double life, for neither side would have recognised me in the other context. I was straddling two very different worlds and felt considerably threatened by the fact that I didn't belong to either. I had a constant sense of being different, which I interpreted as inferiority. I was always aware of the possibility of making a mistake and being exposed as fraudulent. I could not relax in either setting. I had a sense of inferiority within school because I didn't come from such a 'good' background as most of the other pupils. I was always uneasy when people began to parade their status symbols and discuss their father's occupations and where they lived. At school I felt ashamed of my background and attempted to conceal it. My Dad was a manual worker and we were pretty poor and I didn't want my classmates to know this. Nor did I want them to know that I lived in a 'rough' area, in a house that didn't have a bathroom.

At the same time I didn't want my friends in my neighbourhood to know that I was considered clever at school. (It is not of course unusual for some working-class kids who have received scholarships to be diagnosed in this way. One 'clever' working-class student vindicates the whole system and attests to the myth of equality of opportunity. However, it places enormous demands on such students.) In order not to be dismissed by my out-of-school friends I pretended that school was unimportant; I gave the impression that I didn't care about it. This of course demanded many subterfuges on my part. Life was a juggling process. Homework, for example, was difficult for me as I did not want my friends to know that I did it (I could not have preserved the belief that I didn't care about school if I indicated that I conscientiously did my homework). Because I didn't want my friends thinking I was a 'swot' (and withdrawing their friendship as a result) I tried to get all my homework finished before they came to call for me.

With my girlfriends the problems associated with school success were class ones and so that I could retain their friendship I disguised my attitude to school. But there are gender as well as class dimensions to this problem for it wasn't just with my girlfriends that I felt obliged to hide my school achievements. The problem of being seen as clever was particularly acute when it came to having boyfriends. I thought that being regarded as intelligent would make me less attractive to boys. I was always careful, therefore, to make light of my grammar school education and to refrain from mentioning how many O levels I was doing. Again there was the fear of making a mistake for, to me, it seemed that it would be a mistake to be seen as being more clever than a boy.

The pressures on me were conflicting and varied. For quite a while I tried to negotiate two worlds, but the time came when such negotiation was no longer possible. The two worlds proved to be incompatible. The two sets of values ordained different futures and the point came where I had to decide which future would be mine. Eventually the pull of the school was stronger for it held out the promise of social mobility through higher education. Once I decided to stay on at school after the statutory leaving age my fate was sealed. I could no longer pretend that school was unimportant or irrelevant. It was clear to my friends at home that I had marked myself as 'different' and from this point our paths were to diverge. They entered the world of paid work and they left me behind; I could not disguise myself as one of them any more.

I think that my experience shows that working-class values are not readily accommodated within the middle-class culture of schools. It is not possible to incorporate both sets of values, for the conflict between them is too great. In trying to conform to the requirements of the school I ultimately had to live the ideology encompassed within the school and this meant rejecting many of the values of my home. This is not the experience of working-class kids in general because they are not singled out for school success. Realistically, working-class kids have few expectations of education as a means of transforming their lives. They continue to live out the values which will ensure their existence as workers for capitalism.

My experience as a working-class girl contained more contradictions than that of my middle-class peers whose culture more closely approximated that of the school. However, there were contradictions shared and the organisation of the curriculum provides an example of sexist ideology at work. In my school there was an academic ethos and this meant that practical subjects were accorded low status. While this is an aspect of bourgeois ideology which constructs the mental/manual division of labour, it is also an example of patriarchal ideology with its direct relationship to the sexual division of labour in our society. The least desirable subjects in the school curriculum were those associated with traditional female functions, for example, domestic science and needlework. These subjects were for those girls who were not considered to be very clever. Through this mechanism we learned that the skills which were associated with females were not valued. We internalised a hierarchy of knowledge and it was 'male' knowledge which occupied the higher rungs and which was our goal.

Achievement of such a goal, however, was not unproblematic. Certain sacrifices were demanded, among them our femininity. This was the price we had to pay for the acquisition of such knowledge. Those girls who were not of the élite, who did not do academic courses but who were supposed to be satisfied with the traditional female diet, were not required to make a sacrifice: being good at needlework does not rob one of femininity. This was their compensation.

Either choice can be seen as negative. When female skills are undervalued then being good at them does not necessarily count; but attempting to acquire male skills can also be negated because no matter how well a female does she can still be undervalued as only an 'honorary' male. Even within the area of 'male' knowledge, sexist ideology operates so that the female academic élite still learn to choose sex-appropriate knowledge. Although the majority of my teachers were female, the mathematics and physics teachers were, significantly, male. The majority of the girls doing science 'chose' biology: fewer did chemistry and only a tiny minority did physics. In the lower sixth there were two English groups, each of nearly forty students, while there were only three or four students in the physics group.

The ideology of marriage was also a powerful force, even though there were a number of unmarried teachers on the staff. It was used as a rationale for counselling, particularly in relation to those girls who were not defined as academic. The lure of marriage often operated to obscure the female employment position. Those leaving school at sixteen were not encouraged to scrutinise women's employment situation and were given virtually no career advice at all. Marriage was implanted as their aspiration and the prevailing attitude was that 'any old job' would do in that fill-in time until their aspirations were realised.

Those of us who stayed on were pushed towards universities or colleges of education but, even here, the sexist ideology was not challenged. The possibilities for female employment were presented within the confines of what was appropriate to our sex. Limitations operated even for the academic élite, for the role of wife and mother was never lost sight of; it was always taken into consideration when discussing future careers. Those careers which were presented as possibilities were the ones most easily accommodated with the female reproductive role, and were often an extension of the female involvement with children, such as teaching, for example.

The curriculum, career advice and construction of the 'feminine' within the school all served to reproduce the sexual division of labour.

The positioning of individuals is one of patriarchal capitalism's most important means of reproducing itself and my experience of schooling points to the ways in which schools function to reproduce existing social/material relationships via class and sex-specific ideologies.

References

McRobbie, A. and Garber, J. (1975), 'Girls and subcultures', in Hall, S. and Jefferson, T. (eds), *Resistance Through Rituals: Youth Subcultures in Postwar Britain*, London, Hutchinson.

Willis, P. (1977), *Learning to Labour: How Working-Class Kids get Working-Class Jobs*, London, Saxon House.

Part three
Sexual inequalities in educational provision

3.1

Towards a history of women's education in nineteenth-century Britain: a sociological analysis†

June Purvis

The study of women's education in nineteenth-century Britain has received scant attention within the discipline of sociology.[1] This statement is valid even for the 1970s when a number of publications on the education of nineteenth-century girls and women appeared,[2] publications that were mainly written by female historians. However, publications that focus upon the education of nineteenth-century women, rather than girls, tend to localise their interest on the theme of women and higher education in the latter decades of the nineteenth century.[3] By concentrating upon one sector of education, i.e. higher education, upon one particular segment of a specific social grouping of women, i.e. that minority of middle-class women who struggled to enter higher education, and upon a specific historical point in time, i.e. the latter decades of the nineteenth century, major areas of interest in women's education in nineteenth-century Britain have been overlooked. In particular, the education of working-class women has been almost totally ignored,[4] and also the variety of forms of education within which both working-class and middle-class women[5] might participate. The aim of this paper is to provide a general overview of the forms and content of education for both working-class and middle-class women. A major theme of my analysis is that the history of women's education in nineteenth-century Britain can only be understood in relation to wider economic, social, cultural and ideological factors outside the education field, and especially what has been called 'the domestic ideology'. I shall claim that within the domestic ideology we may identify ideals of femininity[6] which helped to shape both the forms and content of education for nineteenth-century women and to pose contradictions for them.

† Source: *Westminster Studies in Education*, Vol. 4, 1981, pp. 45–79.

The domestic ideology and the ideal of femininity: the contradictions that were posed for women

Catherine Hall (1978) has recently emphasised that the period from the late eighteenth to the mid-nineteenth century in England was not only a time of transition from an aristocratic, mercantile, capitalist society to an industrial, capitalist society with a large and influential bourgeoisie, but also a period in which the domestic ideology became established within the dominant, bourgeois culture.[7] Certainly during this transition phase, we find a mass of publications, mainly written by the bourgeoisie, which uphold the notion of separate spheres for men and women. Thus the ideal location for women was represented as within the private sphere of the family as full-time wives and mothers while men were to be located within the public sphere of work whereby sufficient might be earned to support the economic dependants of wife, children and kin. However, though the bourgeoisie were prolific on this subject, this does not mean that other social groupings did not hold similar views nor that there was a dearth of ideologies competing to define the position of women. In particular, few records exist expressing the views of the working class on this matter. However there is evidence to suggest that especially in the latter decades of the century, working-class men came increasingly to take up the domestic ideology through the organisation of the trade union movement: in the 1870s, for example, Henry Broadhurst, a prominent trade unionist, asserted that wives should be in 'their proper place', at home.[8] Though it is sometimes difficult to differentiate the statements made by the working class and bourgeoisie, nevertheless it would appear that in the transition phase that Catherine Hall speaks about, the domestic ideology was especially a part of bourgeois family ideology. Dr John Gregory, for example, in *A Father's Legacy To His Daughters*, first published in 1774 and reprinted as late as 1877, had advised that the domestic economy of a family was entirely a 'women's province',[9] a sentiment that is echoed by Mrs Taylor (1817), in a letter to an imaginary daughter, Laura:

> you are returning 'home'. It is a comprehensive word, my dear Laura. . . . It is chiefly 'there' that the lustre of the female character is discernible; because 'home' is its proper sphere. 'Men' have much to do with the world without; 'our' field of action is circumscribed.[10]

However, the notion of separate spheres for men and women was continually to be articulated in publications throughout the century. One writer, in 1865, asserted:

> Man is formed for the turmoil and the labours of the outer world, woman for the peace and quiet of home.[11]

while Mrs Sarah Ellis, that prolific writer on woman's sphere,[12] claimed, in 1869, that whereas men found their loss and gain in the bank, counting-house or the exchange, women find theirs where they have 'garnered up their souls'.[13] John Ruskin, in the 1860s too, idealised women as beings who exercised 'queenly power' not merely within the household but over all 'within their sphere'.[14]

Embedded in the domestic ideology were three major assumptions. Firstly, the notion of separate spheres was frequently advocated in biological terms as being a 'natural' division between the sexes. Alexander Walker (1840), for example, claimed that the 'natural' pursuits for women were procreation, gestation, delivery, nursing, care of children, cooking and clothing while part of man's existence was the advancement of knowledge.[15] Secondly, since women were to be primarily located within the home as wives and mothers, they were defined in relation to men and children rather than as individual beings with their own, independent, autonomous existence. This view is epitomised in the following statement by Mrs Ellis in *The Women of England* (1839):

> Women, considered in their distinct and abstract nature, as isolated beings, must lose more than half their worth. They are, in fact, from their own constitution, and from the station they occupy in the world, strictly speaking, relative creatures.[16]

The relative nature of women's existence was given verbal support throughout the century. In 1799, Hannah More asserted that the main benefit of study for women was that it would regulate her mind and make her 'useful to others', Mrs Taylor (1817) reminded Laura that every day would afford an opportunity of making an 'effort', 'sacrifice' or 'allowance' for the behaviour of others, Ruskin (1865) claimed that a woman should know a language or science only in so far as it enabled her to sympathise in her husband's pleasure and in those of his best friends, Trollope (1868) pronounced that it was woman's duty to utilise man's earnings and minister to his comfort and Samuel Smiles (1871), while admitting that the mind and character of women should be cultivated with a view to their own well-being also insisted that women should be educated with a view to the happiness of others.[17] Though the relative nature of women's existence was questioned by many feminists, particularly in the second decade of the century,[18] it was inevitably linked to the third assumption embedded in the domestic ideology – namely, that women were inferior to men. Mrs Ellis (1842), for example, claimed: 'As women, then, the first thing of importance is to be content to be inferior to men'.[19] Such an assumption was, of course, a reflection of the patriarchal[20] nature of nineteenth-century society, and especially the patriarchal structure of the family. As one writer commented in 1851:

> We underestimate the character of woman, and keep her in a state of forced submission to man: who, in all his transactions with her, treats her as an inferior. She has no legal rights. She is not supposed to exist as a citizen. Her personality is merged in that of man. She

is always a minor, never reaching majority. She still takes rank, in the eye of the law, among man's goods and chattels, and is classified with 'his ox and his ass'. The law defines her, in a state of marriage, as belonging to and the property of man.[21]

The inferiority of the nineteenth-century woman and her subordination within the husband/wife relationship was advocated from a number of viewpoints. A particularly virulent attack on women was that which based itself on biological determinism. Thus one protagonist argued that since the head and brain size of women were, on average, much smaller than those of men, the reasoning power of women was small.[22] The general conclusion he reached, in regard to the relationship between husband and wife, was this:

It is evident that the man, possessing reasoning faculties, muscular power, and courage to employ it, is qualified for being a protector: the woman, being little capable of reasoning, feeble, and timid, requires protection. Under such circumstances, the man naturally governs: the woman as naturally obeys.[23]

Biological differences between the sexes and the supposed inferiority of woman's intellect were used too as arguments to oppose the entry of women into higher education in the 1860s and after. Thus the right wing newspaper *The Saturday Review*, asserted in 1871, that these were 'bad times' for women and asked: 'what will be gained by further unsexing them, and encouraging their less muscular frames and smaller brains to a competition with men . . .?'[24]

Similar arguments were advocated by the medical profession. Thus Dr Withers Moore, who took the theme of the higher education of women as the topic of his presidential address to the BMA in 1886, argued:

From the eagerness of woman's nature competitive brain-work among gifted girls can hardly but be excessive, especially if the competition be against the superior brain-weight and brain-strength of man. The resulting ruin can be averted – if it be averted at all – only by drawing so largely upon the woman's whole capital stock of vital forces and energy as to leave a remainder quite inadequate for maternity . . . her reproductive system will more or less have been atrophied: she will have lost her womanhood's proper power. . . . Unsexed it might be wrong to call her, but she will be more or less sexless. And the human race will have lost those who should have been her sons. . . . That one truism says it all – women are made and meant to be, not men, but mothers of men.[25]

Religion provided the base for the other main powerful viewpoint that advocated the inferiority of women and their subordination within the conjugal relationship: this time, of course, the arguments frequently refer to a divine order rather than to biological differences. Thus John

Burgon, Dean of Chichester, in a sermon delivered in Oxford in 1884, preached:

> Behold then, at the very outset, the reason of Women's creation distinctly assigned. She is intended to be Man's 'help' – Man's 'helper'. The expression 'meet for him' implies that she is to be something corresponding to him – a second self. Yet not a rival self, for, as the SPIRIT pointed out some 4000 years later, 'the Man was not created for the Woman, "but the Woman for the Man" ': and from this very consideration the SPIRIT deduces Woman's inferiority.[26]

Burgon reminds his congregation that St Paul's persistent requirement of 'subordination, submission, obedience' for women is something that no-one can forget and that married women have consented to obey in their marriage vows.[27]

To sum up so far then, we might say that despite the existence of a strong minority tradition that questioned the definition of women as relative creatures who were inferior and subordinate to men,[28] the establishment of the domestic ideology within the dominant bourgeois culture was such that the social construction of the female gender came to be identified, in society at large, with domesticity. And this was something that both middle-class and working-class women, through the category of their common sex, held in common. But there the link between the women of these different social classes weakens since within the broad identification of femininity with domesticity we find that the bourgeoisie upheld ideals of femininity that were class specific – in other words, they upheld a double standard in that what was considered appropriate, relevant and attainable for middle-class women was inappropriate, irrelevant and unattainable for working-class women.

Within the domestic ideology, the ideal form of femininity that was held to be applicable to middle-class women was the ideal of the 'perfect wife and mother'.[29] This ideal was the cornerstone of the many contemporary writings about woman's position in society: the 'perfect wife and mother' was to provide a well-organised, stable, supportive environment for her husband and children though, as Banks & Banks (1964) have stressed, this reflects what the middle classes believed their women ought to do and be, even if individual middle-class women did not always match precept with practice.[30] [. . .]

In the performance of her duties, therefore, the 'perfect wife and mother' was expected to display certain Christian virtues such as self-denial, patience, resignation and silent suffering.[31] And, in addition, she was also expected to be ladylike. Being ladylike involved three fundamental assumptions. First of all, it was ladylike to be a manager of a household but not to engage in the routine, manual work involved: a 'lady' could afford to employ servants to perform such tasks.

Secondly, it was ladylike to engage in unpaid, philanthropic work but never to engage in waged labour. As Mrs Ellis stated in 1869:

> As society is at present constituted, a lady may do almost anything from motives of charity or zeal. . . . But so soon as a woman begins to receive money however great her need, or however glorious the escape from degrading dependence which she thus attains, so soon as she makes money by her own effort, and lays by a little store acquired by the work of her own hands, the heroine is transformed into a tradeswoman, and she must find her place in society as such.[32]

Thirdly, being ladylike involved not only wearing appropriate apparel,[33] but also learning a complex ritual of etiquette.[34] In particular, the 'perfect wife and mother' would, in bringing up her daughters, emphasise the importance of the system of chaperonage: it was considered a mark of gentility for young, unmarried middle-class women to be accompanied by a chaperone, often an older, married female, when they mixed in the world outside the private sphere of the home.[35]

In contrast to the prescriptive ideal of femininity for middle-class women, the ideal of femininity for working-class women, as evident in the contemporary writings, reveals quite different standards held by the middle classes for their 'social inferiors'. The ideal for working-class women was that of the 'good woman': like the 'perfect wife and mother', the 'good woman' was located within the home, but a much greater emphasis was placed upon her practical domestic skills as a housekeeper, wife and mother. The 'good woman' could have no pretensions to the ladylike behaviour of the 'perfect wife and mother' who employed domestic servants for the manual work within the home. Thus Sarah Austin (1857) quotes with approval a Mr Johnson who asserted:

> We want good servants and good wives; women who know the value of a clean, well-regulated Christian home: for such alone can make 'men' sensible of the real merits of a home, the inestimable blessing of a good wife and tidy obedient children.[36]

while some two years later James Booth (1855) outlined even more clearly the importance of the practical domestic skills that were considered necessary for the 'good women' of the working classes:

> how are the daughters of the working classes brought up to fit them for their lot in life, to be the wives and mothers of men in their own station? . . . Why should not 'young women' be taught a knowledge of those common things with which she will have to deal the whole residue of her life? Why should she not, for example, be taught to light a fire, to sweep a room, to wash crockery and glass without breaking the half of them, to wash clothes, to bake bread, to dress a dinner, to choose meat or fish or vegetables, and to know how to keep them when bought; what clothes are most economical

– cheap, showy tawdry rags, to those which are perhaps more expensive but cheaper in the end? Why should she not be taught the use of savings banks and the results of thrift?[37]

The ideal for working-class women was seen as a solution to many of the problems of the working-class family. Middle-class commentators spoke of the 'slatternly habits' of the working-class women, their inability to make their 'husbands' homes comfortable' and their general 'miserable deficiences'.[38] Thus working-class women were frequently blamed for a host of social problems such as alcoholism, crime, the spread of disease and a high infant mortality rate. A number of contemporary commentators such as W. R. Greg and Fredrick Engels[39] linked such failure to the inadequate training and socialisation of working-class girls in domestic skills. Engels (1892), for example, complained that girls who worked in the mills from the age of nine-years-old knew little about domestic work and proved inexperienced and unfit as housekeepers:

They cannot knit or sew, cook or wash, are unacquainted with the most ordinary duties of a house-keeper, and when they have children to take care of, have not the vaguest idea how to set about it.[40]

As Davin (1979) has recently commented, the explanation of disharmony and malfunction in society was explained in relation to the failure of the working-class family, and, we may add, especially the working-class wife. As Basch (1974) has noted, the working-class wife's ignorance of domestic matters was one of the most powerful arguments used by opponents of waged labour for women:[41] the middle-class solution was to reaffirm the domestic ideology and insist that woman's sphere was in the home where she would be economically dependent. Not unnaturally, *The Saturday Review*, in 1859, gave its opinion on the matter:

Women labourers are a proof of a barbarous and imperfect civilisation. We should be retrograding in the art and science of civilization were more women encouraged to be self-supporters. And the reason is plain enough. Wherever women are self-supporters, marriage is, 'ipso facto', discouraged. The factory population is proof of this. In the manufacturing districts women make worse wives and worse helpmates than where they are altogether dependent on the man. And where there are fewer marriages there is more vice.[42]

The ideal of the 'good woman' may be seen, therefore, as an attempt by the bourgeoisie to solve the various social problems associated with industrialisation and urbanisation. The 'good woman' was a dilution of the higher status ideal of the 'perfect wife and mother' and thus it may be interpreted as a form of 'intervention' into working-class family life, an attempt to convert and transmit that part of bourgeois family ideology that insisted that a woman's place was in the home, that she was responsible for the quality of family life and that her domestic skills were more important than say vocational skills that might be used in waged labour. The 'good woman' was, therefore, a form of class cultural control,[43] an attack upon the patterns of working-class motherhood and parenthood as perceived by the middle classes.

The two bourgeois ideals of femininity formed part of the context within which educational institutions were founded and reformed: after all, most of the formalised educational provision offered in the nineteenth century was the result of middle class voluntary effort.[44] Even when the state became increasingly involved in educational provision in the later decades of the century, those who formulated educational policies were mainly drawn from the middle classes. Of course not all educational practice was homogeneous in assuming that women were primarily to be full-time wives and mothers, that they were relative creatures who were inferior and subordinate to men and that they were biologically incapable of learning. But such assumptions would appear to be pervasive, though probably held in varying degrees. Within an educational context therefore, the bourgeois definitions of femininity posed a number of problems, contradictions and dilemmas for women of both social classes. For middle-class women, the linking of femininity with domesticity posed the contradiction that when they sought to improve the standard of their education, especially from the 1870s when they fought for access to the ancient universities of Cambridge and Oxford – universities that had been exclusively for men – they ran the risk of being labelled 'unfeminine' or 'unsexed'.[45] As Stephen (1927) commented, the popular idea of a well-educated women at this particular point in time was that she was a 'ridiculous monster'.[46] Middle-class women who fought for access to higher education had, therefore, to break away from the specifically male, bourgeois definitions of women and in demanding equal educational opportunities, they presented a new ideal of middle-class femininity – the 'new woman'. As Vicinus (1972) has noted, the 'new woman' struggled to enter higher education, engaged in waged labour and fought for improved legal and political rights.[47] It is likely that the challenge to the dominant ideal of the 'perfect wife and mother' came particularly from those daughters of the professional and business classes who saw education as a form of wealth, a passport to an elite occupation. The new ideal was, of course, partly a result of the demands of the bourgeois 'women's movement' for greater economic, political and social freedom[48] and partly a result of the demographic fact that there was a surplus of single, economically unsupported females. But other broader social and economic changes were occurring too that made the ideal feasible: for example, industrialisation was creating new types of employment in which women might participate while the process of political democratisation was placing greater emphasis upon the individual.[49] Within the context of higher education, therefore, the attempt to establish the 'new woman' ideal was essentially a gender struggle, but a struggle that was contained within the middle classes since few working-class women fought for the right to gain access to the universities. In demanding equal educational opportunities with men, the 'new women' were engaging them in a feminist struggle but not a class struggle.

The bourgeois definition of femininity as domesticity posed, however, rather different problems for those working-class women seeking an education since such women became involved in both class and feminist struggles. As suggested above, the bourgeoisie claimed that social stability and social order necessitated that working-class women should be full-time wives and mothers with practical, efficient domestic skills. In such a way, working-class women would service the capitalist economy by supporting and nurturing a healthy workforce through their care of menfolk within the family and through the rearing of strong children. The most fundamental tension that working-class women faced therefore was the friction between the demands of such an ideology and the realities of a capitalist economy which utilised and exploited them as a source of cheap, female labour. Most working-class women would, at some time in their lives, be forced to engage in some form of waged labour in order to survive,[50] and the conditions of their work would be such as to hinder the fulfilment of their domestic duties as idealised by the bourgeoisie. In addition, since most of the formalised educational provision was organised by the middle classes, working-class women seeking education had to continually confront the rhetoric and content of education offered by their 'social superiors'. But such an attempt at class control is only one facet of patriarchy. As I have previously suggested, during the second half of the nineteenth century in particular working-class men, through their trade unions, began to take up certain aspects of bourgeois domestic ideology when they campaigned for a family wage. As Foreman (1977) comments, to be able to support a wife at home became a sign of working-class strength, of prosperity, of better days to come.[51] And, of course, as Maria Gray (1879) has highlighted, the fact that women were regarded as an 'inferior caste' only intensified trade union opposition to the admission of women on equal terms to certain occupations.[52] Working-class women as women had, therefore, to struggle against the definitions imposed upon them by both sexes within the bourgeoisie and by their own menfolk. And those women who sought some form of education had to struggle against the exhaustive demands made upon their time for family responsibilities and endless childbearings[53] in a patriarchal society which facilitated the entry of their husbands and brothers, rather than themselves, into a variety of forms of adult education. As we shall see, in the latter decades of the century, when working-class women began to organise themselves and provide both formal and informal education through the single sex organisation of the Women's Co-operative Guild, a new ideal of working-class femininity began to emerge – that of the 'home-maker and peaceful reformer'. Unlike the bourgeois ideal of the 'good woman', the new ideal was constructed by working-class women themselves even though the structural location of working-class women was still upheld as being ideally within the home, as full-time wives and mothers.

To sum up so far, then, my main theme is that the domestic ideology which linked femininity with domesticity, together with the class-specific ideals of femininity, were to be important factors shaping the forms and content of education for the nineteenth century woman – an issue I shall now explore in greater detail.

Education for Women of the Middle Classes

Educating middle-class girls and young women for the dominant ideal of middle-class femininity, that of the 'perfect wife and mother' who enjoyed a ladylike, leisured life style, usually involved, especially in the first half of the nineteenth century, a privatised education within a familial domestic setting. Thus most middle-class girls were educated at home and sometimes in a small, private school.

The principle of segregation between the sexes was not always adhered to when the children were young, but once the boys were old enough to be sent to school, the education of middle-class girls was usually contained within the home where teaching might be undertaken by the parents, or a governess, or both. Whichever variant of the home education theme was followed, the basic principle remained the same – girls were to be educated in a cloistered environment for a separate and different life style from that of boys. Sometimes a girl might attend a small private school, usually managed by middle-class women. For example, Mary Marshall, born in 1850, the daughter of a country vicar, recollects that when about thirteen years old, she and her sister went once a week to a 'select school' for young ladies: the school was managed by two maiden women who taught 'Mangnall's Question', the 'use of the globes' and 'deportment'. As she comments, after this experience, her education was considered 'finished'.[54] Such an experience was probably common for middle- and upper-class girls. Since they were defined as potential wives and mothers who would be economically supported rather than independent wage earners, the content of their education tended to stress ornamental knowledge that might attract a husband. As Mrs William Grey said in a paper read before the Society of Arts, on 31st May 1871:

There is a pretty theory abroad, which is always brought forward when women's education is talked about, i.e. that they are educated to be wives and mothers. I do not know a more fallacious one. They are 'not' educated to be wives, but to get husbands. They are 'not' educated to be mothers. . . . They are 'not' educated to be the mistresses of households. . . . What they are educated for is to come up to a certain conventional standard accepted in the class to which they belong, to adorn (if they can) the best parlour or the drawing-room, as it may be, to gratify a mother's vanity, to amuse a father's leisure hours, above all, to get married. And here I must mention the cruel result of this fixed idea in men's minds that their daughters are to be provided for by marriage. No other provision is made for them, nor are they trained or allowed to provide for themselves.[55]

The emphasis upon social priorities in the education of middle-class girls necessarily meant a low standard of education in comparison with that offered to middle-class boys, and this was the general conclusion reached by the Schools Inquiry Commission in 1867–68. Thus after noting the 'general indifference' of parents to girls' education, both in itself and compared to that of boys,[56] the Report went on to say that the deficiencies in girls' education included:

Want of thoroughness and foundation; want of system; slovenliness and showy superficiality; inattention to rudiments: undue time given to accomplishments, and those not taught intelligently or in any scientific manner; want of organisation.[57]

Such a poor standard of education inevitably influenced both the forms and content of education for adult middle-class women. Women were largely denied access to higher education and were ill prepared for it anyway. Male cultural hegemony maintained the universities as 'strongholds of masculine privilege'.[58] There were isolated examples where women were admitted access to various institutions of higher education though they were usually denied the right to take the same course and examination as men. In Scotland, for example, John Anderson, Professor of Natural Philosophy at Glasgow University, died in 1796 leaving an eccentric will that asked for the establishment of a rival university within which, at least once a year, a 'Ladies' Course of Physical Lectures' should be given.[59] Anderson hoped that such courses would make the women the 'most accomplished Ladies in Europe'. He was careful to add, however, that no women who were 'giddy or incorrect in their manners'[60] should be admitted. Such an experiment foreshadowed the development of the university extension movement in the late 1860s. In England, from 1828, women could attend the lectures at both King's and University College, London,[61] but as Alicia Percival was to comment in 1939, the standard of education was such that the colleges were inaccessible to all but exceptionally gifted or exceptionally placed women: even then, to share lectures with men students was considered too advanced and unladylike for most women.[62]

The first important attempt to provide some form of higher education for women was Queen's College, London, established in 1848 largely through the influence of the Rev. F. D. Maurice, a Professor at King's College.[63] Since it was founded to improve the education of governesses and was, in addition, a separate institution outside the university sector, it aroused little opposition and much support from male university academics.[64] As Emily Davies (1896) was to remark, even the name 'college', as associated with women, seemed to require apology.[65] Initially, 'young ladies over twelve years of age'[66] were admitted and one of the first tasks of the Committee was to appoint 'Lady Visitors' who would chaperone the scholars to the various lectures and classes.[67] The dominant ideal of femininity for middle-class girls demanded that they should be supervised in this way: it would appear that, in this particular case, chaperonage offered some protection to these young scholars who came into contact with the men's sphere of learning and scholarship. In 1849, another separate college for women was founded in Bedford Square. Its establishment was largely due to the efforts of Mrs Reid who claimed that the new college was to 'provide for ladies, at a moderate expense, a curriculum of liberal education'.[68] Though both colleges really provided education of a secondary school standard, both were drawn into university work after 1878 when women were admitted to London University degrees.[69]

The struggle for women to enter higher education became mobilised particularly in the 1860s and subsequent decades. However, though an account of such a struggle is important in a history of women's education in nineteenth century Britain, it is also important that our attention to that struggle does not obscure the fact that other major forms of education were available to middle-class women, e.g. lectures organised by certain cultural societies and lectures and classes within the mechanics' institutes. Since these two forms of education were primarily for men, participation by women was often marginal – though it did vary considerably, as we shall see.

Hume (1847), in his classic study of learned societies, notes that they consist of: 'intellectual men, voluntarily united, for the purpose of promoting knowledge generally, or some particular branch of it'.[70] In other words, learned societies were mainly for men of the middle and upper classes. Numerous scientific and cultural societies were established in Britain during the first half of the nineteenth century. It would appear that women were usually automatically excluded from the scientific societies in particular: the paucity of their knowledge did not, of course, facilitate their entry but, more importantly, the assumption that femininity was synonymous with domesticity made it incredibly difficult for women to enter such male centres of learning. In 1869, for example, women were banned from the scientific meetings of the Ethnological Society.[71] However, it would appear that it was particularly in some of the cultural societies that one might find participation by middle-class women. Thus the London Anthropological Society (1873–75) both admitted women and invited them to give papers.[72] But it was probably in the numerous literary and philosophical societies that the greatest number of middle-class women might be found. For example, it was decided at the first General Meeting (10th January

1823) of the Sheffield Literary and Philosophical Society that 'ladies or young men under eighteen years of age' who were of the family of the 'proprietors' (those who were elected by ballot and who paid an entrance fee of two guineas plus an annual subscription of the same amount) could be admitted to the lectures given by the Proprietors and to the public lectures given by guest speakers [. . .] and some time later, three women gave lectures – thus Miss Mary Kingsley spoke on 'West Africa', Mrs Basil Rose on 'Modern Russian Music' and Miss E. Rowland on 'French Canadian Folk-Songs', with vocal illustrations.[73] Women gave lectures at other literary and philosophical societies too: thus at the one at Nottingham, in 1871, Emily Davies read a paper on 'College Education for Women'.[74] Evidence such as this does illustrate that women did participate in the proceedings of certain male, bourgeois societies, even if that participation was limited. As we have already suggested, the subordination of women to men was an important ingredient of the domestic ideology and it found full expression in those patriarchal structures outside the sphere of the home. Thus women had to struggle to gain admission to forms of education intended primarily for men, and even when they were admitted, rarely were they given equality of membership. Nowhere is this more evident that in the mechanics' institutes, often regarded as the major form of adult education in the nineteenth century.

The first mechanics' institutes were established in the 1820s. It would appear that the aims of the institutes were both class and sex specific, i.e. the diffusion of scientifically useful knowledge to working-class men.[75] Though there is some controversy about both the aims and the social class membership of the institutes,[76] the target audience was men, not women. Gradually, however, and often reluctantly, we begin to hear, from the 1830s onwards, of the admission of women.[77] It is highly probable that the female clientèle was largely of middle-class origins, especially in those institutes in Southern England, though a much higher proportion of working-class women might be found in some of the northern institutes. The entry of women into the institutes reinforced their subordinate status within the wider society since they were usually given junior membership status akin to that for youths and apprentices. At Plymouth Mechanics' Institute, for example, the membership rate in 1851 was 8s. per annum for 'Juniors' and 'Ladies' and 10s. for 'Seniors', i.e. adult males.[78] Such differential subscription rates were indeed common. In addition, men were often classified according to the achieved status of their occupation while women were always classified according to the ascribed status of their sex.[79] Though women were usually allowed to attend the lectures and use the libraries within the institutes, it appears to have been common practice to exclude them from the more 'subversive' reading rooms and newsrooms. It is not until the 1860s, when various women's organisations begin to gather strength, that we hear of their admission to the newsroom at a large institute such as that at Manchester.[80] The subordinate status of women within the institutes is reflected too in the fact that they rarely enjoyed the right to vote, to participate in general decision making or hold an official position. At Thornton Mechanics' Institute, for example, as late as 1871, women were forbidden to use the refreshment rooms and to vote in the election of officers.[81]

The inequalities that women experienced in regard to access to facilities within the institutes is also evident in the content of their education in the various classes that were provided. The notion of separate spheres for men and women pervaded the organisational structure of class provision so classes were usually segregated on the basis of sex. Classes for women rarely offered the curricular range available to men especially in the large institutes, such as those at Manchester and Leeds, where separate female departments were established. At Manchester in particular, where a deliberate attempt was made to attract the daughters of the lower middle class – 'shop-keepers', 'respectable classes of mechanics', those who had 'risen in the world a little' and those who had been 'reduced in circumstances'[82] – we find the ideal of middle-class femininity influencing curricular content. Thus, in 1846, a curriculum was offered which included not only instruction in subjects such as English, geography, arithmetic, French literature, natural philosophy and chemistry, but also the teaching of various accomplishments such as piano playing, landscape, flower and figure drawing, the modelling of flowers and fruit in wax and plaster, and speaking French.[83] Such an emphasis upon accomplishments might, hopefully, improve one's chances in the marriage market as well as provide certain skills that might occupy the leisure time of the 'perfect wife and mother'. No sex differentiation is evident though in the lecture programmes since the lectures were open to men and women alike. Though the range of topics was wide, both within any one institute and between institutes, one contemporary observer has suggested that by the middle of the century, the original emphasis upon scientific subjects had given way to dramatic readings and musical entertainments.[84] Nevertheless, despite such a trend, women could attend lectures on a variety of themes. Thus, at Leeds Mechanics' Institute in 1852, Samuel Smiles lectured on 'Self-help in Man', while, at Beverley Mechanics' Institute in 1852, Mr J. F. Wynn spoke on 'Love and Marriage, or Woman's Mission'[85] – themes that illustrate well the prevailing ideology about differences between men and women.

Kelly (1957) estimates that by 1851 698 mechanics' and literary and scientific institutes were in existence with a heavy concentration of institutes in the West Riding, South-East Lancashire and the adjoining corner of North-East Cheshire.[86] It is impossible to give an exact figure of the number of female members though Tylecote (1957) estimates that in 1849 in the Yorkshire and Lancashire institutes alone, there were about 1200 and 600 female members respectively.[87] At Liverpool, for example, the female membership was mainly middle class and in 1845, 560 'Ladies' and 107 'Daughters of Members' are recorded out of a total membership of 3763.[88] In some of the southern institutes where female membership was likely to be predominantly middle-class, women sometimes formed more than half of the total membership. At Chelmsford Literary and Mechanics' Institution, for example, 300 female and 450 male members are recorded in 1851.[89]

In terms of sheer size of numbers therefore, the extent of female membership in the mechanics' institutes by far outshone that minority of middle-class women who fought to gain access to the male preserve of higher education. Yet the struggle of the former group of women to gain access to the male-oriented mechanics' institutes has tended to be forgotten since the struggle of the latter was that much fiercer. The universities, those male bourgeois institutions, could offer something the mechanics' institutes could not – the promise of full-time, systematic study leading to the high status award of a degree. Such an attack, by women, upon the dominant male cultural system that reserved such high status awards for men, would inevitably meet fierce opposition. It is significant that the first major attempt by women to enter the universities, through part time, university extension classes, was welcomed whereas the second major attempt, which would involve women becoming full time, university students, met with resistance, especially in the collegiate system of Oxford and Cambridge.

In 1867, various associations of middle-class women invited James Stuart, a Cambridge don, to deliver a course of lectures, in Liverpool, Manchester, Sheffield and Leeds. Since a number of the women were involved with teaching and wished to improve the standard of women's education generally, they asked for lectures on the theory and methods of education.[90] However, Stuart felt unable to talk about 'an abstract subject of that kind' and offered instead the history of astronomy.[91] Thus the movement to offer part time higher education to adults through university extension was initiated, and the women's movement, especially the North of England Council for Promoting the Higher Education of Women, was an important – though not the only – pressure group in bringing about such a scheme. Though the movement did not arise just to meet the demands of middle-class women or of the middle classes generally but also to aid the working classes in their struggle to be educated,[92] the presence of so many middle-class women 'indelibly'[93] shaped the movement. In particular, the ideal of middle-class femininity, especially the emphasis upon ladylike behaviour, influenced directly the form of the university extension classes. Kelly (1962) has noted that three features of the movement which later became characteristic of university extension teaching were the printed syllabus, the written work and the discussion period.[94] Both the printed syllabus and the written work, devised as pedagogic tools to assist Stuart in his teaching, result directly from the fact that his early audiences were middle-class women. Thus, since the education of his students was deficient, Stuart attempted to advise on note taking by giving each student, initially at the end of the first lecture, a syllabus of the content of his talk. Later, Stuart found it more useful to give such a printed handout at the beginning rather than the end of his lecture since it aided understanding of the lecture content. The introduction of written work as a pedagogic device is best told in Stuart's own words:

> I had circulated . . . a letter amongst those intending to attend the lectures, suggesting several suitable books to be read, and stating that an opportunity would be given after the lectures for questions. But I found that a considerable amount of excitement prevailed on the impropriety of a number of young ladies asking questions of, or being questioned by, a young man. . . . I solved the difficulty by bringing to the first lecture three or four questions in print, which I distributed with the statement that if answers were sent to me by post, two clear days before the next lecture, I would then return them corrected. Thus all the dangers attaching to personal intercourse would be avoided. I expected twenty or thirty answers, but from the four centres, which consisted of about six hundred pupils, I got about three hundred answers. . . . This was the origin of the questions which have since accompanied all University Extension lectures.[95]

Middle-class women continued to be the main stalwart of the movement for the rest of the century. Sadler estimated that they formed two-thirds of the Oxford Extension classes in 1888–89,[96] and such a general pattern is confirmed by a number of accounts written by early extension lecturers. [. . .]

Within the women's movement, Emily Davies became concerned that part-time, university extension would become a substitute for full-time, university study: she wanted colleges for women that were fully integrated within the university structure rather than the separate, second best education that university extension might offer.[97] Her general position on such an issue is well stated in a letter she wrote dated January 6 1869:

> all separate schemes for women are objectionable . . . with Ladies' Committees, Ladies' Associations, Lectures to Ladies, and the rest, one does not quite see why we should not soon have also Ladies' Churches and Chapels, in which the duties of women as such should be specially inculcated . . . it is discouraging to see so many of the new things for women started on the basis of separation. It seems like getting more of a 'system' of separateness, and it makes one suspicious of anything like a step in that direction.[98]

This was a fundamental statement from which Miss Davies did not defer. She sought for equal educational opportunities for women within the universities and, as Stephen (1927) has noted, took a feminist rather than an educational view of the matter.[99] Thus the gender struggle against the prevailing bourgeois definition of middle-class women as 'domestic', 'relative' and 'inferior' beings began in earnest. A new ideal of middle-class femininity had to be fought for and established, that of the 'new woman' who could study the same subjects as men and enter paid, professional employment. The issue of whether women should follow the same or separate educational courses to men, and whether they should take the same or separate examinations, was, however, a dividing factor amongst those early pioneers who struggled to enter the universities, and especially the ancient universities of Cambridge and Oxford, as full-time students.

Largely due to the initiative and hard work of Miss Davies, the 'first genuine women's college'[100] was formally opened at Hitchin, Herts, in October 1869.[101] The aim of the College was to prepare female students for the examinations of Cambridge University and in October 1873, the College moved to a site much closer to the university, at Girton. The scheme was experimental in that female students were to enter a domain of learning that had been preserved for men within the monastic, collegiate, university structure. But even though the women's college was outside, rather than integrated into, this structure, it was essential for the success of the scheme that the behaviour of the students should be above criticism. Miss Davies insisted therefore on ladylike behaviour and especially chaperonage.[102] This was essential in order to win the support of two groups necessary for the success of the venture – male, university scholars who would be willing to teach and examine the female students, and middle-class parents who were willing to pay the fees for the education of their daughters.[103] Yet despite the insistence upon ladylike manners, these students were advised to study such 'unfeminine' subjects as maths and classics, subjects that were part of the traditional male university curriculum.[104] As Delamont (1978) has argued, the students were caught in a snare of double conformity – conformity to certain rituals of behaviour and to the dominant, male, cultural system.[105] The social cost of Miss Davies' insistence on 'the same' educational opportunities for male and female students was, however, social isolation. Thus Louisa Lumsden, a tutor at Girton for 'two lonely and difficult years'[106] in the early 1870s, recollects that the difference of opinions held by Miss Davies and those of the creators of another Cambridge women's college – Newnham, separated her and Miss Davies from the social life of Cambridge.

Newnham was the outcome of principles different to those of Miss Davies since the antecedents to its foundation were largely based on the theme of 'separate and different' education for women. In the late 1860s, the North of England Council, of which Miss Clough was secretary, were of the view that identical examinations for women and men were not desirable and thus a memorial was sent to Cambridge University asking for an examination for women over 18 years of age: the request was granted and in 1869, 36 candidates sat the examination. In 1870, mainly through the efforts of Henry Sedgwick, a Cambridge don, special lectures for women were established in order to prepare them for the Women's Examination.[107] The students needed a place of residence and in 1871, Miss Clough was asked to take charge of a house at 74 Regent Street (Newnham Hall was not erected until 1876). From its very beginnings, therefore, Newnham was totally different in orientation to Girton. Whereas the latter wished to prove that women were capable of the 'same intellectual work as men', the former considered such a view 'undesirable' in the 'interest of the individual students' who were intellectually ill-prepared for such a hurdle.[108]

Such a compromising attitude towards women's education at Newnham, an attitude which did not fully challenge the dominant ideal of middle-class femininity but still upheld the notion of separate examinations for women, typically 'feminine' subjects such as history, English language and literature[109] and links with the typically 'feminine' occupation of school teaching[110] met with less fierce resistance than the Girton principles. The dominant middle-class ideal of femininity is evident too in the philanthrophy that Miss Clough encouraged amongst her students. A 'noble enthusiasm' for social service flourished at Newnham and found concrete expression in ventures such as teaching working men.[111] Even so, Newnham students like their Girton sisters were encouraged to conform to ladylike behaviour, especially in the early days when Miss Clough was nervous lest any eccentricity in dress or conduct should attract attention:

> If a girl wore shorter dresses than she liked, she would seize the opportunity of her wearing a slightly longer one to say how much she liked it, and why. If a girl wore her hair in a fringe (a fashion Miss Clough abhorred), she would put it aside with her hands and say, 'I like to see your forehead'. . . . At a debate, a student, noted for throwing bombs in conversation, advocated knickerbockers for women as a much cleaner and tidier mode of dress. Miss Clough listened with a face of horror. A few days later this reformer came to speak to her, dressed in a long, handsome cloak. Miss Clough took hold of it, 'What a nice cloak you've got, my dear!' and then, in a low confidential tone, 'Much nicer than knickerbockers'.[112]

Though many students resented such interference,[113] the 'new woman' in higher education often conceded to such restrictions. It was only gradually, during the next few decades, that such restrictions were slowly eroded.

Women's colleges were to be established too at Oxford University, though once again, not without a struggle.[114] In 1881, women students at Cambridge were formally admitted to degree examinations, though they could still not be awarded a degree: similar conditions prevailed at Oxford where examinations were gradually opened to women from 1884. The first university to admit women to degree examinations on equal terms with men was London University, in 1878. During the next two decades, a number of other universities also allowed women to be awarded degrees, e.g. Victoria University in 1880, the Scottish universities in 1892 and the University of Durham in 1895.[115] But the ancient universities of Cambridge and Oxford refused to yield. Thus, as Holcombe (1973) notes, despite repeated attempts by the feminists, the struggle for women to be awarded degrees at Oxford and Cambridge did not end until 1919 and 1947 respectively.[116]

The experience of higher education for women facilitated their entry into certain forms of waged labour, and paid work became a legitimate area of activity for middle- and upper-class women, a goal to be aimed for, if desired. The entry of women into higher education had, therefore, profound implications for their subsequent social placement within the economic structure. By the beginning of the twentieth century, we find a new, female educated élite who were concentrated in certain kinds of employment. Amongst the students who took the Hygiene Course at Bedford College, for example, was Miss Maud Hartland, who became, in 1913, one of the first women Inspectors under the National Insurance Act and Miss Hilda Martindale who became Deputy Chief Inspector of Factories in 1921 and then Director of Women's Establishment, HM Treasury, from 1933–37.[117] But this new female élite was especially concentrated in teaching posts in the expanding, fee-paying, middle-class girls' schools established by the Girls' Public Day School Trust.[118] Thus ex-Newnham students such as Edith Creak and Miss F. R. Gray became headmistresses – the former at a GPDST school in Brighton and the latter at St Paul's Girls' School.[119] The presence of such well-educated teachers within the GPDST schools helped, of course, to increase the pool of recruits for the women's colleges and thus a cyclical relationship was established between the two kinds of educational institutions. Generally, college educated women avoided teaching in the state financed, elementary sector that catered almost exclusively for working-class children: there was in fact much debate about whether it was 'genteel' for middle-class women to enter elementary school teaching.[120] Some of the women students eventually became college or university lecturers themselves. Miss Welsh, a Girton student, became a mistress at that college from 1885–1904, while Margaret Murray, a student, in the 1890s, of Egyptology at University College, London, became a member of the academic staff there.[121] However, the number of college educated women entering occupations in industry and business was very small.[122]

To sum up then, we might say that though by the end of the nineteenth century a minority[123] of middle- and upper-class women had struggled to enter the masculine stronghold of higher education and thereby resisted the conventional, bourgeois, male definition of what a middle-class woman should be, such changes were impregnated with conservatism in that the majority of this new elite entered an occupation that was traditionally linked with women – teaching. As Pedersen (1974) aptly says:

> it would seem that the reforms in women's secondary and higher education in 19th century England served more effectually to give

liberally educated woman an edge in competing with other women for plum positions in occupations long open to women (especially teaching) than to encourage large numbers of women to compete with men for less conventional employments.[124]

The entry of women into higher education further served, then, to polarise the differences between this educated female élite and other women generally, especially working-class women.

Education for Women of the Working Classes

Before the advent of the 1870 Education Act which made full time elementary education for working-class children a possibility, working-class girls might experience co-education in a variety of forms e.g. dame schools, charity schools, day schools of the British and Foreign School Society (largely supported by religious dissenters) and of the National Society for Promoting the Education of the Poor in the Principles of the Established Church, Sunday schools and industrial schools. In contrast to the accomplishments curriculum for middle-class girls, with its emphasis upon social priorities, working-class girls were offered a basic curriculum that might comprise reading, writing and practical, utilitarian skills such as plain sewing and knitting. Such subjects might teach working-class girls not only literacy but also certain skills, such as mending or the making of clothes, which could be used in both the domestic situation and in various forms of waged labour, especially domestic service and dressmaking. Though the quality of education obviously varied greatly, it is highly probable that the overall standard was very low. For example, Mary Smith (1892) the daughter of a shoemaker, attended a succession of schools and recollects that when she was about seven-years-old, she was sent to another dame school where the knowledge of the dame was: 'very small. The girls had a lesson once a day in the New Testament, and the little ones read out of the "Reading Made Easy". But knitting and sewing occupied nearly the whole time of the girls'.[125]

It is not surprising to find, therefore, that for most of the century, the literacy rate of women, especially working-class women, was lower than that for men.[126] In the eyes of the bourgeoisie, therefore, the femininity of working-class girls and women lacked that 'finesse' that was expected amongst middle-class females: in particular, the experience of waged labour, both before and after marriage, cast a blemish on their femininity. Working-class females were defined by the bourgeoisie as ignorant and incapable of learning anything but the most basic knowledge. In addition, the bourgeoisie upheld the domestic ideology as particularly important for such women since it was believed that their inadequacies as wives and mothers accounted for many of the social problems associated with the working classes. Since most of the formalised educational provision was organised by the middle classes, the ideal of the 'good woman' necessarily involved therefore, an emphasis upon the 3 Rs (reading, writing and arithmetic) and practical domestic skills. These are indeed common themes, as we shall now see, in the rhetoric that justifies the forms and content of adult education for working-class women in nineteenth century Britain.

In the early nineteenth century, adult Sunday schools for working-class men and women began to flourish. The movement developed particularly from the Bristol area where from February 1812–March 1813, nine schools for men and nine schools for women were established.[127] . . . By 1815, adult Sunday schools were established in at least 20 towns in England[128] and a report as late as 1831 reveals that many middle-class individuals hoped that such schools would 'reform' and 'civilise' working-class families into more acceptable ways of living:

> It must be extremely gratifying to the Conductors and Teachers . . .
> to find persons in their humble cottages reading the Bible with
> meditation and prayer, and thanking God that they ever attended
> an Adult School. Formerly they spent their Sabbaths in lounging,
> in walking in the fields of pleasure, in vain conversation, or in public
> houses: now they attend the public worship of Almighty God, wait
> at the posts of wisdom's doors, and receive instructions in the way
> of righteousness. In time past their families were in want, in
> wretchedness, and disorder: now they have food and raiment, and
> are taught to be there with content.[129]

As I have argued elsewhere,[130] though the manifest function of adult Sunday schools was teaching people to read the Bible, the latent functions may have related to class cultural control. In middle-class eyes, the working classes were culturally deficient: one way to improve them was to use adult education as an agency for socialisation into a different group of values. For working-class females, the ideal of the 'good woman' involved the hope that they should become 'better wives'.[131] But in addition to such an attempt to change their way of life, working-class women also had frequently to face a gender struggle within their own immediate family. Thus a woman who had diligently attended one of the Bath Adult Schools was, on that account:

> roughly treated by her husband, who had been a seafaring man, and
> much addicted to drunkenness and swearing; this obdurate man
> threatened his wife, that if she continued to go to the school or to
> meeting, he would break her bones.[132]

Though not all working-class women experienced such opposition to their attempts to gain access to education, we do find, as we shall see, some recorded instances of such a gender struggle.

The adult schools declined in importance as alternative forms of adult education offering subjects other than basic literacy began to develop. One such alternative form were the mechanics' institutes. But as we have already seen, the aims of the institutes were both class and sex-specific. Since the institutes generally failed to attract the mass of unskilled, male workers[133] it is hardly surprising to find that they failed to attract large numbers of working-class women too.[134] Working-class women were most likely to be found in the smaller, northern mixed-sex institutes and in the two large single-sex institutes at Huddersfield and Bradford. At the small, mixed-sex institute at Northowram, for example, the membership in 1861 was 79 males and 42 females:[135] weekly subscriptions are usually a reliable indication of working-class background and at this institute, the number of males paying 2d. and the number of females paying 1½d. weekly was 29 and 34 respectively. Within the mixed-sex institutes that particularly attracted working-class scholars, we tend to find that education was organised along principles similar to those forms of education attended by the bourgeoisie, i.e. segregation on the basis of sex. Thus in regard to the instruction provided within the classes, we tend to find a female section and a male section, based on the separation between the domestic sphere and waged labour. Thus at Gomersal Mechanics' Institute, in Yorkshire, the Committee regret, in their annual report for 1859, that the female class which meets on Tuesday and Thursday evenings has not succeeded to the extent:

> commensurate with the necessity and importance which the proper education and improvement of the minds of the 'gentler sex' demands for qualifying them, in some respects, for more efficiently discharging the important duty incumbent upon all who have the training of the rising generation.[136]

But while adult education for working-class women within the institutes is justified in relation to domesticity, the education for working-class men is justified in terms of its vocational value. For example, the new class in mechanical and freehand drawing introduced at Northowram Mechanics' Institute in 1857 is justified as being 'useful' and 'serviceable' to the young male members such as 'joiners, masons, mechanics, and designers' in their respective trades.[137] The emphasis upon the domestic sphere for working-class women is continually reiterated in the rhetoric that justifies their presence within the institutes, and the implications of this rhetoric for the kinds of curricula that working-class women might be offered relate to the ideal of the 'good woman'. Thus an educational diet of the 3 Rs and selected, practical skills such as sewing is all that is considered necessary since such a curriculum might improve the quality of domestic work, the standard of family life and solve generally the social problems associated with the working classes. This viewpoint is epitomised in the statement made in 1859 by Mr Barnett Blake, Agent and Lecturer of the Yorkshire Union of Mechanics' Institutes:

> Little space has . . . been left to direct attention to the great importance of female education as one of the surest means of

achieving social amelioration. As the first lessons of instruction, whether for good or evil, are derived from the mother, it is evident that our young females should not be neglected. Upon their training depends much of the future, and indeed it has been asserted that if attention were exclusively applied to the education of the female portion of our population, all the rest would follow as a matter of course. To reading and writing, with the simple rules of arithmetic, should be added the indispensable art of plain needlework so necessary to the comfort of the working-man's household, and the good effects would be felt in succeeding generations.[138]

Working-class male supporters of the mechanics' institutes movement frequently upheld the rhetoric of the domestic ideology too. For example, Rowland Detrosier, the working-class radical, when addressing fellow institute members in 1829 asks them whether it was not essential to 'the comfort of man' that young women of the working classes should be taught 'the duties of housewifery'.[139] And bourgeois female supporters, such as Fanny Hertz, who was on the committee of the Bradford Female Education Institute, though complaining that the education of women within the institutes should not be considered from the viewpoint of the duties of wives, mothers, mistresses and servants, nevertheless argued that the education of female factory operatives within the institutes would help them to become 'suitable and worthy helpmates for the educated and intelligent working men, who are the glory of England'.[140]

Working-class women were thus bombarded on all sides with the basic assumptions of the domestic ideology – reaffirming their 'relative', 'subordinate' and 'inferior' status. Within this bombardment, bourgeois women participated in the imposition of class ideology upon their sisters in the lower social orders as well as bourgeois men. But, as the above quotation from Detrosier illustrates, the struggle of working-class women to obtain an education within the institutes may be interpreted as not only a class struggle but also a gender struggle within their own social grouping. As Elizabeth Wilson (1977) has commented, the reactionary attitude to women adopted by many male, working-class radicals has been one of the saddest and most persistent themes in the history of socialism.[141]

The two main all-female institutes at Bradford and Huddersfield did offer a wider range of curricula than the 3 Rs and plain sewing common to a large number of the mixed-sex institutes that attracted working-class women. At the Huddersfield Female Institute, for example, where the students were mainly milliners, dressmakers, domestic servants or women living at home with their parents,[142] the curriculum in 1860 covered reading, writing, arithmetic, grammar, dictation, history, geography, and singing.[143] Yet even so, little more than 100 pupils are enrolled in 1862: the Committee, in their annual report for that year, speak of the 'many obstacles' preventing females attending the evening classes and in particular mention the obstacles arising from their 'home duties'.[144] Unlike many bourgeois women, working-class females could not afford to employ domestic servants: even when they were employed in waged labour, therefore, they still had to meet the 'double load' of engaging in such work and performing these domestic tasks expected of their sex. It is little wonder that they failed to attend such institutes in large numbers. The Bradford Female Education Institute was, in fact, the larger of the two main female institutes: in December 1861, 570 female members were recorded of whom 267 were spinners and other factory workers while a further 129 were weavers.[145]

Another major attempt by the middle classes to educate their social inferiors was through the working men's college movement. A number of influential middle-class men, such as the Rev. F. D. Maurice, a prominent Christian socialist, felt that the mechanics' institutes had failed to attract a large number of the working class and that democratic control within the institutes had been frustrated by middle-class control amongst the boards of directors. In particular, Maurice felt that the curriculum of the institutes had aimed at popularity and did nothing more than 'graze the surface of men's minds than penetrate into them'.[146] The aim of the colleges was to provide, therefore, an 'enrichment of personal life'.[147] However, as the name implies, the working men's colleges were, in their original conceptions, both class and sex specific. The first college, the People's College, Sheffield, established by the Rev. R. S. Bayley in 1842, did in fact admit women, but it was regarded by even the most 'ardent' supporters of popular education as a great 'novelty'.[148] Maurice, who had held several meetings with other interested parties drew up, in 1854, an outline for a London 'College for Working Men' and point 3 of this plan illustrates how marginal women were to the whole enterprise:

3. It was agreed that adult males (that is to say, at all events, not younger than 16) should be contemplated first and chiefly in our education; though it was thought desirable that provision should in due time be made for the teaching of boys and of females.[149]

Once again it would appear that working-class women would have to struggle to survive within such male-oriented colleges. As we have already noted, within a patriarchal society where the domestic ideology located women within the private sphere of the home and men to those public spheres outside the home, the entry of men into various institutionalised forms of educational provision would be facilitated and that of women restricted: in addition, of course, the sexual power basis of society was such that women, especially working-class women, were rarely involved in those power structures within which important policy making decisions about adult education might be made. Thus the 'Committee of Teaching and Publications' that helped Maurice to draw up the plan for the proposed London college were all males and included such notable figures as the Rev. Charles Kingsley, J. M. Ludlow and E. Vansittart Neale – both barristers.

Maurice, in the 1854 plan, upheld the principle of sex segregation for certain classes, especially the more abstract and controversial subjects such as ethics and politics while the low status, recreational subjects such as languages, drawing and music might be shared: he also stated that women ought to have lessons in 'social life and order' and 'health' since the 'domestic life' was their prime location.[150] Once again, a differential curriculum for working-class women was justified in terms of their domesticity. As Sadler was to comment in 1907, the co-educational plan that had been adopted at the Sheffield People's College did not commend itself to Maurice.[151] The question of the admission of women was in fact an important dividing issue between the opinions of Maurice and another bourgeois supporter of the new college – the philologist Frederick James Furnivall, son of a physician.[152] The issue of whether women should be educated in separate or co-educational classes had profound social implications. Once women were offered separate rather than integrated education with men, there was always the risk that women's education would develop into an inferior, second best system outside and distinct from the dominant, male, cultural world: a double educational standard could then be more easily created and maintained. If, on the other hand, women at least shared the same educational facilities – if not the same curricula – as men, then there was always a chance that sex segregation and sex based inequalities could break down. The London Working Men's College, founded in 1854, and the dozen or so other Colleges established between 1855 and 1868, illustrate only too well some of the problems associated with this issue. Nowhere is this more evident than in those working men's colleges, such as the one at Halifax, where a separate female institute was founded.

The 1859 official annual report of the young women's Institute at Halifax reveals quite clearly that the curriculum embodies utilitarian, domestic skills such as plain cooking, the making and mending of clothes – skills that were considered necessary for the ideal of the 'good woman', the efficient, practical housekeeper:

In the young women's Institute great progress has been made. A school of cookery has been instituted in which young women are taught the art of plain cooking, such as will increase the comforts of the home of the working-man, and economise his limited means. They are also taught the art of cooking for the sick, which not only teaches them a lesson of charity, but also provides them with the means of usefulness in their own homes when sickness visits them. There is no idea of training them for domestic servants. The classes for vocal music are well attended, as well as the sewing classes. In these classes also, great care is taken to teach them only what is useful, viz., making and mending their own dresses, & c.[153]

The emphasis upon the 'usefulness' of the curriculum contrasts sharply with the 'useless' accomplishments commonly taught to middle-class girls and to the more theoretical, abstract subjects which those upper- and middle-class women might study who entered university-oriented colleges. Within the men's division at the Halifax Working Men's College, the curriculum included basic literacy, theology, geometry, book-keeping, French and science.[154] It would appear then that once a separate female section became established within a college, the female scholars tended to become isolated: it was much easier to impose the prevailing domestic ideology and class-specific ideal of femininity under such conditions.

Some entirely separate colleges for women were established in London and it would appear that the curricula here was much less directly related to domesticity than is evident at Halifax. In 1865, the Working Women's College was founded in Queen's Square, Bloomsbury with the intention of being a counterpart to the London Working Men's College.[155] Arthur J. Munby, the poet and barrister, who was actively involved in the initial discussions about the College, notes that they hoped to attract 'teachers, shopgirls, and even servant maids' as members and pupils: the College was largely successful in this aim since by 1866 the majority of the students were milliners, shopgirls or young women living at home.[156] However, the issue of co-educational classes eventually divided the College in two. The Working Women's College became 'The College for Men and Women' and remained at the original site while a new institution, 'The College for Working Women' established itself in Fitzroy Street in 1874. The curriculum at the new college included not only the 3 Rs but also bookkeeping, drawing, French, German, geography, English history, English literature, physics, hygiene and singing[157] – as well as 'cheap cookery' classes.[158] But even though the range of subjects was much wider than that previously offered by many middle-class individuals, it did not embrace a number of subjects taught at the London Working Men's College, e.g. public health, algebra, geometry, natural philosophy, astronomy, machinery, and law.[159] As these examples illustrate, by the 1870s, the wider stratification of knowledge had a well-established sexual base.

Throughout the century, a number of other attempts were made by the middle classes to educate working-class women through various forms of part-time evening schools. For example, some middle class 'ladies' opened an evening school for working-class women in Birmingham, in September 1847: they offered instruction in reading, writing, arithmetic, sewing and Biblical knowledge and hoped eventually to teach also subjects such as cookery and vocal music. The scholars, most of whom were married, are described as 'Poor things' who are ignorant of 'household business'.[160] It is particularly in the advocacy of arithmetic, sewing and cookery that we can see the way such middle-class women tried to impose the domestic ideology and the ideal of the 'good woman' upon their working-class sisters:

They (the scholars) have a good deal of reckoning to do every day, – most of them. . . . They do learn arithmetic to some purpose: and they learn something else by means of it: – nothing less than that it answers better to some of them to stay at home and keep house, than to earn wages in the manufactory. . . . With great satisfaction, a wife . . . now finds herself able to check . . . mistakes. When, added to this, she has become a reasonable thinker and planner, can understand her business, – can make and mend, and buy and economise, and suit her ways to her means; she may easily find that it answers better, as regards mere money, to stay at home, than to work at the factory. The great truth will be more evident still when the kitchen is opened, and the world of economy and comfort belonging to that department is revealed to minds at present wholly dark in regard to it. The young women think they can cook, as before they thought they could reckon and could sew. They will soon see.[161]

It is difficult to estimate how many such evening schools, organised privately by the middle classes, were established: at the above school in Birmingham, for example the scholars had to pay thirteen pence plus an extra penny for the copybook in which they practised their exercises. The 1851 Census tells us that the vast majority of evening schools taught only the 3 Rs and that of the 1545 schools from which information was obtained, more than half the total number of scholars are male – thus 27,829 male but only 11,954 female scholars are recorded.[162] As the state began to increase the extent of grant aid for evening schools, the number of scholars expanded. By 1902–03, 657,594 scholars are recorded of whom 403,629 are male and 253,965 are female.[163] Working-class women were increasingly drawn into such state financed classes where they were concentrated particularly in 'Division V' type subjects – 'Home Occupation and Industries'. Under this broad heading came subjects such as needlework, dressmaking, domestic tailoring, millinery, embroidery, lace making, domestic economy and cookery.[164] The link between femininity and domesticity became further institutionalised. But before state aided evening classes expanded in the latter decades of the nineteenth century, a new challenge to the dominant middle-class ideal of the 'good woman' came from amongst working-class women themselves, through the organisational structure of the Women's Co-operative Guild.

The Women's Co-operative Guild (originally called the Women's League for the Spread of Co-operation), established in June 1883, has been described by Gaffin (1977) as the first separate organisation for working-class women.[165] The majority of members were married women, full-time wives and mothers, whose husbands were of the artisan class – weavers, mechanics, railway men, Co-operative employees etc.[166] Even so, in the early years in particular, a number of upper- and middle-class women were influential in both the initiation of the Guild and in its organisational structure. Mrs Alice Acland, for example, the daughter of a Minister and wife of an Oxford don, was the first General Secretary of the Guild: as Gaffin (1977) points out, the values that she upheld for Guildswomen, in these early days, were simple and moralistic – a woman's place was in the home, keeping herself busy, learning to be a better household manager and a better cooperator.[166] It would appear then, that Mrs Acland, like many other middle-class ladies before her, upheld the ideal of woman as the home-maker, who through her own efforts, could improve the quality of home life. In particular the 'good' Guildswoman was expected to express her loyalty to the Co-operative Movement through buying only at Co-operative Stores, even if the price of the products was more expensive than elsewhere: the interest paid out to members in the form of the 'divi' encouraged, of course, values such as self-help, saving and thrift – qualities considered necessary for the running of an efficient house-hold. One Guildswoman, for example, was so keen in building up her 'divi' that she walked two miles to Co-operative Stores every time she wished to buy a few things.[168] It is difficult, of course, to determine to what extent the 'good' Guildswoman ideal was imposed upon the Guildswomen by their middle-class leaders, by their own menfolk or created by the women themselves: we have already noted that the domestic ideology was deeply embedded within the working-class, male trade union movement.

Particularly in the early years of the Guild, educational activities revolved around domestic subjects. For example, the annual report for 1889 notes that five branches had lecture courses on dressmaking and two had lecture courses on sick nursing, though classes were also held in basic skills such as reading and writing: single lectures during the year covered topics such as 'Political Economy', 'Money', 'The Air we Breathe', 'The Industrial Revolution' as well as the more predictable 'Domestic Economy', 'Food', 'Clear-starching' and 'Ironing'.[169] It would appear that working-class women were still primarily defined as domestic beings. However, when Margaret Llewelyn Davies became Secretary of the Guild, from 1889–1921, a clear change of direction in guild policy becomes evident.

Miss Davies was one of that élite of educated women who had attended both Queen's College, London and Girton College, Cambridge. For Miss Davies, the chief aim of the Guild was to educate women and to give them 'a wider life',[170] i.e. to extend interest from outside the sphere of the home to broader social and political issues. Under her guidance, and presumably with the support of the majority of Guildswomen who were organised in democratic, self-governing branches, a new ideal of working-class femininity was upheld – that of woman as 'homemaker and peaceful reformer'. Miss Davies hoped that the democratic structure of the Guild, whereby all who joined enjoyed equal voting rights, would ensure against middle-class domination. It does appear that at long last, working-class women were in an organisational structure where they had the power to decide, through the vote, on various policy matters, including the content of their own education. The ideal of the 'homemaker and peaceful reformer' reflected both the reality of their own lives, as full-time wives and mothers, and also an increasing self and social awareness. The double edge of 'homemaker' and 'reformer' is well reflected in the curricular provision of the 1890s. Thus for the year 1893–94, 93 Guild branches held classes in domestic subjects while discussions included the topics of free education, old age pensions, sick benefit societies and socialism.[171] With the home as the base, many Guildswomen began to engage in activities as diverse as pensions for widows, divorce law reform, the ending of half-time education for children, trade unionism for women and the campaign for women's suffrage.[172] Other Guildswomen prepared and read papers at conferences. At the Autumn Conference of 1907, for example, Mrs Gasson read a paper on 'Wives' Savings' in which she argued that a wife should have a legal claim to a part of the family income.[173] Through the solidarity of a single-sex organisation, working-class women were 'finding a voice'.[174] The consciousness raising that Guild activities developed is evident in accounts such as that of Mrs Scott, a felt hat worker, who notes that the Guild taught working-class women to become articulate and ask for the things they needed.[175]

The development of self and social awareness was not won without a feminist struggle though, at both the organisational and familial levels. At the organisational level there was the thorny question of equality of membership for women within the Co-operative Movement. In some societies only one person in a family could be a member and this was usually the husband. A few societies excluded women too while others demanded the husband's permission for his wife's membership.[176] Such patriarchal structures had to be fought against and Guildswomen pressed for, and won, on the issue of open membership. The increase in membership – some 1,700 in 1889 and 57,874 in 1927[177] – brought renewed strength. But the possible gender struggle on the more personal, individual level, within the family and home, was probably the most difficult to encounter. G. J. Holyoake, the prominent cooperator, once claimed that a law should be passed deeming any young woman ineligible for marriage unless she possessed a certificate of having cooked a mutton chop to the satisfaction of the clergyman of the parish![178] Though many male cooperators would probably not hold such extreme views, it is very likely that care of the children and housework were regarded as woman's sphere and that women were expected to be subordinate within the husband/wife relationship. In particular, Guild activities could challenge the latter assumption. Mrs Layton, for example, who saved sufficient money for a deposit for a house and obtained the mortgage in her own name, found that her husband blamed the Guild for her assertive attitude.[179]

By the end of the century, then, the education of working-class women was such that their social placement within the economic structure would reflect their low level of educational attainment. Though a variety of forms of education had been offered to working-class women throughout the century, the content of their education tended to reflect the same basic curriculum of the 3 Rs, some limited general knowledge and certain domestic skills such as sewing and cookery. The standard of education of working-class women was directly related to the standard of education they received as girls: as late as 1899, MacNamara could still claim that as the present law stood, a child might leave school at 11-years-old to work 'half time' in a factory or workshop or 'full time' outside a factory, workshop or mine, provided a certain educational standard had been attained.[180] Thus Sarah Reddish who became a radical suffragist in Lancashire, left school at the age of 11, in 1861, and after winding silk at home, worked as a winder and 'roll coverer' in a cotton mill. Another suffragist, Ada Nield, left school in 1881, at the same age as Miss Reddish, and after helping to bring up her seven younger brothers, became – at the age of nineteen or twenty – an employee in a clothing factory at Crewe, a job that she stayed in for only three weeks.[181] A Guildswoman, whose anonymous account was published in 1913, and who wished she had been 'better educated', had left school at 10-years-old and gone into farm service.[182] As Sterns (1972) has noted, at the turn of the century, most working-class women still lived in a 'culture of poverty'[183] – a poverty that is reflected in their poor material conditions and in their standard of education. For working-class women, therefore, the part-time education offered through state aided evening classes or Guild meetings could be an invaluable means of retaining and improving that basic education already received. Even so, for most working-class women, marriage was still the ideal end state and before marriage, most engaged in forms of waged labour that were shunned by their middle-class sisters – domestic service and various kinds of factory work such as manufacturing, food processing, clothing.[184] Generally their lives were lives of toil in which not only the demands of waged labour had to be met but also the demands considered appropriate for their sex – the demands of home and family responsibilities.

Conclusion

In conclusion I would like to make four main points. Firstly, I have tried to illustrate how the domestic ideology, which located women within the home as full-time wives and mothers, helped to shape both the forms and content of education for nineteenth-century women. The domestic ideology which defined women as relative, inferior and subordinate beings whose femininity was linked with domesticity, became a part of the dominant, male, bourgeois culture but it was also increasingly taken up by working-class men, especially in the second half of the century. However, since the bourgeoisie were the main providers of formalised education, their class-specific ideals of femininity – that of the middle-class 'perfect wife and mother' and that of the working-class 'good woman' – tended to be the dominant ideals which provided part of the context within which educational institutions were founded and reformed. Secondly, both middle-class and working-class women used education as a form of struggle against male, bourgeois definitions of women. For middle-class women the struggle was essentially a feminist struggle which particularly gathered force when they attempted to enter the most prestigious, male, bourgeois institutions – the universities. Their attempt to establish the ideal of the 'new woman' who could enjoy equal opportunities in higher education and engage in various forms of professional work was an attempt, therefore, to break free from the bonds of domesticity and to create a definition of woman as a careerist, someone who could be dedicated to her work, professionally trained, financially independent and therefore not in need of the economic support that a husband might provide. However, for working-class women, for much of the century, the struggle was both a class and feminist struggle that was contained within low status educational institutions. Their attempt to establish the ideal of the 'homemaker and peaceful reformer' never broke with the bond of domesticity – though such a bond was re-defined, it was also re-affirmed. Thirdly, by the 1900s, the educational changes that had occurred during the course of the nineteenth century served only to reinforce and polarise the differences between middle-class and working-class women. Lastly, though this paper has concentrated upon the feminist and social class struggles encountered by some nineteenth-century women within the educational context, we must not forget that such issues are still of relevance for the present day. Just as we need much more research into the historical struggles that women encountered, so we need much more research into the present day situation. Within such studies, the past can inform the present and the present can help us to interpret the past.

Acknowledgments

The research upon which this paper is based is part of a continuing project being financed by the SSRC, and I would like to express my grateful thanks for this financial support. I would also like to thank Madeleine Arnot, Lecturer in Educational Studies at the Open University, for the many helpful suggestions and constructive criticisms she made on the first draft of this paper. Her constant flow of ideas has been an invaluable help to me in ordering my own thoughts. Any inadequacies in this paper are, however, my own.

This paper was first presented at the International Sociological Association Conference 'The Origins and Operations of Educational Systems', Paris, August 7–8 1980.

Notes and references

1 The few references include Marks, P, 'Femininity in the classroom: an account of changing attitudes' in Mitchell, J. and Oakley, A. (Eds) *The Rights and Wrongs of Women* (1976) Penguin Books; Delamont, S., 'The contradictions in ladies' education' and Delamont. S., 'The domestic ideology and women's education' in Delamont, S. and Duffin, L. (Eds) *The Nineteenth-Century Woman: Her Cultural and Physical World* (1978) Croom Helm; Purvis, J., 'Working-class women and adult education in nineteenth-century Britain', *History of Education*, 9, No. 3, 1980, pp. 193–212; Purvis, J., 'Women and teaching in the nineteenth century' in Dale, R., Esland, G., Fergusson, R. and Macdonald, M. (Eds) *Education and the State*, Vol 2 *Politics, Patriarchy & Practice* (1981) Falmer Press; and Purvis, J., ' "Women's life is essentially domestic, public life being confined to men" (Comte): separate spheres and inequality in the education of working-class women, 1854–1900', *History of Education*, 10, No. 4, 1981, pp. 227–243.

2 In addition to those cited above, the list of publications includes Kamm, J., *Indicative Past: A Hundred Years of the Girls' Public Day School Trust* (1971) Allen & Unwin; Burstyn, J., 'Religious arguments against higher education for women in England, 1840–1890' in: *Women's Studies*, 1, No. 1, 1972, pp. 111–131; Turner, B., *Equality for Some: the Story of Girls' Education* (1974) Ward Lock Educational; Pedersen, J. S., 'Schoolmistresses and headmistresses: elites and education in nineteenth century England', *Journal of British Studies*, 15, 1975, pp. 135–162; Pedersen, J. S., 'The reform of women's secondary and higher education: institutional change and social values in mid and late Victorian England', *History of Education Quarterly*, 19, 1979, pp. 61–91; McWilliams-Tullberg, R., *Women at Cambridge: a Men's University – Though of a Mixed Type* (1975) Victor Gollancz; Borer, M., *Willingly to School: a History of Women's Education* (1976) Lutterworth Press; Dyhouse, C., 'Social Darwinistic ideas and the development of women's education in England, 1880–1920', *History of Education*, 5, No. 1, 1976, pp. 41–58; Dyhouse, C., 'Good wives and little mothers: social anxieties and the schoolgirl's curriculum, 1890–1920', *Oxford Review of Education*, 3, No. 1, 1977 pp. 21–35; Dyhouse, C., 'Towards a "feminine" curriculum for English schoolgirls: the demands of ideology 1870–1963', *Women's Studies International Quarterly*, 1, No. 4, 1978 pp. 297–311; Burstyn, J., 'Women's education in England during the nineteenth century: a review of the literature, 1970–1976', *History of Education*, 6, No. 1, 1977, pp. 11–19; Davin, A., ' "Mind that you do as you are told": reading books for Board School girls' *Feminist Review*, 3, 1979 and Bryant, M., *The Unexpected Revolution: A Study in the Education of Women and Girls in the Nineteenth Century* (1980) CUP, Burstyn, J., *Victorian Education and the Ideal of Womanhood* (1980) Croom Helm; and Dyhouse, C., *Girls Growing Up in Late Victorian and Edwardian England* (1981) Routledge & Kegan Paul.

3 See, for example, Burstyn, J. 1972 *loc. cit.*, McWilliams-Tullberg 1975 *op. cit.*, Delamont 1978 *loc. cit.* and Burstyn, J. 1980 *op. cit.*

4 The major exception here is Purvis, J. 1980 *loc. cit.*

5 The working class was a highly diversified grouping and distinctions were often made between the poorest, the poor and the artisan sections – though the latter often merged into the lower middle class. Those not

engaged in manual waged labour, who could afford to keep a wife full-time at home and employ a number of domestic servants, were usually seen as 'middle class'. By the end of the century, the divisions between the working and middle classes on the issue of the employment of domestic servants appears to have been pronounced. Seebohm Rowntree, for example, when he conducted his survey of York in 1899 took the 'keeping or not keeping of domestic servants' as the dividing line between 'the working classes and those of a higher social class' – cited in Horn, Pamela (1975) *The Rise and Fall of the Victorian Servant*, p. 17 (London, Gill & Macmillan).

6 I am using the term 'femininity' in the way outlined by Oakley, A., *Sex, Gender and Society* (1972), Temple Smith, pp. 158–9, where she argues that 'sex' refers to the biological differences between males and females while 'gender' refers to the psychological and cultural aspects that distinguish masculinity and femininity. 'Femininity' is thus a socially constructed category.

7 Hall, C., 'The early formation of Victorian domestic ideology', in Burman, S. (Ed.) *Fit Work for Women* (1979), Croom Helm, pp. 18–19.

8 Quoted in Ramelson, M., *Petticoat Rebellion: A Century of Struggle for Women's Rights* (1967) Lawrence & Wishart, 1976 ed., p. 103.

9 Gregory, Dr J., *A Father's Legacy to His Daughters* (1774), W. Strahan, London, p. 169, the page number here refers to the 1823 edition by John Anderson, Edinburgh.

10 Taylor, Mrs & Taylor, Jane, *Correspondence between a Mother and her Daughter at School* (1817), Taylor & Hessey, London, p. 140.

11 Oxiensis, 'The education of women', a review of F. Power Cobbe: Essays on the Pursuits of Women (1863) in the *Christian Observer*, July 1865, p. 547.

12 Her writings include, *The Women of England, their Social Duties, and Domestic Habits* (1839), *The Daughters of England, their Position in Society, Character and Responsibilities* (1842), *The Mothers of England, their Influence and Responsibility* (1843) and *The Wives of England, their Relative Duties, Domestic Influence and Social Obligations* (1843) – all published by Fisher, Son & Co., London.

13 Ellis, Mrs, *Education of the Heart: Woman's Best Work* (1869), Hodder & Stoughton, p. 35.

14 Ruskin, J., 'Of Queen's Gardens' in *Sesame and Lilies* (1865), Smith, Elder & Co., p. 122.

15 Walker, Alexander, *Woman Physiologically Considered as to Mind, Morals, Marriage, Matrimonial Slavery, Infidelity and Divorce*, 2nd edn. (1840), A. H. Baily, London, pp. 43 & 47.

16 *op. cit.*, p. 149.

17 More, H., *Strictures on the Modern System of Female Education with a View of the Principles and Conduct prevalent among Women of Rank and Fortune* (1799), Vol. II, T. Cadell, London, p. 2; Taylor, Mrs & Taylor, Jane (1817) *op. cit.*, p. 19; Ruskin, J. (1865) *op. cit.*, p. 161; Trollope, Anthony, 'Higher education of women' (1868) in Trollope, A. *Four Lectures*, ed. by Parrish Morris (1938), Constable, p. 75 and Smiles, Samuel, *Character* (1884), John Murray, p. 57.

18 Such a questioning did not necessarily mean that marriage and the family were regarded as unnecessary for women. See Bryant, M. (1979) *op. cit.*, pp. 118–119, where she argues that the family could provide a secure economic and emotional centre, a supportive rather than restrictive base from which women could articulate new demands.

19 Ellis, Mrs, *The Daughters* . . . (1842) *op. cit.*, p. 3.
20 Beechey, V., 'On patriarchy', *Feminist Review*, 3, 1979, p. 66, suggests that patriarchy refers to male domination and to the power relationships by which men dominate women. Further discussion of the concept is to be found in Eisenstein, Zillah R. (Ed.) *Capitalist Patriarchy and the Case for Socialist Feminism* (1979), Monthly Review Press, New York.
21 'Treatment of women', *Eliza Cook's Journal*, Saturday, August 9, 1851, p. 225.
22 Walker, Alexander, *Woman Physiologically*. . . . (1840) *op. cit.*, p. 13.
23 Ibid, p. 129.
24 'The probable retrogression of women', *The Saturday Review*, July 1, 1871, pp. 10–11. For a general discussion of the biological arguments regarding brain size and the intellect of women see Burstyn, 1980, *op. cit.*, chapter 4.
25 'British Medical Association: Fifty Fourth Annual Meeting, held at Brighton, 1886' *The Lancet*, August 14 1886, p. 315. For a general discussion of the medical arguments advanced to oppose the higher education of women see Burstyn, J. 'Education and sex: the medical case against higher education for women in England, 1870–1900', *Proceedings of the American Philosophical Society*, 117, No. 2, April 1 1973, pp. 79–89.
26 Burgon, John William, *To Educate Young Women like Young Men, and with Young Men – a Thing Inexpedient and Immodest* (1884), Parker & Co., London, p. 15. For a general discussion of the religious arguments advanced to oppose higher education for women see Burstyn, J. (1980) *op. cit.*, chapter 6.
27 Ibid., p. 17, 29.
28 Perhaps the best known of such statements are Wollstonecraft, M. *A Vindication of the Rights of Women* (1792), London; Thompson, W., *Appeal of One Half the Human Race, Women, against the Pretensions of the Other Half, Men* (1825), Longman and Mill, J. S., *The Subjection of Women* (1869), Longmans.
29 See the useful discussion offered in chapter 5 of J. A. & O. Banks, *Feminism and Family Planning in Victorian England* (1964), Liverpool University Press.
30 Ibid., p. 58.
31 Dyhouse, C., 'The role of women: from self sacrifice to self-awareness' in Lerner, L. (Ed.) *The Victorians* (1978), Methuen, p. 175.
32 Ellis, Mrs, *Education of the Heart* . . . (1869) *op. cit.*, p. 14.
33 The quality and style of dress would, of course, always distinguish a 'lady' from other women. As we shall later see, those women who entered higher education from the 1860s were expected not to be 'dressy' or 'crude' in their taste in clothes. Even in the early twentieth century, Miss Penrose, the Principal of Somerville College, Oxford was 'shocked' when Dorothy Sayers appeared one morning at breakfast with a three-inch-wide scarlet riband around her head and ear-rings which reached almost to each shoulder and contained scarlet and green parrots in gilt cages. Miss Penrose asked a student to persuade Miss Sayers to remove the 'offending bedizenment' – quoted in Brittain, V. *The Women at Oxford* (1960), George Harrap, p. 123.
34 See, Davidoff, L., *The Best Circles: Society, Etiquette and the Season* (1973) Croom Helm, especially chapter 3.
35 Ibid., p. 50.

36 Austin, Mrs, *Two Letters on Girls' Schools, and on the Training of Working Women* (1857), Chapman & Hall, p. 41.
37 Booth, James, *On the Female Education of the Industrial Classes* (1855), Bell & Daldy, pp. 12–15.
38 Ingestre, Lord Viscount, *Social Evils: Their Causes and Their Cure* (1853), William Parker, p. 12; Greg, W. R., 'Why are women redundant?' in Greg, W. R., *Literary and Social Judgements* (1868), N. Truber & Co., p. 373 and Austin, Mrs, *Two Letters . . .* (1857) *op. cit.*, p. 34.
39 Greg, W. R., 'Why are women . . .?' (1868) *loc. cit.*, Engels, Frederick, *The Condition of the Working Class in England* (1845) reprinted by Panther Books, 1969.
40 Ibid., 1969, reprint p. 175.
41 Davin, Anna, 'Mind that you do. . . .' (1979) *loc. cit.*, p. 90. Basch, Francoise, *Relative Creatures: Victorian Women in Society and the Novel 1837–67* (1974) Allen Lane, p. 50.
42 'Queen bees or working bees?', *The Saturday Review*, November 12, 1859, p. 576.
43 This term is discussed in Johnson, R. 'Notes on the schooling of the English working class 1780–1850', in Dale, R., Esland, G. & MacDonald, M. (Eds), *Schooling and Capitalism* (1976), Routledge & Kegan Paul, pp. 44–54.
44 The extent of middle-class provision is a controversial issue. For example, Lacqueur, Thomas, *Religion and Respectability: Sunday Schools and Working Class Culture* (1976) Yale University Press, claims that Sunday schools, a popular form of working-class education, were largely founded and staffed by the working classes themselves. For a critique of Lacqueur see Dick, Malcolm, 'The myth of the working-class Sunday school', *History of Education*, 1980, 9, No. 1, pp. 27–41.
45 See, for example, Maudsley, H., 'Sex in mind and in education', *Fortnightly Review*, 1874, pp. 466–483.
46 Stephen, Barbara, *Emily Davies and Girton College* (1927), Constable & Co., p. 13.
47 Vicinus, Martha, 'Introduction: the perfect Victorian lady' in Vicinus, M. (Ed.) *Suffer and Be Still: Women in the Victorian Age* (1972), Indiana University Press, p. ix.
48 Perhaps the best known history is Strachey, Ray, *The Cause: a Short History of the Women's Movement in Great Britain* (1928), G. Bell. For an account of the part that working-class women played in the suffrage movement see Liddington, J. & Norris, J., *One Hand Tied Behind Us: – the Rise of the Women's Suffrage Movement* (1978), Virago.
49 See, for example, Williams, R., *The Long Revolution* (1965) Pelican Books, chapter 3.
50 Alexander, Sally, 'Women's work in nineteenth-century London: a study of the years 1820–50', in Mitchell, J. & Oakley, A. (Eds) *The Rights and Wrongs of Women* (1976) Penguin Books, pp. 59–111 provides a recent account on some aspects of this issue. See also Pinchbeck, Ivy, *Women Workers and the Industrial Revolution 1750–1850* (1930) George Routledge & Sons and Margaret Hewitt, *Wives and Mothers in Victorian Industry* (1958) Rockliff.
51 Foreman, Ann, *Femininity as Alienation: Women and the Family in Marxism and Psychoanalysis* (1977), Pluto Press, p. 92.
52 Gray, Maria H., 'Men and women', *The Fortnightly Review*, 26, New Series July 1 to December 1 1879, p. 681.
53 In his classic essay, 'The position of women', in Titmuss, R. H., *Essays*

on 'The Welfare State' (1963, new edn) Allen & Unwin, Titmuss states that the average size of the mid-Victorian working-class family was six or more (p. 89), a figure that does not reflect the number of pregnancies that resulted in still-births, miscarriages and deaths (p. 91). See the moving accounts written by working-class women about their experiences of childbirth and child rearing in Davies, M. Llewelyn (Ed.) *Maternity: Letters from Working Women* (1915, reprint by Virago 1978).

54 Marshall, Mary Paley, *What I Remember* (1947), University Press, Cambridge, p. 7.

55 Grey, William Mrs, *On The Education of Women*: a paper read at the Meeting of the Society of Arts, May 31st 1871 2nd edn (1871) William Ridgway, pp. 19–20.

56 *Reports from Commissioners: Schools Inquiry Vol. 1.* (Session 19 November 1867–31 July 1868), p. 546.

57 Ibid., pp. 548–549.

58 Kelly, Thomas, *A History of Adult Education in Great Britain* (1962), Liverpool University Press, p. 228.

59 Muir, Professor James, *John Anderson: Pioneer of Technical Education and The College he Founded*, edited by Macaulay, James M. (1950), John Smith & Son, Glasgow, p. 147.

60 Ibid. p. 147, 148.

61 Kamm Josephine, *Hope Deferred: Girls' Education in English History* (1965), Methuen, p. 175.

62 Percival, Alicia C., *The English Miss To-Day and Yesterday* (1939), George Harrap, p. 124.

63 See, for example, Kamm, J., *Hope Deferred . . .* (1965) *op. cit.*, p. 173.

64 Burstyn, J., *Higher Education for Women . . .* (1968) PhD thesis, *op. cit.*, p. 15.

65 Davies, Emily, *Women in the Universities of England and Scotland* (1896), Macmillan & Bowes, Cambridge, p. 4.

66 Stanley, Lady H. M., of Alderley, 'Personal recollections of women's education', *The Nineteenth Century*, August 1879, p. 309.

67 Percival, Alicia C., *The English Miss. . . .* (1939) *op. cit.*, p. 126.

68 Quoted in Tuke, Margaret J., *A History of Bedford College for Women* (1939), Oxford University Press, p. 21.

69 Kamm, J., *Hope Deferred. . . .* (1965) *op. cit.*, p. 176 makes the point, however, that unlike Bedford, Queen's College was not destined for university status.

70 The Rev. Hume, A., *The Learned Societies and Printing Clubs of the United Kingdom* (1847), Longman, p. 3.

71 Burstyn, J., *Higher Education for Women. . . .* (1968), PhD thesis, *op. cit.*, p. 61.

72 Ibid., p. 238.

73 Porter, William Smith, *Sheffield Literary and Philosophical Society: a Centenary Retrospect 1822–1922* (1922) Northend, Sheffield, pp. 14–16, 67, 71.

74 Stephen, Barbara, *Emily Davies. . . .* (1927) *op. cit.*, p. 261.

75 Purvis, J. 'Working-class women and adult education. . . .' (1980) *loc. cit.*, p. 198.

76 Inkster, Ian, 'The social context of an educational movement: a revisionist approach to the English mechanics' institutes, 1820–1850', *Oxford Review of Education*, No. 3, 1976, p. 280 suggests that the origins, motivations, provisions and social class membership of the institutes was marked by variety rather than uniformity.

77 For example, at the London Mechanics' Institution, a decision was made in 1830 to admit female relations and friends of members to the lectures and circulating library on the same terms as sons and apprentices – Kelly, Thomas *George Birkbeck: Pioneer of Adult Education* (1957), Liverpool University Press, p. 126.

78 *Census, 1851: Education Section: List of Literary and Scientific Institutions from which Returns were Procured at the Census of 1851*, p. 457.

79 Most of the women are listed as 'Ladies' in the various reports of the institutes.

80 Manchester Mechanics' Institution, *Annual Report* (1862), p. 13.

81 Dyer, John, 'Nineteenth century community centres Part 1 Thornton Mechanics' Institute', *Adult Education*, 1948–49, Vol. 21, p. 19.

82 Manchester Mechanics' Institute, *Annual Report* (1846), p. ix.

83 Ibid., pp. 41–42.

84 Hole, James, *An Essay on the History and Management of Literary, Scientific, and Mechanics' Institutions* (1853), Longman, p. 29.

85 *Report of the Yorkshire Union of Mechanics' Institutes, held in Skipton, June 2, 1852* (1852), pp. 67, 42.

86 Kelly, T., *George Birbeck*. . . . (1957) *op. cit.*, p. 259.

87 Tylecote, Mabel, *The Mechanics' Institutes of Lancashire and Yorkshire Before 1851* (1957) Manchester University Press, p. 265.

88 Hudson, J. W., *The History of Adult Education* (1851), Longman, p. 100.

89 Quoted in J. Purvis, 'Working-class women and adult education. . . .' (1980) *loc. cit.*, p. 200.

90 Stuart, James, *Reminiscences* (1911), printed for private circulation at the Chiswick Press, London, p. 157.

91 Ibid., p. 158. Kelly, T., *A History*. . . . (1962) *op. cit.* mentions, however, that the course was advertised as being on 'The History of Science' and included subjects other than astronomy.

92 Jepson, N. A., *The Beginnings of English University Adult Education: Policy and Problems* (1973), Michael Joseph, pp. 44–45.

93 Harrison, J. F. C., *Learning and Living 1790–1960: a Study in the History of the English Adult Education Movement* (1961) Routledge & Kegan Paul, p. 231.

94 Kelly, T., *A History*. . . . (1962) *op. cit.*, p. 220.

95 Stuart, J., *Reminiscences* (1911) *op. cit.*, p. 162.

96 Quoted in J. Jepson, *The Beginnings*. . . . (1973) *op. cit.*, p. 104.

97 Jepson, N., *The Beginnings*. . . . (1973) *op. cit.*, p. 41.

98 Stephen, Barbara, *Emily Davies*. . . . (1972) *op. cit.*, p. 195.

99 Ibid., p. 194.

100 Kamm, J., *Hope Deferred*. . . . (1965) *op. cit.*, p. 174.

101 Stephen, Barbara, *Emily Davies*. . . . (1927) *op. cit.*, p. 218.

102 Burstall, Sara, *Retrospect and Prospect* (1933), Longmans, p. 86 recollects that the social rules for women students were very strict in her student days at Girton (1878–1881). Women students could be chaperoned to men's college parties only by some lady known at home, independently of Cambridge. For an insightful analysis of these points see Delamont, S., 'The contradictions. . . .' (1978) *loc. cit.*

103 Pascoe, Charles Eyre, *Schools for Girls and Colleges for Women: a Handbook of Female Education* (1879) Hardwick & Bogue, p. 144 notes that the charge for board, lodging and instruction at Girton was £35 per term, paid in advance.

104 Stephen, Barbara, *Emily Davies*. . . . (1927) *op. cit.*, p. 232. Miss Davies allowed no extra time for the ignorance of her students but 'scorned' all

compromises and insisted that if men prepared for the Tripos in three years and one term, then female students must conform to the same rule (p. 231).

105 S. Delamoni, 'The contradictions . . . .' (1978) *loc. cit*, p. 160.

106 Lumsden, Louisa Innes, *Yellow Leaves: Memories of a Long Life* (1933) William Blackwood, London, p. 58.

107 Clough, Blanche Athena, *A Memoir of Anne Jemima Clough* (1897) Edward Arnold, pp. 129–130.

108 Ibid., p. 175.

109 Ibid., p. 169 notes that Miss Clough encouraged the students to begin with familiar subjects, such as arithmetic, history, English language and literature, and then to study whatever was of most interest.

110 Ibid., p. 177. See Purvis, J., 'Women and teaching. . . .' (1981) *loc. cit.*, for a discussion on the link between femininity and schoolteaching.

111 Glendinning, Victoria, *A Suppressed Cry* (1929), Routledge & Kegan Paul, p. 52.

112 Clough, Blanche Athena, *A Memoir. . . .* (1897) *op. cit.*, p. 232, 240. For the debates, the students wore evening dress! – see Sidgwick, Ethel, *Mrs. Henry Sidgwick: a Memoir by her Niece* (1938), Sidgwick & Jackson, p. 75.

113 Clough, Blanche Athena, *A Memoir. . . .* (1897) *op. cit.*, p. 196 – most of the students 'were old enough to have already tasted some amount of liberty'.

114 See, for example, Rogers, Annie, *Degrees by Degrees* (1938) OUP and Brittain, V., *The Women at Oxford* (1960), *op. cit.*

115 Sidgwick, Mrs Henry, 'The higher education of women', in Roberts, R. D. (Ed.) *Education in the Nineteenth Century* (1901), CUP, p. 203.

116 Holcombe, Lee, *Victorian Ladies at Work: Middle-Class Working Women in England and Wales 1850–1914* (1973), David & Charles, p. 49.

117 Tuke, Margaret, *A History of Bedford College for Women* (1939) *op. cit.*, pp. 159–160.

118 The Girls' Public Day School Company was founded in 1872 with the aim of providing, at a moderate cost, sound, secondary education for middle-class girls. See Kamm, J., *Indicative Past. . . .* (1971) *op. cit.* for a detailed account.

119 Hamilton, Mary Agnes, *Newnham: an Informal Biography* (1936) Faber & Faber, p. 114.

120 Purvis, J., 'Women and teaching. . . .' (1981) *loc. cit.*, p. 371. A study that explores this issue is Widdowson, Frances, *Going Up Into The Next Class: Women and Elementary Teacher Training, 1840–1914* (1980), Women's Research and Resources Centre Publications.

121 Stephen, Barbara, *Emily Davies. . . .* (1927) *op. cit.*, p. 314. Murray, Margaret, *My First Hundred Years* (1963), William Kimber, pp. 93–96.

122 Sanderson, Michael, *The Universities and British Industry 1850–1970* (1972) Routledge & Kegan Paul, pp. 328–329.

123 It is difficult to give an exact total of the number of women who had entered higher education or taken degree examinations. Mrs Henry Sidgwick, 'The higher education. . . .' (1901) *loc. cit.*, p. 207 estimates that, by 1901, the number of women who had taken Honours at Newnham and Girton was 1036. If we add to this the female students taking university degrees elsewhere, the total is probably in excess of 2000.

124 Pedersen, Joyce Senders, *The Reform of Women's Secondary and Higher Education in Nineteenth Century England: a Study in Elite Groups*, PhD thesis, University of California, Berkeley, 1974, p. 592.

125 Smith, Mary, *The Autobiography of Mary Smith, Schoolmistress and Nonconformist, a Fragment of a Life* (1892) Bemrose & Sons, Carlisle, pp. 24–25.
126 The issues of defining and measuring literacy in the nineteenth century are, of course, highly problematic. In this section of the paper I draw particularly upon my own article, 'Working-class women and adult education. . . .' (1981) *loc. cit.*
127 Hudson, J. W., *The History*. . . . (1851) *op. cit.*, pp. 3–5.
128 Hudson, J. W., *The History* . . . (1851) *op. cit.* p. 12.
129 Ibid., p. 14.
130 Purvis, J., 'Working-class women and adult education. . . .' (1980) *loc. cit.*, p. 198.
131 Pole, Thomas, *A History of the Origins and Progress of Adult Schools* (1816, 2nd edn), C. McDowall, Bristol, p. 19.
132 Ibid., p. 29.
133 Kelly, T., *A History*. . . . (1962) *op. cit.*, p. 128.
134 Tylecote, M., *The Mechanics' Institutes*. . . . (1957) *op. cit.*, p. 265, suggests that this was even so in those institutes in Lancashire and Cheshire.
135 *Report of the Yorkshire Union of Mechanics' Institutes held in Scarborough, 22nd May, 1861* (1861), p. 103.
136 *Report of the Yorkshire Union of Mechanics' Institutes held in Rotherham, 15th June, 1859* (1859), p. 79.
137 *Report of the Yorkshire Union of Mechanics' Institutes held in Huddersfield, 29th July, 1857* (1857), p. 102.
138 *Report of the Yorkshire Union*. . . . (1859) *op. cit.*, p. 21.
139 Detrosier, R., *An Address* delivered at the New Mechanics' Institution, Pool-Street, Manchester, on Wednesday evening December 30 1829 (n.d.), T. Forest, Manchester, p. 12.
140 Hertz, Fanny 'Mechanics' institutes for working women, with special reference to the manufacturing districts of Yorkshire', *Transactions of the National Association for the Promotion of Social Science 1859*, p. 354.
141 Wilson, Elizabeth, *Women and the Welfare State* (1977) Tavistock Publications, p. 26.
142 Hertz, Fanny, 'Mechanics' institute. . . .' (1859) *loc. cit.*, p. 352.
143 *Report of the Yorkshire Union of Mechanics' Institutes, held in Otley, 30th May, 1860* (1860) p. 93.
144 *Report of the Yorkshire Union of Mechanics' Institutes held in Batley and Dewsbury, 23rd April, 1862* (1862) p. 103.
145 *Report of the Yorkshire Union*. . . . (1862) *op. cit.*, p. 83.
146 Harrison, J. F. C., *A History of the Working Men's College 1854–1954* (1954) Routledge & Kegan Paul, pp. xvi, xvii.
147 Ibid., p. 26.
148 Rowbotham, T., 'Account of the origin and progress of the People's College at Sheffield', *The Working Men's College Magazine 1859*, No. 1, p. 71.
149 Furnivall, F. J., 'History of the London Working Men's College', *The Working Men's College Magazine 1860*, p. 146.
150 Ibid., pp. 147–148.
151 Sadler, M. E. (Ed.) *Continuation Schools in England and Elsewhere* (1908, 2nd edn), University Press, Manchester, p. 41.
152 Harrison, J. F. C., *A History*. . . . (1954) *op. cit.*, p. 39.
153 *Report of the Yorkshire Union*. . . . (1859) *op. cit.*, p. 84.
154 *Report of the Yorkshire Union*. . . . (1862) *op. cit.*, p. 94.

155 Harrison, J. F. C., *A History.* . . . (1954) *op. cit.*, p. 108.
156 Hudson, D., *Munby, Man of Two Worlds* (1972) John Murray, pp. 177, 215.
157 Martin, Frances, 'A college for working women', *Macmillans Magazine*, 1879, p. 487.
158 Harris, R. M., 'Frances Martin College', *Further Education*, Vol. 1., 1947–48, p. 225.
159 Sadler, M. E. (Ed.), *Continuation Schools.* . . . (1908) *op. cit.*, p. 44.
160 'The new school for wives', *Household Words*, 1852, pp. 85–86.
161 Ibid., p. 88.
162 *Census, 1851: Education Section: Evening Schools for Adults*, pp. 80–81.
163 Sadler, M. E. (Ed.) *Continuation Schools.* . . . (1908) *op. cit.*, p. 111.
164 Ibid., p. 108.
165 Gaffin, Jean, 'Women and cooperation', in Middleton, Lucy (Ed.) *Women in the Labour Movement* (1977) Croom Helm. p. 114.
166 Davies, Margaret Llewelyn, *The Women's Co-operative Guild 1883–1904* (1904), the Women's Co-operative Guild, Kirby Lonsdale, p. 148.
167 Gaffin, Jean, 'Women and cooperation' (1977) *loc. cit.*, pp. 113–114.
168 Layton, Mrs, 'Memories of seventy years', in Davies, Margaret Llewelyn (Ed.) *Life as We have Known it* by Co-operative Working Women (1931) reprint by Virago, 1977, p. 38.
169 Webb, Catherine, *The Woman with the Basket* (1927), Co-operative Wholesale Society's Printing Works, Manchester, p. 52.
170 Davies, Margaret Llewelyn, *The Women's Co-operative Guild.* . . . (1904) *op. cit.*, p. 73.
171 Webb, Catherine, *The Woman.* . . . (1927) *op. cit.*, pp. 55–56.
172 Ibid., pp. 100, 101, 107, 98–99.
173 Ibid., p. 100.
174 Davies, Margaret Llewelyn, *The Women's Co-operative Guild.* . . . (1904) *op. cit.*, p. 103.
175 Scott, Mrs, 'A felt hat worker' in *Davies*, M. L., *Life.* . . . (1977 reprint) p. 101.
176 Davies, Margaret Llewelyn, *The Women's Co-operative Guild.* . . . (1904) *op. cit.*, p. 98.
177 Webb, Catherine, *The Woman.* . . . (1927) *op. cit.*, pp. 30, 49.
178 Holyoake, G. J., *The History of Co-operation in Halifax: and of some other Institutions around it* (n.d. B.L. stamp 1867) London Book Store, p. 37.
179 Layton, Mrs, 'Memories. . . .', in Davies, M. L. (Ed.) *Life.* . . . (1977 reprint) pp. 47–48.
180 MacNamara, T. J., 'Joints in our educational armour', *Fortnightly Review*, June 1899, p. 921.
181 Liddington, Jill, & Norris, Jill, *One Hand Tied Behind Us: the Rise of the Women's Suffrage Movement* (1978) Virago, pp. 93, 106.
182 'I think a lot', in Davies, M. L. (Ed.) *Maternity.* . . . (1978 reprint) *op. cit.*, p. 74.
183 Sterns, Peter 'Working-class women in Britain, 1890–1914' in Vicinus, Martha (Ed.), *Suffer and Be Still* (1972), Indiana University Press, p. 106.
184 Ibid., pp. 109–110.

3.2

The importance of being Ernest . . . Emma . . . Tom . . . Jane . . . The perception and categorization of gender conformity and gender deviation in primary schools†

Katherine Clarricoates

Present-day research on primary schools in England has usually dealt with the descriptive field (i.e., curricular materials, inequalities of staff ratio by sex, subject specialism) rather than the analytical, although there have been some analyses of teachers' expectations.[1]

I should like to concentrate [. . .] upon the constructs of 'femininity' and 'masculinity' within primary schools and how these differ according to class and the catchment area. In all four schools I observed, 'masculine' and 'feminine' are seen as immutable characteristics of normal proper behaviour. But contradictions emerge. Just as there is a capricious inconsistency of sex-role attributes accorded to males and females in varying cultures,[2] so what is considered normal in some schools is abnormal in others.

Differing patterns of sex-role socialization are by no means a new concept in feminist scholarship: Pauline Marks, in her paper on 'Femininity in the Classroom', discussed the class-specific notions of femininity which underlie the existing educational model (1976, p. 180):

It is fascinating to discover that their [girls'] 'femininity', that supposedly biological and absolute characteristic, is dependent on the viewpoint of the observer; different social origins and intellectual abilities alter the meaning of 'femininity', which is thus not a fixed concept in educational thinking.

Belotti, in her book *Little Girls* also states (1975, p. 126):

Those who have had the opportunity to make comparisons because they have taught in schools encompassing different social groupings, admit that this [masculinity and femininity] phenomenon is much

† Source: R. Deem (1980) (ed.), *Schooling for Women's Work*, London, Routledge & Kegan Paul, pp. 26–40.

more pronounced in village or small-town schools where masculine and feminine stereotypes are more rigidly differentiated.

Although I agree in principle with Belotti's hypothesis, I question her generalization. To begin with, the situation is more complex than she suggests and her contrasts (village and small-town schools) are oversimplified. I hope to show that, despite the variations in sex-role stereotypes, it is not that some schools are less authoritarian or discriminatory to girls; rather the pattern, not the degree, of socialization changes to accommodate so-called 'liberal' attitudes to women. This could be defined as a 'divide and rule' philosophy. Sue Sharpe points out that the values and attitudes of sex differentiation do not develop in an arbitrary way, but are influenced by the nature of the economic structure of a society and 'the division of labour that has been developed around it'.[3]

My research is based on eighteen months' observation in four totally different primary schools, encompassing diverse social groups (for the purpose of this report individuals and schools will be given fictitious names in order to retain anonymity).[4]

A   A traditional working-class school of Dock Side, set in the heart of an urban area and fishing port, due for demolition and usually termed 'a northern industrial slum'.[5] It is characteristically comprised of terraced housing – 'tunnels-to-backs' – which are poorly maintained by private landlords.

B   A modern suburban 'rural' middle-class school of Applegate, opened eleven years ago to meet the needs of an expanding population due to development of what Pahl called 'the rural fringe' (Pahl, 1965). Within easy commuting distance of the small Minster town, it serves mainly settled, prosperous, home-owning professional parents.

C   A council estate school of Long Estate which is an early example of the new, spacious primary school built in the early 1960s. It serves children of parents who have been rehoused from the old decaying urban areas, situated five to six miles outside the city centre.

D   A very small rural primary school in the village of Linton Bray in an agricultural area. House-types vary from the country stone cottage and farmhouse to the row of newly developed ranch-style bungalows of the 1970s. Although the basic economics of the community are no longer totally agrarian (lorry drivers, workers in light industry, garage mechanics, etc.), nevertheless family farms dominate the area.

[. . .] The bewildering variety of organized spatial practices and social expectations reveals the diverse attitudes to sex-role stereotyping; but there is some overlap and this makes it difficult to keep assumptions – and results – discrete.

It was through the recognition of divisions set up by the schools and the teachers (and in turn accepted by the children) that the polarization between the sexes was revealed. As stated before, though many aspects were similar in all four schools, a pattern did emerge revealing significant differences in gender deviation and gender conformity. By studying the appropriate behaviour required from each of the sexes within each school, I was able to make some judgments about the value structure of 'femininity' and 'masculinity' within the specific catchment area. My research has led me to believe that models presented to the children, with their demarcation between masculine and feminine, are based on ecological factors which pertain to that school, i.e. the value structure of the school in relation to the community values.

The urban traditional school revealed behaviour which was considered 'typical' of the two sexes, behaviour and norms that were sharply differentiated. This was due to the school's reinforcement of stereotypes and the children's learning and development experienced within the community. Dock Side has all the hallmarks of a male culture (this is not to say that middle-class communities do not), consisting of norms interpreted through a masculine-feminine polarization. O'Neill, in his research of the actual community, states: 'The tendency towards stereotyping and compartmentalization characterise the authoritarian elements of traditional working-class life' (1973, p. 195). A rigid conformity existed in social relations, with a preoccupation towards fixed masculine qualities of strength, toughness, dominance and bravery; whereas women were seen in direct contrast: submissive, weak, with 'their place' emphatically in the home. There does, however, appear to be a contradiction here, for there was a large number of women who were employed.[6]

Segregation begins in the street outside, and one must assume that girls and boys have been socialized within families which express a sharply defined sexual division of labour, so that the children learn from an early age to steer clear of each other. Boys are aware of what is expected of them and avoid 'feminine' things at all cost; social deviance of any form in a pervasive working-class community is likely to meet firm resistance and to be finally suppressed.[7]

Girls will make their way to school in separate groups from their brothers, and through this process the stereotypes are solidified and reinforced. It is a land of working men's clubs, or 'men only' bars where landlords encourage sex segregation. To be seen too often with women would undermine a man's 'maleness'. The young males join their fathers at this form of social club, with women invited only on specific days.

School does not offer any alternatives. Separation begins in early infancy with separate playgrounds, separate toilets, separate lines, even separate lists on registers. This serves as something of a reminder of Victorian morality, and suggests that if boys and girls come together they somehow become immoral. Conformity to sex-roles is strictly adhered to, whilst deviation is rigidly avoided. The school, like its surroundings, is impoverished of grass, space and playing fields; the high walls bordering it are covered in graffiti announcing the ever-youthful optimism of the local football team (this despite its struggles in the lower half of the Third Division). Above the doorway are those ominously familiar letters: BOYS.

Appropriate gender behaviour is expressed in all aspects of school life. High academic achievement is neither highly valued nor expected; at best it is only hoped for by the teachers. For girls it is expected that they follow the traditional line of 'doing well anyway' as part of their conformity to institutional expectations; in fact their 'achievement' is seen as part of the 'feminine' stereotype.[8] When asked who tends to get the best results, the teachers' most common reaction is to explain in sex differentiated terms:

'Oh the girls, naturally; you can always rely on them to do their work properly.'

'The girls ask the right questions simply because it's expected of them.'

'Definitely the girls, but I think it's more to do with wanting to please rather than being intelligent.'

But the general expectations for these children were revealed in the following way:

'There isn't much opportunity round here for these kids anyway.'

'Change and opportunity hardly filter down here . . . parents want their sons to follow the traditional jobs like fishing.'

'Higher hopes are not the sort you would expect in this type of area.'

'To be realistic and when you think of the jobs and what 90 per cent of these children are going to do, you know, I'm very glad I've got the intelligence not to have to do that kind of job.'

'I think of the kind of life and the job that they're going to have just by having these parents.'

'I can't actually change the system; most of these kids will finish up in semi-skilled or unskilled jobs.'

Academic norms among the children can easily be distinguished when observing and listening to them:

'Girls always try to answer the questions first.'

'Yeah, they think they're a bunch of cleverclogs.'

'We sit quiet, we don't have to do anything 'cos the girls will answer the teachers' questions.'

'Boys always make a noise and try to stop you working. . . . I like doing sums. . . . I got three stars today.'

'They don't do their writing properly like we do.'

'See that girl there, Wendy Hagan . . . she's the best in the class.'

Tables by rote, and regurgitative 'singing' in order to memorize knowledge, were the order of the day. Girls were eager to 'succeed' in this one sphere that was allowed them, but even then they were not given the credit for creative potential.[9] Expectations (or lack of) exacerbated the divisions between the sexes; in a game of general knowledge girls and boys were constantly pitted against each other. If the boys won there was a loud triumphant uproar. The girls frowned upon Ian who was exceptionally good at general knowledge: 'We would win if it wasn't for him,' stated Debbie, pointing at him. The academic expectations of the teachers towards this social group were reflections of a belief in the stereotypical qualities.

Physical aggression was much more accepted in this school than in others:

'It comes from home.'

'They've no idea of discipline in the home.'

'We have a lot of "humdingers" in this school; mind you, I blame it on the parents.'

'You can't expect anything better from these kids, coming from an area like this.'

But they did expect girls to set a good example in behaviour, and in fact they thought they got such behaviour (though this could well be a product of their own perceptions which dichotomize the behaviour of girls and boys so that even the same activity may be evaluated differently according to the sex of the actor):

'Girls are better behaved, boys are louder.'

'The boys are more aggressive, whilst the girls are typically feminine.'

'Boys are the ideal of what males ought to be.'

'Girls are more bitchy towards each other.'

'Girls are more fussy.'

'I think boys tend to be a little more aggressive, and on thinking about it the male is the same in the animal world. . . . We are animals basically.'

This was despite the fact that the girls were as verbally aggressive (particularly in terms of swearing) as the boys. When asked what lay behind these differences, most teachers agreed it was 'conditioning' or 'socialization' within the family, and there was general recognition that parents' expectations were different for girls and boys. But this did not prevent these same teachers from going right back into the classroom and reinforcing the sex-role stereotypes by their expectations and toleration of different standards of behaviour between the sexes, instead of trying to eradicate the previous conditioning.

> Craig, a five-year-old, spent a good deal of his time in harassing his classmates. He took a great delight in breaking up their games, bombarding any hapless child who happened near him with marbles, and was a constant source of irritation to the girls, whom he maliciously attacked – either verbally or physically – and all this within the confines of the class and to the non-reaction of the teacher. On the other hand, Sarah was prone to outbursts of temper, either screaming or letting loose a barrage of insults at her offender. I was present at a time when she let fly a quantity of paint at Lynsey, who promptly burst into tears. Sarah's behaviour was met with severe rebuke in public by the teacher: 'Little girls do not do that,' amongst other things; and thereafter she was nicknamed the 'paint-dauber'.

The teacher then proceeded to justify her own behaviour by telling me how Sarah was a problem child; for example, annoying her classmates. It seemed to escape her attention that this was the very same behaviour that Craig was allowed to get away with. Not only were different standards of tolerance applied, but also the same behaviour was categorized differently depending on the sex. Many times I observed children involved in play, and in many instances I was aware of the use of this double standard:

> Craig and Edward were involved in a game of Plasticine and both are seized with a fit of laughter. They are allowed to carry on. But, parallel to this, when two girls were caught up in a similar game and became noisy the teacher classed it as 'giggling hysterically' and told the girls to 'calm down'.

And yet in this particular instance there was no real distinction between the girls' or the boys' behaviour. It can be seen that there is a subtle interaction between the teachers' observations and the teachers' beliefs.

As stated before, the phenomenon of masculine and feminine behaviour differed between urban traditional, suburban middle-class, council estate and village school; this fact of necessity leads to a brief discussion of the value structure and norms of the catchment areas, indicating the different patterns of male dominance arising from the social relations of production and consumption.

Applegate reflected the space, green fields and high aspirations that Dock Side lacked. It was representative of middle-class, prosperous parents with young children, searching for the 'rural' family life: the new 'rural-urban fringe'.[10] According to O'Neill, the middle-class stereotype of femininity is bound up with occupational status and social prestige.[11] Still implicit in middle-class ideology, however, is the belief that it is preferable for a wife not to work, and that the aspiring husband should be able to earn enough to support his whole family. Most of the children I talked to told me their Mums 'did not work' but stayed at home. Pahl states that the middle classes have high aspirations for their children's education since 82 per cent (against 15 per cent of the working class) wanted their children to stay on until 18 or over. To the working class, extra schooling was seen as a training of some sort, whereas the middle class saw it as a means of urging their children to go to university. The veil of egalitarianism between the sexes is soon lifted when one scrutinizes the values and norms of such a community. Pahl also recognized the significant theme that emerged from his research into the middle-class 'commuter villages': parents tended to discriminate in favour of their sons in regard to university education when they had to pay for it, with the consequence that the education of daughters could well be made to suffer. Justification for this lay in the 'belief' that daughters are not clever enough to study for a degree.[12]

[. . .] Applegate primary school reflected the value structure of high aspirations and academic achievement:

'Most of these children are capable of going to university.'

'We have a very high standard educationally . . . if you compare it with an urban working-class school.'

The high academic goal was projected to the children:

'If you work hard now, chances are you'll get to university without any trouble.'

Whilst at Dock Side pupils were taught 'dates' and 'things', in Applegate rote learning was almost non-existent, and the emphasis was on relationships and processes in most subjects. Boys were required to have the academic norms which were so lacking in the Dock Side boys. In fact they were regarded as the intellectual elite (by both teachers and children), even though girls usually had the highest marks in all subjects right throughout primary school. I was browsing through some poetry displayed on a classroom wall written by top junior children when a girl touched me on the arm. Pointing to a specific poem she told me, 'That's Peter Jenkinson's; he's the brightest in our class,' a statement of fact not said with surprise or envy – just relayed as a piece of information. The teacher informed me:

'On the whole you can generally say that the boys are more capable of learning.'

'Boys are interested in everything and are prepared to take things seriously.'

'They tend to ask the deeper questions, while girls tend to be more superficial about subjects.'

'Although girls tend to be good at most things, in the end you find it's going to be a boy who's your most brilliant pupil.'

The teachers' perception of creativity was underscored by their beliefs in sex-roles. They saw the boys as having much more imagination, and having the real ability.

In this school a high standard of hygiene and dress was expected from both sexes, but particularly from the girls. There was also a verbal double standard, with teachers censuring girls more harshly than boys for using improper language:

When Emma fought to retain a prized book from the school library her self-control faltered and she emitted verbal abuse to the boy who had endeavoured to take it: 'Give me that book back you rotten, lousy . . .' Her words reached the teacher: 'Emma, that is no way for a young girl to speak; go and stand at the back until you decide to improve your language.' Emma does so, and the boy gets away with his misdemeanour.

Aggressive behaviour in general was discouraged in Applegate but, again, more actively for girls than for boys. The teachers informed me (as in Dock Side) that they did not believe that there were any real innate personality differences between the sexes, and all stressed that in no way did they treat them any differently, except of course on an individual basis. They were emphatic that the children were not treated differently. The discrepancy between their stated behaviour and my observations is apparent, for why else would they actively discourage aggressive behaviour more often in girls:

'It's not nice to see a young girl fighting.'

'You would expect it from boys, although I myself wouldn't condone it, rather than you would expect it from girls.'

'I expect a high standard of behaviour from my girls and fighting and swearing is totally inexcusable.'

The children in Applegate were steered to the norms of hard work, self-denial and academic achievement with their ensuing rewards of good prospects, university education and economic competition. (Well, this was the context for boys.)

Sex-segregation was not so distinctively a part of organization at Applegate as at Dock Side. It did not seem so important to keep the two sexes apart, perhaps because other social forces were in operation to do it for the school. It was obvious that there seemed a flexibility and not the fixed polarization between the two sexes which was evident in the urban traditional school:

Paul, a six-year-old, does not need a reason to play with or be in the presence of girls. He consistently seeks their company and enjoys being involved in what is usually referred to as 'feminine' play: as indeed other boys do, but he does not falsify his behaviour as they do. He also withstands the ultimate insults which boys direct against each other expressed in female gender terms like 'sissy' or 'puffy'. Paul's status within the class is indeed quite good, his company being sought by both girls and boys. In Dock Side a boy like Paul would have been shunned, especially by the girls, who tend to deride 'deviant' boys as much as the boys themselves.

Boys who got involved in the Wendy House and were 'caught in the act' took measures to reduce the likelihood of ridicule and belittlement by assuming to comply with appropriate gender behaviour:

Two boys are happily playing in the Wendy House: Edward is setting the table whilst Tom is ironing. The teacher comes forward: 'Aren't you busy? What are you playing?' Edward looks at Tom, both look sheepish. 'Batman and Robin', states Edward vehemently. The teacher smiles and moves away.

In order to cloak any behaviour that might be met with derision by their classmates they falsified their activity, giving it a 'masculine' name: It was significant that this so-called flexibility was much phased out in the older classes of junior pupils where sex-segregation became once more an internal feature of organization within the school. But it was a less dogmatically expressed division than within Dock Side.

Even in Applegate the young children faced many limitations as to what was acceptable gender behaviour and 'deviants' were soon made aware of this. The peer group's attempt to control and ridicule a deviant can be very powerful:

Andy approached me wearing a long, tatty, gold lamé dress, a woollen beret pulled down over his ears, and carrying an old handbag. It was obvious he had been in the 'dressing-up' corner. He stumbled towards me, 'I'm a policeman' he declared. (I don't know what the sociological implications of this are.) During our ensuing conversation another boy dashed past and yelled 'sissy'. All this was being observed by the teacher. Surprisingly, Andy was slightly confused and asked his friend, 'What is a sissy?' 'Someone who dresses up in women's clothes,' came the reply. He hurriedly removed the now offensive clothing and retreated to the other side of the classroom with a hostile look in my direction. One can easily assume he will never don 'women's clothing' again.

The teacher, in allowing the incident to pass without a reaction from her, informed the class that it was acceptable for Andy to be 'checked' for his deviant behaviour. Just as the teacher's interaction with the children (or a particular child) could be perceived as enticing the child to engage or not engage in certain behaviour, so her non-interaction would be construed in a similar fashion.

In my observations of Long Estate primary school the routines of discipline, dress and language were again gender-differentiated. The school caters for the children of parents who have been rehoused from the area around Dock Side. To a certain extent a break comes in the close family ties and, according to O'Neill, there is less pressure to conform to the sharp demarcation between male and female. The inhabitants 'question the existing norms of polarization of masculine/feminine'.[13] Husbands tended to help more in the home, a thing hitherto unheard of in the Dock Side district, which pointed to 'a democratic and participatory attitude towards conjugal relationships'.[14] If one is to discuss egalitarian relationships between men and women, then it is inevitable to define what form power usually takes: how women are socially, materially, and historically dominated by men. The fact that a man helps with the washing-up hardly means an equal relationship in the making. Though there did not exist 'male only' bars, and there was a decline in some of the practices observed in Dock Side, this did not necessarily mean a decrease in male dominance but rather just a change in pattern.

Long Estate school did reflect change: the school, with a female headteacher, did not on first sight reflect the obsessive need to keep the two sexes apart. This was partly due to the fact that the architecture was not spatially organized in such a rigid design as Dock Side. But this did not necessarily preclude the existence of categories of gender deviation and gender conformity. The discouragement of participatory activity between girls and boys was a constant factor. The pattern did vary – in certain aspects it was more contrived than in Applegate and less so than in Dock Side.

Long Estate's conditioned response to sex-role stereotypes was revealed in particular with regard to Michael, a seven-year-old boy in the third-year infants' class:

> Michael, much to the concern of his teachers and to the contempt of his peer group, loved to play with dolls. He liked to bake, and constantly sought the company of girls, despite their insults. He was constantly admonished by his teacher 'to try to behave properly'. But to no avail.

During a conversation in the staffroom about his particular behaviour:

> 'Ah, yes,' said one teacher, 'bionic woman.'
> 'Don't be unkind,' laughed another.
> A well-meaning teacher added, 'His brother is really a nice little boy and quite normal.'
> 'Perhaps when he grows up he'll get straightened out.'

This behaviour is similar to what was accepted in Applegate. Michael is excluded from his peer group and avoided by teachers in answering questions for fear of 'making it more obvious'. When I spoke of the advantages of Michael's behaviour – that he was not a bully, and really an imaginative and pleasing child – I was immediately corrected:

'Oh no, he has all those nasty little ways that girls have.'

'What do you mean?' I asked.

'He's ever so "catty", he bites and scratches and pulls hair.'

Michael's deviant behaviour is obviously very 'bad' for him. He is publicly called 'bionic woman' and many attempts are made to 'guide' him away from his deviancy.

Ms T . . . reads Michael's 'diary' for the morning: 'On Saturday I helped my Mum bake a cake and I made a dress for my doll.' The teacher despairs: 'Couldn't you play football or something?' Taking the doll he is clutching away from him she offers him an 'Action Man' [same toy, different label]. Michael stares at her as if she's gone quite mad and moves over to the other side of the classroom.

'I'm merely trying to protect him from the rest of the class; you know children can be so cruel,' the teacher informs me.

Because it is conveyed to the class that Michael's behaviour is deviant, he is the target of much bullying by some girls and most boys. The headteacher, a kind and progressive woman, remarks that Michael is confused between masculine and feminine roles and she suspects that he has 'feminine genes'. If he is not 'cured' by the time he leaves school, she suggested to me, then the only solution to his 'problem' is that he enter the 'world' of the arts, drama or music, where 'that kind of behaviour' is much more acceptable. The obvious implications in this, is that 'deviant' behaviour is caused by some personality disorder, i.e. a biological malfunction. It is not that Michael is being attacked personally, but rather his behaviour – his identification with the inferior sex, female.

I'd like to focus on the small rural school in Linton Bray, where, as in most agricultural areas, the tendency is towards an enclosed existence, traditional and hierarchical. Here the sexual division of labour is pronounced, partly because farming is considered a man's job and the only occupation for a woman is to be a farmer's wife. Indeed, the children's attitudes to sex-roles were entrenched, due to the limited occupations within the village itself. The only jobs available for women were shop assistant (very limited as there were only three shops and two pubs in the village) or cleaning woman; the only alternative was to travel to Market Heathton some five miles distant to obtain any other job.

The school itself was very small and hence there was little need for lining up or queueing (although this sometimes happened), a practice which usually allows for the physical segregation of the sexes. The lack of amenities required that all pupils had to share, from toilets to sports equipment. But no matter how small the school and how few the pupils it would seem that the all-pervasive phenomenon of gender required segregation. I might have walked into a small-scale Dock Side if it hadn't been for the dramatic change in scenery. The children had specific lines of demarcation: boys and girls did not sit at the same table, they did not stand in the same files in assembly, they did not all play for the football team (girls were mostly excluded). The irrationality of sex-typing the female was ever-present at this school: it was believed that girls are weak, that they cry, that they can't drive tractors (neither can boys at that age). In contrast, it was believed that boys play football, they're tough. There was the same boring, dogmatic and seemingly endless list of 'arbitrary qualities' assigned to the social categories of 'masculine' and 'feminine'. The school in no way questioned these assumptions, and by not questioning it automatically provided implicit approval for such stereotypes.

The illogicality of such views is obvious when you realize that in the country girls are expected to help with the rough and dirty work of the farm:

'When I go home I change into my wellies and help with the chickens.' (Debbie)

'I help my Dad bring in the cows and then I "muck out" with the other helpers.' (Linda)

'There's not much else to do in the village on an evening so I generally help out on the farm like my brothers and sisters do.' (Jenny)

Academic norms are not high, and most of these kids have never even heard of university:

'Most of these children have only been as far as Market Heathton.'

'Their horizon is very narrow, limited within the village.'

And the school does nothing to widen this horizon. According to Eileen Byrne, a less-able girl in a rural school has a triple chance of resource deprivation.[15]

In all the schools the constant exercise of separating the sexes on a consistent level serves to emphasize the assumed sex-role differentiation of girls and boys; and, whether intended or not, it serves to inculcate rivalry and antagonism between them:

'Why don't you boys do as you're told; you don't find the girls behaving like that.'

'Let's have a game of general knowledge: boys against girls.'

When asked why they segregated the girls from the boys most teachers tended to reply with stock answers, which in reality did not even address the question:

'Well, it's easier to mark off girls from boys.'

'It's a common division, isn't it?'

'I'd get confused if they were mixed . . . you know, if another form of division was used.'

'Well, it's the easiest . . . with children they know which are boys and which are girls.'

These statements are from the very teachers who constantly told me that they:

'don't treat girls differently from boys.'

'I treat them all the same.'

'They'll play with each other and not realize they are a girl or a boy.'

In all the schools even the punishment system works against any solidarity between the sexes. The slipper or cane is mainly used on boys for 'serious' misdemeanours (although it is used more often in working-class schools), whilst girls are sent to the senior female teacher for a 'good talking-to' or given some other form of institutionalized school punishment, like being made to stay in at playtimes:

'Girls never get the slipper.'

'They always get away with more things than us.'

'They always get us into trouble.'

In the working-class schools the boys tend to brag about how many times they've 'had the slipper' for it is a sign of being tough. The girls do not share this norm:

'Boys are naughtier than us; they get the slipper from "Sir".'

'They're silly, they show off about getting the slipper.'

The teachers rationalize this demarcation by stating:

'Girls are not as bad as boys.'

"It's not quite right somehow to give girls the slipper or the cane.'

'I would give a swift kick up the boy's backside more than I would a girl's.' (male teacher)

'I suppose on the whole I'm stricter with the boys than with the girls.'

'A lot more trouble comes from the boys than the girls.'

'Girls never seem to be mischievous as do the boys, so I suppose I do overlook the few misdemeanours the odd girl may get up to.' (male teacher)

The speed at which teachers will enumerate the many differences between girls and boys is startling:

GIRLS	BOYS
Obedient	Livelier
Tidy	Adventurous

Neat	Aggressive
Conscientious	Boisterous
Orderly	Self-confident
Fussy	Independent
Catty	Energetic
Bitchy	Couldn't-care-less
Gossiping	Loyal

By providing such ready, stereotyped lists, the teachers betray their own habit of classifying children according to their sex. Any girl who is 'aggressive' or 'independent' and any boy who is 'effeminate' or 'sensitive' are the exceptions, the so-called deviants. The children must change, for there seems little chance of the teachers' stereotypes changing when presented with contradictions.

The girls' internalization of the beliefs that boys are superior whilst they are inferior manifested itself when I talked to both girls and boys about their hopes and aspirations for the future. Girls actually believed that boys were naturally ordained with a profusion of masculine esoteric skills such as being able to drive a car, tractor or helicopter; significantly boys revealed a pattern of oppression already in their young lives, against girls:

Applegate:

> Jennifer informed me her father was a helicopter pilot.
> 'Would you like to be one?' I asked.
> 'Oh no. Women would fall out of a helicopter whereas men wouldn't – they're stronger.'
> 'But don't men fall out?'
> 'No, they hang on better than women.'

> Damian informed me his father was a doctor. He wanted to be a scientist. I asked him:
> 'Don't you think women should be able to do the same jobs?'
> 'No, I don't think too many women should be scientists as they might get hurt.'
> 'What do you mean?'
> 'Well women are more likely to touch things they're not supposed to.'

Linton Bray:

> 'A woman wouldn't be able to drive a tractor; it is too heavy for her.' (Mark)

> 'A man would work on a farm but a girl cannot work on a farm; she is not strong enough.' (Laura)

> 'I would not let my Mum drive a tractor; she would get it dirty and break it.' (Chris)

> 'Women drive the tractor and trailer too fast.' (Samantha)

'A woman can't be a farmer, she can't drive a tractor,' said Sean.

'But men can't either; like everybody else they have to learn,' I replied.

'Yes, but it would take much longer to teach women to learn.'

Irrational they may be, but to these kids these reasons are concrete. They had simply accepted that if a job was categorized as men's work it was obviously not right for a girl to do it. It was tragic to recognize the realism within Dock Side, when asked about their future:

'I suppose I'll work at Birdseye like my Mum and get home in time for when my kids leave school.' (Stephanie, 8 years old)

Stereotypes are not only different for each sex, but also vary according to class, and the symbolic separation between girls and boys is manifested in varying ways. Once women appear to be strong, self-willed, or assertive, they immediately displace the prevailing norms defining what it is to be a man. The two main points of this chapter are: that 'femininity' varies, and does so according to the area in which the school is situated (occupational structure); and that, despite such variations, the subordination of women is always maintained. . . .

Notes

1 See Frazier, N. and Sadker, M. (1973), *Sexism in School and Society*, New York, Harper & Row; Lobban, G. (1978), 'The influence of the school on sex-role stereo-typing' in Chetwynd, J. and Hartnett, O. (eds) (1978), *The Sex Role System*, London, Routledge & Kegan Paul; Weinrich, H. (1978), 'Sex-role socialisation' in Chetwynd and Hartnett (eds) (1978), op. cit.

2 Mead, M. (1935), *Sex and Temperament in Three Primitive Societies*, New York, William Morrow.

3 Sharpe, S. (1976), *Just Like a Girl*, Middlesex, Penguin, p. 62.

4 This research is from a larger project funded by the SSRC.

5 According to the Inland Revenue's assessment of rateable value.

6 There has been a long tradition for women to work outside the home in this seaport area.

7 O'Neill, N. J. (1973), 'Class and Social Consciousness: variations in the social perspectives of industrial workers', unpublished PhD thesis, University of Hull.

8 Clarricoates, K. (1978), 'Dinosaurs in the classroom: a re-examination of some aspects of the "hidden curriculum" in primary schools', *Women's Studies International Quarterly*, vol. 1, no. 4, pp. 353–64.

9 Ibid.

10 Pahl, R. E. (1965), 'Class and community in English commuter villages', *Sociologia Ruralis*, vol. 2, pp. 5–21.

11 O'Neill (1973), op. cit., p. 81.

12 Pahl, R. E. (1963), 'Education and social class in commuter villages', *Sociological Review*, New Series, 2, pp. 241–6.

13 O'Neill (1973), op. cit., p. 97.

14 Ibid., p. 97.

15 Byrne, E. (1973), 'Education, training and equal opportunity' unpublished paper quoted in *Educational Review*, vol. 27, June 1975.

3.3
Privileged, schooled and finished: boarding education for girls†

Judith Okely

Theoretical and methodological questions

The public school[1] has moulded a large proportion of the dominant male élite in British society, as well as their wives and mothers. It has also had a wider influence and has affected, albeit elusively, the alternative state form of schooling. While we find considerable research into public schools for boys,[2] there is little serious investigation of the girls' schools, nor indeed of the larger topic of gender differentiation in education.[3] It is assumed either that girls' boarding-schools are replicas of those for boys, or that they are of peripheral importance. The male and female institutions are not analysed as parts of one system. In addition to the studies of boys' schools, we have a plethora of autobiographies by men, while little comparable information exists from women, since few achieve the status which calls for an account of themselves.[4]

Statements about the educational achievements of 'the middle class' have tended to conceal their gender bias. Certainly some middle-class girls attend schools, boarding or day, of high academic quality, which encourage independent careers for their pupils. But there are other middle- or upper-class girls who are denied this, and *precisely because of their class*. The development of a distinct class consciousness is seen as more important than scholarship and achievement for them, as are beliefs which maintain the boundaries of their class. The girls are protected for a future marriage contract within an elite whose biological and social reproduction they ensure. They have no economic and political power independent of males such as their fathers, and later

† Source: S. Ardener (1979) (eds), *Defining Females*, London, Croom Helm, pp. 109–39.

their husbands and sons. Born into a privileged and powerful élite, the women learn to live ambitions only vicariously through men.

The girls' school may be, invisibly, a preparation for dependence, while the boys' school is more visibly a preparation for independence and power. Some of the lessons of a girls' boarding-school carry uncertainties, or are inapplicable in later life. There is greater continuity for boys who, for example, are not confronted with the marriage-career dilemma which, for girls, becomes a source of conflict within their identity as female. In the boys' education, self-confidence, the experience of leadership and ambitious expectations are what count. Paradoxically, academic qualifications may not be crucial for public-school boys who, even if they do not progress to university, often move into lucrative and prestigious occupations not made available to their sisters with possibly equal potential. The girls' expectations are circumscribed by marriage.

The boys' and girls' educations are not symmetrical but they are ideologically interdependent. That considered female is partly defined by its opposite: that which is considered to be male. The characteristics of one institution are strengthened by their absence in the other. Qualities primarily reserved for one gender will have a different meaning in the institution for the opposing gender. The two educations are also linked in practice since, in adulthood, individuals from the separate institutions will be united in marriage, for the consolidation of their class. As members of the same social class the girls and boys may share similar educational experiences, but as members of different gender categories some of their education may differ. This aspect is also considered below. Little emphasis is placed here on the academic curriculum and the transmission of knowledge associated with it. Instead attention is paid to the kind of instruction received in contexts other than the classroom lesson, but which is nevertheless integral to public-school education.

The ethnographic data for this preliminary enquiry are largely autobiographical, my main informant being myself. Only these resources are explored fully here. In due course they may be synthesised with accounts by other former residents of boarding-schools, including those giving the perspective of the staff, which, of course, will be quite different. Subsequent comparative research will necessarily reveal a diversity of experiences and understanding. Many women will have enjoyed their boarding-schools, especially those who fulfilled the aims of that education. But for some, including myself, it failed to teach its terms. If my sister and I had learnt our lessons correctly, it is unlikely that we should have gone to university. The extent to which my boarding-school is 'typical' of its time, the 1950s, or is similar to any such institution in the 1970s, cannot be examined here.[5] Obviously there will be considerable variations and changes.

I deliberately confront the notion of objectivity in research by starting with the subjective, working from the self outwards. The self – the past self – becomes a thing, an object. Yet this part creates and governs the present and future. Even social anthropologists who usually study other cultures are led back from the other to the self. Indeed Pocock (1973, 1975) has suggested that there is a need to explore the totality of one's 'personal anthropology' and its consequences in order to be able fully to perceive others.[6] This interest in the subjective is no doubt strengthened by my being female and brought up so. Women's language of experience is often distinctly personal, but the general implications are always there to be found. We must therefore explore the abstractions contained in our anecdotes.

A word on the epistemological status of the autobiographical. It is retrospective – unlike a diary which is the record of the present. There will be a loss of memory. Some forgotten experiences may nevertheless affect the narrator unconsciously. The past will have become distorted. Misunderstandings will be revealed later if accounts of events are cross-checked with others who were present at them. But their information will also be skewed. The accuracy of childhood events may, however, be less important than the child's perception of them. They may have important repercussions in later life, some of which may be contrary to the conscious intentions of instructors and parents. The validity of autobiographical material is no different from many presentations by social anthropologists based on data gathered from informants during their field-work. The former is merely one account of what is believed to have existed, whereas the latter often include several autobiographical accounts which have been collapsed into one version.

I am concerned with what I believed happened. My information is based on nine years as a boarding-school girl in the 1950s and on all the subsequent years of retrospective analysis. Participant observation (methodologically crucial to social anthropologists) is perfectly split. In the study of childhood a temporal split between participation and observation is special, and in some instances unavoidable, because children cannot articulate their experiences in the language of adults. Only after childhood can it be thus expressed. When young we found the school world the reality, the norm, the only rationality. That was its power. My mother has often said since, 'But why didn't you tell me?' We, my sister and I, could not discriminate that which now seems bizarre. Whenever I inwardly questioned aspects of this education, I thought myself mad, and identified with the mad and isolated, for example, Nijinsky, van Gogh and other heroes of Colin Wilson's *The Outsider* (1956).

The girls' boarding-school

Boarding academies for ladies existed in the eighteenth century, offering certain 'accomplishments'. But most of the now famous girls' public schools were established at the end of the nineteenth century and later, long after the boys' public schools were founded. Even in the 1920s and 1930s many middle- and upper-class girls, for example Jessica Mitford and her sisters (Mitford, 1977), were kept at home to be taught by governesses, whereas their brothers were sent away to school. My mother had a governess until the age of sixteen. Her five enjoyable terms at the school I later attended were a release from a somewhat claustrophobic home and gave her a chance to meet other girls. Her brothers went to boarding-school at an early age, but her younger sisters never went to school.

The girls' public boarding-schools may have been depicted as a new freedom and advance in women's education, but there were important class interests. Pauline Marks has noted that in 1898 in England, 70 per cent of girls in secondary education were in private boarding-schools 'often in towns where grammar and high schools had empty places'. The advantage of the schools they attended was their social homogeneity: 'eligibility for marriage and not the content of their daughter's education remained the dominant concern of middle-class parents' (Marks, 1976, p. 189). These observations are relevant to at least one girls' boarding-school in the 1950s.

Even though both private and state schools have been affected by various reforms, including sometimes the principle of equality of opportunity for women, they have failed to resolve a persistent dichotomy, the choice for the future for girls between a career and marriage with motherhood. This is reinforced by a sexual division of labour which, both inside and outside the home, perpetuates women's relative economic dependence and insecurity, whatever their social class, and whether married or single. Educational reform alone cannot resolve this. Its confused policies have alternated from an unrealisable attempt at assimilation of female education into the male model, to an emphasis on teaching the qualities supposedly required of women as wives and mothers: other skills being regarded as secondary (cf. Marks, 1976, pp. 185–9).

It is not surprising that the dilemma between a career and marriage scarcely arose in a middle-class and relatively undistinguished boarding-school such as mine. Ideally, marriage was the ultimate vocation. Without records of the stated intentions of my teachers, I reconstruct these from remembered incidents. Some slogans remain: we were 'fortunate to be receiving a good education', and we believed it. Yet if there was academic intent, this was not borne out by the girls' performance, since the majority left after taking a few GCE, 'O' levels. Out of a class containing up to 35 girls, six or less remained to take sometimes a single 'A' level – an accomplishment which simultaneously prohibited university ambition. There is no memory of the word equality. The pattern after school tended to be a year at a private domestic science or finishing school, preferably in Switzerland, and progress to an exclusive secretarial college. The ideal was to be a débutante, before making a 'good marriage'. Another respectable vocation was nursing, and then only at select London hospitals. Teachers' training was *déclassé*. Whereas work as a private secretary or nurse offered contact with a man of the right social class, teaching did not. Few, if any, of the girls entered occupations comparable to their brothers'.

Scholarly achievements and higher education were, nevertheless, reserved for a few girls,[7] possibly marked as vocational spinsters. These had also to conform to the school's ideas of good conduct. Academic proficiency did not guarantee encouragement.

> With 13 'O' levels and while studying for four 'A' levels, I was summoned to the senior mistress. She declared I would be 'selfish to go to University, *even* Aberystwyth', thereby depriving a worthier person of a place. She suggested a career which would make use of my 'A' levels in French and Art – by training as a designer of corsets and lingerie for a famous company in Switzerland.

Separations

The British boarding-school is marked by its forms of separation from urban culture, from other social classes, from family and home, and from the opposite sex. Anthropologists have devoted much attention to *rites de passage*, ceremonies associated for example with birth, adulthood, marriage and death. In the transition of persons from one status to another, a frequent element is the separation of the individual (socially, spatially and temporally), from 'normal life' and from the community at large. In some initiation rites marking the transition from childhood to adulthood, the neophytes are grouped together, separated from the village, perhaps in the forest, and subjected to painful physical experiences, such as circumcision. They are instructed by selected adults in the sacred mysteries of their culture, by the use of special songs and sacred masks. Their pain is mingled with drama and beauty. They return with new knowledge and are reintegrated. A lasting bond is created between the neophytes who shared the same terror. The boarding-school can also be seen as a *rite de passage* from childhood to adulthood.[8] The separation from 'normal' life lasts many years. Although separations exist for both boys and girls, the differing consequences for each sex will become apparent.

1 Geographical and cultural
British public schools nowadays are almost invariably set in rural areas, distant from urban concentrations, the threatening proletariat and metropolitan culture. Originally the boys' public schools were not so organised. But from 1850 they were increasingly concentrated in large buildings, and some were moved out of London, and 'set in large houses, cut off by great oceans of land from the outside world' (Gathorne-Hardy, 1977, pp. 103–5). The girls' schools followed suit.

Apart from the efficacy of isolation and its greater control, the choice of the countryside was consistent with the current British belief that open spaces and fresh air improve moral, as well as bodily, health.

Our instructors never initiated us into nature's beauties, but only marched us through the landscape, two by two. Yet nature in the form of wild scenery was a fortuitous compensation. This was the only sacred knowledge acquired – from the downs, pine trees, woods and the uncontrollable south coast sea. Nature with its lack of discipline confounded their rules. It nurtured our souls.

Compared to boarding-school boys, it seems that girls are permitted even less contact with the world outside the school grounds.[9] For us, the nearby town was banned, taboo, except for perhaps a termly shopping trip under strict surveillance and with our few shillings handed out on Saturdays. We retained our coppers for Sunday chapel collection. Money found on us on any other days brought the severest punishment. Thus we were withdrawn from commerce, from earning and purchase.

We left the grounds about twice a week in 'crocodile' on set rural routes, skirting the town. Over-fifteens could go out for 'walks in threes' on certain days. Parents came and 'took us out', perhaps once a term. Written contact from and to the outer world was overseen. Outgoing letters not to parents were placed in unsealed envelopes for checking, incoming mail was examined, steamed open, even confiscated in some cases.

> My sister was crazy about Elvis Presley. Her friends paid for her subscription to the Presley fan club. Nothing arrived. Weeks later, the senior mistress summoned her and showed her the pile of Presley literature. My sister was told, 'You are fit only to dance at Hammersmith Palais!' The papers and pictures were destroyed.

Presley, sexually insinuating, was part of that proletarian culture from which we were to be protected. Yet even tamer forces threatened. Except for the *Illustrated London News* and *Punch* in the library, comics and magazines were banned, even *Woman's Own*, which we read secretly in the lavatory, where its torn pages were hung by matron for wrapping our dirty sanitary towels. All personal books had to be checked and signed by staff. Our storage drawers and our mattresses were searched for any offending literature which might have come from that far, urban world. Like the neophytes, the girls were bound together as partners in pain, or we detached ourselves in shared humour, and laughed at our custodians.

2 Class

Geographical seclusion was matched by our separation from all other social classes in the strange English hierarchy. Parents of middle- or upper-middle-class children demonstrate a desire to protect them from any classes below, and from contamination in what were euphemistically called the 'local' schools. Families may see themselves as randomly scattered and without sufficient contact with others of the same class pretensions, thereby risking inter-class familiarity. The boarding-school solves the technical problem. Offspring are concentrated with their kind and simultaneously separated from others. That is the meaning of 'exclusive' when applied to these institutions. When the children are home for the holidays, their parents can control their friends and contacts.

The children in such schools don't need to be told they are different and superior, since they are able to perceive it, learn it, know it for themselves. The children are isolated from any alternative life and the ways of others become the more alien. Stereotypes take form. We despised the grammar-school children we had to encounter at county music competitions. They were unknown, frightening and inferior, and the males of course were unmarriageable. Henceforth we could never treat anyone from another 'background' as equal. The differentiation was epitomised in the 'accent'. Here we received support from the dominant ideology of the larger society of which we were a necessary ingredient. The children in a boarding-school pool their parents' accents. Differences in a minority of girls in my school, such as the few scholarship girls, were ridiculed and mimicked until repressed. The public-school accent, just as the pronunciation of any language, must be constantly reinforced through childhood. Our inner ears or class tuning forks were sensitised by years of sounds in words. If the school teaches nothing else, it stamps the child with a way of speaking and the awareness of deviation. Style spoke before content. We need only utter a few words – any assortment – to mark ourselves. The consequences of our separation would go for ever with us when reintegrated into British society. The accent is a sign and a weapon.

Along with our accents went a pooling of prejudices and values, and ways of eating and moving – even our handwriting conformed. When I arrived, aged nine, from my Lincolnshire school, my ornate looped writing had to be unlearnt; it was too proletarian. A distinct set of manners was acquired.

Many years after leaving, I met an old school friend who commented on another former inmate who appeared to have slipped down the class ladder: 'She wrote to me on lined paper. I know when a friendship has to stop.'

We were taught that we could give charity but never receive it, thus defining precisely our class position:

A dormitory mate, whose parents were abroad, asked her relatives to forward a parcel of discarded holiday clothes. Several of us shared out the luxurious dresses, skirts and sweaters. The parcel had aroused the curiosity of the authorities. We were summoned, rebuked for 'accepting charity' and bringing shame on our parents, then ordered to repack and send the items to an East London mission.

I managed to conceal a skirt and pair of shoes in the recesses of the games corridor until the end of term.

3 Family and home

Ironically the fifties witnessed the popularity of Bowlby's claims that early separation from mothers would produce unstable children. The arguments were extended to schoolchildren of working mothers. The cry went up of 'latch-key' children. It was really directed at working-class mothers. The upper middle classes continued to despatch their children from home, depriving them of affection though guaranteeing twenty-four-hour custodial care. In some cases boarding-school has been justified as the solution after divorce or widowhood. The loss of one parent is thereby compounded by separation from the other.

Unlike prison or Borstal, we were there because our parents loved us. Prisoners and Borstal offenders know they are incarcerated in order to suffer for their own misdeeds. Their relatives and parents may lament and oppose their sentences. Even if the parents of a Borstal offender assisted the authorities, it would be apparent that they had failed as parents or rejected their offspring. The trick for us at boarding-school was that we were not ostensibly there as a punishment. We could not take responsibility for what our unconscious might tell us. Parents were wholly in collaboration with our fate. The school song made us declaim: It is well understood/We are here for our good/So our parents/And mistresses say/And I fancy that we/Are inclined to agree./Though we mean it/A different way.

After each verse, the refrain concluded:

> Your lot's not a bad one at all./
> NOT AT ALL!

The last line was shouted – one of the few occasions when the girls were encouraged, and indeed expected, to raise their voices.

The boarding-school can appropriately be defined as a 'total institution' (Goffman, 1968). The holiday intervals with parents are part of a continuous moral universe, since the parents are responsible for boarding their children and demand that they succeed there. Accepting, conforming and surviving can be a duty to the parents whose financial contribution is translated as love and sacrifice for the child's greater good. Whereas Borstal offenders may be able to nurture revenge against the establishment which sentenced them, public-school children dare not think through the ultimate blame upon their parents. The 'double bind' is complete.[10] In contrast to Borstal inmates' attempts to escape, running away from school can only be an emotional appeal to the parents who made the initial decision and may merely send their child back.

We were orphans but did not know it. Ironic that each child was encouraged to have a collection box in the shape of a house – a Dr Barnardo's home. Here we placed our pennies for the 'real orphans'. 'Family Favourites' on the Sunday radio fascinated us. We unconsciously identified with the messages sent between relatives apart. Our separation meant, indeed, the loss of a personal relationship with any adult. The ratio of staff to child within the school made it technically impossible. Moreover, at least from my experience, the demands of the institution overrode even the memory of family relationships. For individuals facing the crisis of the death of a parent or relative few, if any, allowances were made.[11] Misbehaviour arising from these circumstances was punished. We defied the rules to comfort our friends in the dormitory at night.

Denied personal access to adults, we were also constrained in rigid peer groups. Friendships, even prolonged encounters, were not permitted between persons of different forms – since they threatened the rigid hierarchy with its ascending privileges and status. Only love could undermine it. Friendships between different ages were deviant and passionate, though rarely expressed in physical terms. For the authorities such relationships were seen as a dangerous emergence of sexuality, and of course a perversion. There were strict regulations also on intimacy between equals. No two girls were ever allowed to be together alone in the bathroom, lavatory or small music rooms. Thus any loving relationship possible was taboo. Two girls were actually expelled, allegedly for mingling their blood from cut wrists and swearing friendship on the Bible.[12]

There appears to be a difference in the age when boys and girls in England are sent away from home. Boys are more likely to be boarded before eleven or even eight years of age (Lambert, 1975, p. 35), while girls are more likely to be boarded from eleven or later (Ollerenshaw, 1967, pp. 128–9; Wober, 1971, pp. 44–5).[13] A minority of us were younger when we joined our school. This difference between boys and girls may have consequences for each gender's responses and expectations in adult relationships. I suggest tentatively that boys seem to be required to repress 'childish' emotional dependence sooner, and thus more violently, than girls. Boarding for a 'prep' school boy entails an early severance from the mother and her emotional power, and absorption into a future where authority is vested in men. The fearsome school matron is no mother substitute. In other societies, male initiation rites express most dramatically this break with the mother. For the girl who may be at home longer, intimacy and identification with the mother become clearly established. It is at the onset of puberty, when her social and biological virginity must be protected, that she is sent from home and the local school. By contrast, a boy's virginity is of little or no consequence. Thus both boys and girls are separated from home and parents, but not always for the same reasons.

4 Gender

Along with the hierarchy of class, another major division of British society is the segregation of the sexes. For girls, separation from boys and men will have meaning and consequences not symmetrical to that of boys in single-sex schools. Compared to the boys, girls are subjected to greater restrictions and less autonomy.[14] Female adolescence, if not childhood, is socially prolonged in such schools, for this is a dangerous time for girls who are sexually mature, but considered too young for a marriage contract. This is especially true of a girl of a wealthy class, since her prospective spouse must be well established in his occupation, and have property, either transmitted or acquired. So the boarding-school offers safe segregation for girls from males of all social classes. Ollerenshaw hints at this:

> Some parents and headmistresses feel that there is advantage for some girls in their being withdrawn during the schoolday or at boarding schools for the school term from the emotional turmoil of relationships with boys so that they may develop poise and self confidence (1967, p. 29).

Boys, it will be argued, are likewise segregated from females,[15] and are deprived of heterosexuality. Unlike girls, however, they are not separated from the vision of political power. Indeed, separation from women and the domestic sphere consolidates patriarchy. By contrast, girls in a boarding-school are deprived of both heterosexuality and education for power, our glimpse of which would always be vicarious, would always be through males. Like the disease of haemophilia, as Helen Callaway once said, power can be transmitted through females but is only manifest in males. In schools such as mine, we were separated from those destined to monopolise certain political and economic spheres – those who were to acquire lucrative occupations and earn our living for us. Our own exclusive education, unlike theirs, was not for a career.

The school consisted almost entirely of females – the Head, matrons, teaching and domestic staff – most of whom were resident. The males usually seen within the school grounds can be listed:

the school chaplain;
two non-resident gardeners;
the boiler-man;
two elderly retired male teachers, for German and English 'A' levels, who visited perhaps one day a week;
the part-time tennis coach who appeared in my last two summer terms;
the headmistress's male dachsund.[16]

The majority of girls only directly heard the voice of one male, that of the chaplain. On Sundays we occasionally had a visiting preacher. If we were lucky enough to have a wireless we could hear male voices transmitted from the outer world. Yet men lurked somewhere, unseen. The Board of Governors consisted almost entirely of men – for example, a lord, a Tory MP, JPs and bishops.[17]

[. . .] Famous men, not women, were to be our heroic models. The school was divided into four cosmological 'houses', not represented by buildings but as groups of girls competing for cups in sports; conduct, drama and deportment – but not academic performance. The houses were named Shackleton, Scott, Livingstone and Rhodes, after male explorers and chauvinists of the colonial kind whom we, as Penelope to Ulysses, could never imitate. We could only marry and beget these kind of men [. . .]. Aspirations were stimulated which were simultaneously shown to be impossible for women to attain. Our impotence was confirmed. Even our classrooms were named after male, not female, writers: Shakespeare, Cowper, Kingsley (not Brontë, nor Eliot, certainly not Wollstonecraft). The choice of famous men indicates how completely an alternative, potentially revolutionary, female ideology was suppressed.[18]

With no heroines with whom to identify, heroism was always located in the mysterious 'other', from which we were to choose just one man as spouse. The male/female category was not learnt and created by observable opposition, as was possible for those in mixed schools or living at home, but by an absence or omission. There was no way either to become as men, or to find an independent female way. Our lives and potential were presented as those of failed men. We knew and learnt that women were beneath men in that hierarchy in which we ourselves believed. Only a male could confirm us, preach to us. Marriage offered the only release from this multiple separation. Without a husband, we knew we could not maintain our financial hold in the class system, however exclusive our accent and manners. Our privileges were at the mercy of men.

We learnt this also from the teachers. An exclusively female community does not necessarily have feminist aspirations, nor do its custodians provide models of ideal independence. The majority of our teachers were unmarried[19] and, apart from a few proud and self-sufficient ones, they presented themselves as victims of misfortune – so many tales of fiancés killed in the war – perhaps to justify self-confessed failure. They did not teach us to emulate themselves. We recognised our teachers as of a lower social class, some by their accents. In so far as the girls upheld beliefs in their exclusive background, they could not easily identify with women who came from the stigmatised state schools. Wober's data on girls' boarding-schools in the 1960s confirms that only a minority of staff had themselves been boarded, the majority, 63.6 per cent, had been to day school (1971, p. 40). Women from boarding-school do not wish to return there as teachers, because the desired destiny of most was a marriage which excluded a career. The same is not the case for men. Lambert's study of boys' public schools notes that: 'Most teachers . . . come from social groups which correspond to their pupils . . . Over 70% of staff in public schools were themselves educated at public schools and about 10% of them were educated in their own schools' (1975, p. 54). Thus the boys can more readily identify with their teachers.

Containment and powerlessness

It is sometimes said that girls' boarding-schools are more 'homely' than boys'. Certainly there were feminine touches for us (the rose garden, the floral curtains and coloured bedspreads) and the main building was more a country house than a utilitarian edifice. Wober notes the visual beauty of the girls' boarding-schools and seems almost to justify them in the name of that beauty (1971, pp. 282–3). But within homely or domestic quarters life may still become oppressive. We longed for love and approval from these substitute parents, our custodians, but they were not mothers with relaxed affection and visible femininity. Nor were they like fathers, for we saw how they deferred to male visitors. Girls, in contrast to boys, were addressed by their first names, a practice which states, among other things, that surnames were merely passing premarital stamps of identity. The use of the personal name may not reflect kindness though it speaks of intimacy, which in the boarding-school is not reciprocated between the child named and the adult namer. Some intimacy facilitated greater control. Privacy could be thus invaded. Further research is required into variations between male and female boarding-schools in the extent of control exercised. From the evidence now available, it seems that girls are more rigidly confined within the precincts of the school and subject to greater control (cf. Gathorne-Hardy, 1977, pp. 241, 246). Ollerenshaw hints at the demands made by the invisible fathers who delegated control of their daughters. The girls' schools 'had to establish the academic capabilities of women . . . with the approval and support of Victorian parents – in particular Victorian fathers. Rules of behaviour and deportment were therefore strict' (1967, p. 20).

The ethnography of the school I describe includes the limitations on the girls' movement in space and time, and on their sounds and speech. Movement *beyond* the school grounds was minimal. Only the five or six prefects could ever go out alone. Control *within* these boundaries was infinitely detailed. The focus on minutiae demanding all our concentration impeded the thought of, reduced the possibility of, bolder action. What counted as crime for girls may seem petty, especially when compared to the misdemeanours of boys. But its very triviality affirmed the pervasiveness of control. For instance, to be 'out of bounds' was almost unimaginable. It rarely occurred, and carried the risk of being expelled. Our triumphs were less dramatic, although meaningful to us – when on a 'walk in three', for example, taking the lift instead of the many steps from the beach, and having the pennies to pay for it. (I still have that lift ticket in my album.)

At any time of the day and night, any day of the week, our exact location was ordained. Summer alone gave free range of the garden in the limited play periods. Otherwise we traversed the grounds on set paths to outhouse and games field. Within the buildings, we moved along the corridors to specified rooms. Rules established that each location, such as dormitory, dining-room and common room were out of bounds when the timetable demanded our presence elsewhere. As we moved according to the lines of the timetable, we could neither hurry nor linger:

No running in the passage
No talking in the passage

were cardinal rules.

Just as space, so was time subjected to a changeless grid. An electric bell rang at half-hour intervals, or more often. There was no unorganised time for doing what we wanted or going where we wanted, even at weekends. No way to decide for ourselves the next move. After lessons our prep was supervised: often seventy silent girls sat in one long room. We had no private studies. One of the very few times when the girls were not within sight of an adult was 'after lights out' in the dormitory. The punishment for talking or being found out of bed was therefore the severest. We defied the invasions of our privacy which surveillance implied by hiding in the lavatory or bathroom. I would climb on to the roof at night. A former inmate confessed that she even went for moonlit walks in the grounds. The constraints on space and time were further compounded by the rules imposing silence during the ten or so hours between lights out and the morning bell, also when lining up and entering the dining-room, moving from chapel to 'roll call', indeed in all passages and inevitably in lessons. Not only were our words limited, but at all times sound was abated.[20]

Not being expected to choose, to decide and to make statements, the girls had to exercise extreme self-discipline, especially when they complied with orders which seemed either small-minded or incomprehensible. The notion of 'character' was contrasted favourably by our instructors with 'personality' – a negative trait because it carried the notion of individuality. Leadership of sorts was expected from seniors, not charisma, but the ability to lead others into a conformity to maintain a *status quo* predetermined by adults.

In contrast, in boys' public schools, seniors and prefects assume dictatorial powers, including the right to inflict corporal punishment, to have 'fags' (junior boys as servants) and to establish rules. They thus acquire near-adult authority before they leave school. Cyril Connolly has compared the position of senior boys at Eton to 'feudal overlords' (1961, pp. 194–5). Lambert describes how, in the 1960s, the boarding pupils at the top of the boy's public-school hierarchies exercised 'more real power over others than sometimes the junior teachers . . . and many other teachers in day schools'. Day pupils did not experience 'this dual training in responsible authority on the one hand and obedience on the other' (1975, p. 241). For girls, obedience rather than authority is emphasised. Present evidence suggests that girls' prefect power is weak compared to that of their male counterparts. Certainly the fagging system is non-existent. Wober found that girls gave low priority to being a prefect (1971, p. 78), and that houses in girls' schools were rarely residential entities 'with separate authority and privilege systems' (1971, p. 116). The vertical social grouping found in boys' schools coincides with the extensive supervision of juniors by seniors. The horizontal social grouping of girls coincides with the reduced authority of seniors over juniors.[21]

In girls' schools, authority is placed beyond both the pupils and teaching staff in a single individual: the headmistress.[22] This is described by Gathorne-Hardy as 'the dictator headmistress tradition' (1977, pp. 241–4). The position of the headmistress in my school appeared extremely powerful. Even the school magazine was edited by her. The staff had some authority, but the girls always had to defer to both staff and head. The seniors had no powers to initiate rules, they could not even give out 'bad marks' in the punishment system. The responsibilities of the 'junior sergeants', 'sergeants', 'sub-prefects' and 'prefects' consisted mainly of keeping the other girls silent in the passages and when lining up for meals, serving out the food at each long table, and reporting misdemeanours to staff. The head girl – the most coveted station for a pupil – performed mainly symbolic functions. When the entire school filed in silently to the dining room, she stood in the passage in a focal position raised four inches in a doorway. She announced the 'notices' after lunch (usually timetable changes). At the end of 'roll call' she marched out first to the military music. She helped the headmistress put on her MA gown in the vestry before daily prayers. At Sunday evensong she held the cross, processing before the chaplain. She sat on the headmistress's right at lunch on high table – her confidante, a ritual handmaid, but no innovatory leader. She had 'character', usually also an ability at games, and academic mediocrity. The closest description of this ideal type is provided in Angela Brazil's *The Nicest Girl in the School* (1909, pp. 20–1).[23]

Punishment by exposure

In boys' schools, punishment includes the cane – often wielded by other boys. Paradoxically the girls abdicate more freedoms without the terror of corporal punishment. How are they controlled when there is this apparently greater leniency? Foucault (1977) has demonstrated how direct and spectacular attacks on the body by public torture and execution before the eighteenth century were replaced by the more 'humane' methods of imprisonment. These controls were more effective because they entailed intervention in every aspect of the criminal's existence. Girls too are controlled not by material and metonymic weapons upon the flesh, but through intangible and metaphorical routes to the soul.

The system of punishment plays on the behaviour expected of girls, among whom self-control and self-negation take special forms. From infancy they are made modest, passive and withdrawn compared to boys. The pattern is already set before school, but there it is exploited, reinforced and elaborated. I use again the ethnographic example of my boarding-school. The required behaviour, and that which brought the precious reward of non-interference, included modesty, deference and submission. After a misdeed, part of the punishment was a 'row' from a member of staff and later the house captain. Humility, an apologetic stance, downcast eyes – possibly tears of defeat – were the correct forms. Any appearance of pride or dignity provoked further rebukes. Self-defence was rebuked with 'Don't answer back.' The 'right attitude' was rewarded, in that the girl was permitted to merge into the group. Our 'total institution' had all the elements which Goffman has described as 'stripping' (1968, p. 29), by which he means loss of personal identity. Here we see a closed circuit. The more a girl successfully complied with and internalised modesty, humility and the invisibility of the self, the more devastating the threat of their opposites.

We were given a number, useless, but printed on name tapes and stamped in nails on the soles of our shoes. But there was a worse kind of 'stripping' than that described by Goffman for us: being exposed before others as deviant, and regaining individuality as a wrongdoer. Both formal and informal methods of punishment had this common ingredient – public exposure, or individual visibility. To be picked out and stared at, was to be stripped as naked, with feminine reticence denied. This threat seems recurrent in girls' upbringing.[24] Control in our school was maintained not by the ultimate threat of cane marks but by disembodied conduct marks engraved on the collective mind. Whereas there was only one reward for good conduct, a 'good house-mark', our crimes were minutely subdivided (cf. Foucault, 1977, p. 98). Running or talking at the inappropriate place or time and other vaguer acts of 'insolence' earned a 'disobedience' mark (or 'disso'). The slightest delay brought a 'late' mark. 'Order' marks were given for the misplacement or loss of items like uniform or books, and for offences so trivial I cannot remember. Untidiness, even poor darning, brought a 'bad housemark'. We were bound in spiders' webs of fine rules and constraints until spontaneity seemed to be a crime. On the last morning of each holiday I would lie in bed wishing that I could foresee and avoid all my future misdeeds, for their consequences were frightful.

The stage was set at daily 'roll-call' where, in the presence of the entire school and staff, a girl with a 'disobedience', 'order' or 'late' had to announce the mark instead of saying 'present'. Hearts thumped as names came nearer. After a disobedience the headmistress would always ask. 'What's that for?' and the girl would have to detail her crime. While the rest of the school was sitting cross-legged on the floor, she might be asked to stand up and repeat her crime loud and clear. This public confession was also a symbolic variant of the public execution, with its necessary witnesses among whom fear of a similar fate would be generated. At 'fortnightly marks' the headmistress would read out the percentages of each girl's academic performance in the pre-

ceding weeks. We learnt that obedience and good conduct were insepar-
able from and superior to the intellect and academic knowledge. From
our total percentage received for classwork, two points were deducted
for a disobedience and one point for a late or order. The term culmin-
ated in 'Marks and Remarks' where every girl received a conduct
comment, again read aloud by the headmistress to staff and school.
Ideally it was 'good', but terrifying if different and among the few like
'a poor term', 'Jane resents criticism', or worse. After this ordeal a girl
might weep as I did, in the lavatory.

Conduct marks were given textual form, emblazoned in a public
record of crime or obedience. In the main passage at the chapel
entrance, for all to see, were four boards, one for each house (Rhodes,
Livingstone, Scott and Shackleton). A large sheet of paper bore the
name of each house member at one edge, with columns marking each
day and week of the term. A 'disso' earned a black cross, as did a bad
housemark. A 'late' or 'order' brought a nought, a good housemark a
vertical stroke. Every week ended with an additional column and an
individual square, for painting according to individual conduct. The
house colour (red for Rhodes, yellow for Livingstone, blue for Shackleton or green for Scott) was painted in for 'good' or 'normal'. There
were different intermediate gradings for bad conduct, the squares being
half white and half coloured, or all white, or half white and half black,
in order of severity. The worst was a completely black square with the
word 'disgrace' printed alongside. Thus the performance of each girl
for each week of the term was mapped and open to scrutiny by
everyone. The black squares generated the most curiosity and excitement and the recipient would be picked out wherever she went. At the
end of term, the house with the best score in conduct would be awarded
the school 'house cup', so each deviant knew the multiple consequences
of her misbehaviour. A miniature cup was awarded by each captain to
the 'best' girl in the house.

Informal methods of exposure were also used by staff and senior
girls. A girl who talked and who failed to respond to the sergeant or
prefect while lining up for the dining-room was made to stand in the
main passage, her back turned, not seeing those who filed past, but
conspicuous to all. A miscreant might be ordered to stand in the aisle
of the dining-room, or made to stand up at her table throughout a meal
while the entire school sat eating. The final humiliation was standing
on high-table, again with back turned, but abjectly visible. One matron
would punish a girl by making her sit under the table in the surgery,
while she had afternoon tea above.

Thus we were punished by the very terms they demanded of us. If
modesty were not pre-existent or not enforced, exposure would be no
terror, but instead would call for the bravado so often found among
boys. The girls who rejected modesty, submission and shame were
impervious to exposure. Only deprivation (such as detention on
Saturday after tea and no weekend sweets) might work for them. For

one, it was whispered, the slipper was used; the corporal punishment was resorted to because she behaved as a boy. Such girls were eventually expelled. For the rest of us, the more successful our conversion, the more we eliminated individuality, the more terrifying the punishment for any deviation. We were both rewarded and punished for our complicity.

In some contexts public exposure occurred without opprobrium and in pride. Like the duties of the head girl, they were mainly in ritual, in chapel. Girls would be chosen as servers at Holy Communion and for the daily Bible reading from the chapel lectern. They could speak with authority while reading the Holy Word, God's word, not mouthing their own. Here we could expose ourselves, for we were clothed in righteousness, especially on Sundays when our heads were covered by a blue veil, and we were muffled and purified. Prize-giving demanded a brief public walk, before disappearance back into the crowd, protected by the mass applause. Such exposure was different. First, because there were many prize-winners and second, because prizes were rewards for conformity. Some rewards in the form of privileges such as promotion to sergeant, sub-prefect or prefect, came with age, combined with the 'right attitude', and were welcomed. Indeed, not to be promoted with your age group meant further exposure (for instance, having to line up and sit with younger girls in the dining-room). Your state of promotion, or lack of it, was doubly visible, since felt embroidered badges of authority were sewn on the uniform, together with games team membership. There were no badges for academic achievement or intelligence – that which celebrates individual and original thought, and which can subvert.

The body: subjugated and unsexed

The concern with demeanour and carriage is one aspect of a total view of the body which reflects the extent of the institution's invasion and the ambivalences of its intentions. Mauss (1936) has discussed the ways different societies, groups and forms of education make use of the body. These may change over time and there are individual variations. Mauss isolates three factors: social, psychological and biological.

> In all the elements of the art of using the human body, the facts of education are dominant . . . The child, the adult, imitates actions which have succeeded and which he has seen to succeed among persons in whom he has confidence and who have authority over him (1936, p. 369).

In the girls' boarding-school, the pupils must acquire such movements. They may give the longed-for anonymity, as well as conspicuous selection as a team member. Within our school there could be no 'natural' movement which might contradict what the authorities considered correct. 'Bad' ways we had learnt elsewhere had to be changed. We did not merely unconsciously imitate movements and gestures, we were consciously made to sit, stand and move in uniform ways. We were drilled and schooled, not by those in whom we had confidence, but by those who had power over us. Our flesh unscarred, yet our gestures bore their marks.[25] Even when outside the classroom or off the games field, we were to sit, stand and walk erect, chin up, back straight, shoulders well back. At table when not eating, our hands were to rest in our laps. During the afternoon rest period matrons ordered us not to lie on our backs with knees bent. The games mistresses watched girls at meals, at roll-call and in chapel, and would award good and bad 'deportment marks', recorded on a chart, and with house cups. If you were consistently upright you won a red felt badge, embroidered with the word 'Deportment'. This, sewn on your tunic, was a sign of both achievement and defeat. Our minds and understanding of the world were to reflect our custodians. With no private space, we could not even hide in our bodies which also had to move in unison with their thoughts.

The authorities observed accurately the language of the body. However much a girl might say the right things, do and act within the rules, and however in order her uniform may be, her general carriage, her minutest gesture could betray a lack of conviction, a failure in conversion. I remember (after yet another term's anxious waiting for promotion) being called to the headmistress who said that I needed to improve my 'attitude' before I could be made a sergeant. I was baffled because I thought I had successfully concealed my unorthodoxy. I had said and done what appeared to me to be in order. But they must have seen through me, just by the way my body spoke. It also had to be tempered. I eventually won my deportment badge, and then soared from sergeant, to sub-prefect, to prefect. But my conformity over-reached itself; the games mistress took me aside and said I was now sitting and walking too stiffly, too rigidly. I was becoming conspicuous again.

Eventually the imitating child becomes the part. To survive in a place which beats down diversity, the victim has to believe in the rightness of his or her controller. Children and adolescents are most vulnerable, their minds and growing bodies may be permanently shaped. Apparently insignificant details such as bearing and posture are emphasised because, to use Bourdieu's words, the body is treated 'as a memory'. The principles of a whole cosmology or ethic are, 'placed beyond the grasp of consciousness, and hence cannot be touched by voluntary, deliberate transformation' (1977, p. 94). At an Old Girls' meeting, I talked with an old form-mate who had tried to train as an opera singer, but who could never breathe deeply enough. She spontaneously laid the blame on her schooling – her chest had, as it were, been too rigidly encased, and later she couldn't free herself, couldn't project her voice. In our bodies, we carried their minds into the future.

The presence of corporal punishment in boys' schools and its absence in girls' schools indicate differing attitudes to bodily display and contact, and possibly a differing consciousness of sexuality. Connections have been made between the childhood beatings of English males and their adult predilections for flagellation in brothels.[26] Although our deportment was continually viewed, our corporal modesty nevertheless stayed intact. In punishment, the girls were fully clothed and untouchable. In this sense, our bodies were invisible, anaesthetised and protected for one man's intrusion later.

As skeletons, we were corrected and straightened, ordered to sit and stand in upright lines. As female flesh and curves, we were concealed by the uniform. Take the traditional gym slip – a barrel shape with deep pleats designed to hide breasts, waist, hips and buttocks, giving freedom of movement without contour. My mother wore such a tunic. Previously women wore clothes which revealed the 'hour-glass' shape, but one made rigid and immobile by 'stays' or corsets. From the gym slip of the 1930s, we had graduated to the tunic of thick serge ('hopsack' we called it), without pleats, but again skilfully flattening the breasts and widening the waist. While my mother's legs had been hidden and desexualised by thick black stockings, we wore thick brown ones, 'regulation shade', and called them 'bullet-proofs'.

In those days before tights, our movements were further constrained lest we expose our suspenders beneath our short tunics. There was no risk of any greater exposure. We had to wear two pairs of knickers – white 'linings' and thick navy blue baggy knickers complete with pocket.[27] For gym we removed our tunics and any girl in linings only was shamed and punished. In summer the navy knickers were replaced by pale blue ones.

> A friend still recalls being given a 'disobedience' for doing handstands and, unknown to her, exposing her knickers to a nearby gardener. She was told only to say, 'for handstands' at roll call.

Thus her unmentionable exposure was effectively treated by psychological exposure. For games, our shorts concealed the existence of a split between the thighs. Two deep pleats in front and back made them like a skirt, but one which did not lift and reveal the thighs or buttocks as we ran or jumped. The lower abdomen retained its mystery.

This was the fifties when the dominant female fashion meant long full skirts. Yet our tunics had to be 'three inches above the knee when kneeling' (note the supplicant pose), even for girls aged 17 years. I have been informed by a girl at another boarding school in the 1960s, when the mini-skirt symbolised fashionable femininity, that her tunic had to be '*touching* the floor when kneeling'. Thus the girls' schools demand the opposite to the notion of sexuality in the world outside. Our appearance was neutered. Our hair could not touch the backs of our shirt collars; in effect we were given the male 'short back and sides'. The crucial inspection time was the daily march-past at roll call. The dilemma was whether to bend forward and be rebuked for 'poking' the head (and not marching in the male military fashion) or whether to straighten up and risk being summoned for mutilation by the hairdresser. We were caught between conformity to the school, and saving our female sexuality as symbolised by longer hair.

The girls' uniform also had strange male traits: lace-up shoes, striped shirts, blazers, ties and tie pins. Unlike some of the boys' uniforms, ours was discontinuous with the clothes we would wear in adulthood. To us the school tie had no significance for membership of an 'old boy network'. We were caught between a male and female image long after puberty, and denied an identity which asserted the dangerous consciousness of sexuality. Immediately we left school, we had to drop all masculine traits, since a very different appearance was required for marriageability. Sexual ripeness, if only expressed in clothes, burst out. The hated tunics and lace-ups were torn, cut, burnt or flung into the sea. Old girls would return on parade, keen to demonstrate their transformation from androgeny to womanhood. To be wearing the diamond engagement ring was the ultimate achievement. There was no link between our past and future. In such uncertainty our confidence was surely broken.

Exercise: games and marching

Bodily exercise of a distinct kind competed with and usually triumphed over academic study. For 220 girls there were two hockey pitches, six netball courts converted for tennis in the summer, along with two grass courts, a gymnasium and a swimming pool. The library, an old glass conservatory, half the size of a netball court, with three entrances linked to the main buildings, was little more than a draughty passageway. The games mistresses enjoyed at least equal and, in some cases, higher status than the academic staff. Boys could admire and model themselves on athletes. The games mistresses, however, even more than the academic staff, presented a model we were not willing to emulate either at the time, or after leaving school – the boyish hair style, shorts, aertex shirt, muscular unstockinged legs and sandals on all occasions. Games were compulsory every weekday. On Saturdays those girls selected for teams played in matches, while the rest of us took our compulsory exercise in walks. The timetable also demanded gym lessons twice a week, and those whom the games mistresses decided had flat feet or round shoulders devoted evenings to 'remedials' (stretching, balancing on tip-toe, or hanging on rib stools).

Pressure of exams meant no release from the daily obligation to play hockey or netball in winter and spring, and tennis, swimming and rounders in summer. Sometimes I would bandage my ankle and dare to put my name on the 'non-players' list, hoping no one would confer with my matron – the final authority on my bodily health.[28] Then I would lie on the cold lino under my bed, secretly reading. Before 'walks in threes', we would stuff books in our knickers so as to study in the fields. After 'lights out' we would revise for 'A' levels in the lavatories or in lit passages off the matron's beat. Knowledge and academic success were acquired by stealth.

It can be argued that physical exercise is essential, that youthful energy must be unleashed and directed. This does not explain the special form our exercises had to take. They were not merely to satisfy physiological needs, but another route to the mind. Those traditional 'female' accomplishments, dance, ballet and riding, at which we could excel as women, and which some of us preferred, were 'extras' to be paid for above the basic fees and then only available one hour a week. Games, on the other hand, were compulsory and free. We marched as soldiers out of roll-call but alternative movement to music was absent from the official curriculum. Our gymnastics were not of the modern kind, feminine and flowing, but instead freakish masculine jerks. Hockey and netball captured mind and body, because they concentrated group mentality, required whistle-blown attention and imprinted rules on the imagination.

[. . .] Popular images of the girls' boarding-school sometimes give important hints of the ambivalence and contradictions in these institutions. Ollerenshaw refers to the image of St Trinian's, with its 'whisky-swigging, hockey-stick-hacking, little horrors', and that of 'seminaries for nice girls where daughters can be safely locked up for the greater part of their troublesome teenage years' (1967, pp. 21–2). She concludes that no girls' school fits either image. I suggest that elements of both may be found together in the institution. On the games field we were expected to show a certain aggressive muscularity which in no way undermined the simultaneous demand that we be chaste and feminine.

There are indeed certain male and female sports. Those exclusively for boys include rugby, football and boxing. Those mainly for girls include netball, hockey, lacrosse and rounders. Tennis, swimming and sometimes cricket are found in both. The association of 'hockey-stick-hacking' with girls sometimes elicits laughter. Apparently incongruous for females, hockey is yet considered insufficiently masculine to count as a major sport for British boys,[29] and is absent or marginal to the basic curriculum.

What differences exist between male and female sports? First, rugby permits the use of the arms as weapons to hold or push opponents. Boxing depends on an even more forceful drive and punch of arms and fist. In the rugger 'scrum' the players are obliged to cling to each other. There are 'running tackles'; and the players throw themselves at each other. Netball, rounders, hockey and lacrosse do not permit holds and pushes with the arms, fists or body. If you knock or hold an opponent this is a 'foul'. As in the punishment system, there is no bodily contact. The only institutionalised body contact in exercise at our school took place in ballroom dancing lessons (paid for as an 'extra'), or during the Saturday evening dances. In those quicksteps and waltzes, the partners were surrogate man and woman, permitted the one tactile premonition of adulthood.

Other differences between the male and female sports concern the use of the legs, feet and hands. The aggressive use of the legs (kicking, and thus opening or raising the legs forward to expose, metaphorically, the genitals) is not permitted for girls. They must not touch the ball with the foot, must not kick any male ball. Modesty is retained.[30] Thus the 'weaker sex' is made weaker, being forbidden aggressive and defensive use of the arms, legs and feet. All the female sports demand manual dexterity in throwing, catching, hitting, 'dribbling' (hockey), or 'cradling' (lacrosse) the ball. This inhibits speed in running. Rounders is freer in some ways in that players can hit and swing with the full force of their bodies, with both arms raised. Sports, like cricket and tennis, more especially, are permitted for women because they have none of the characteristics of the exclusively male sports discussed above.

Although rugger, football, lacrosse and hockey pitches are of comparable size, movement for girls in that space is at all times encumbered by holding a stick. The rugger and football players can at times run free and fast, hurtling through space. Even the rugger player's flight is not greatly impeded by embracing the ball. For girls, only in netball is movement permitted free of stick, but restricted within the smaller space, and the player holding the ball is rendered immobile. The proximity of lines and many players require delicate avoidance within what amounts to a cage. I understand more clearly now why I would gaze out through the wire mesh of the netball court, repeating Shelley's words:

> Oh, lift me as a wave, a leaf, a cloud!
> . . .
> A heavy weight of hours has chained and bowed.
> One too like thee: tameless, and swift, and proud.

Despite the rationale for games as being for exercise and development, netball was experienced by me as an endeavour to domesticate, slow down and humiliate us. In the girls' games speed is reduced, the body peculiarly controlled or burdened. When playing hockey or lacrosse, an intermediary was required between our feet and the ball, between our arms and the ball, between our bodies and the opponent. Off the games field the limited, aggressive skill we had acquired was useless without our tools. We were rendered powerless, impotent without our substitute phallus.

Gathorne-Hardy notes that a girls' game 'however well done, looks unconvincing' (1977, p. 251). He suggests that girls are more sensitive than boys to purposeless activities, and that games reinforce the contradiction whereby girls are educated to be like boys and then expected

to be subservient to them later. He examines neither the gender differentiation in games nor their form, whereas I suggest that the contradiction is embedded in the rules of the games and enacted and reaffirmed
in each performance. The girls' bodies are extended and constrained
in this choreography of their future which they learn unconsciously in
legs, arms, hands, feet and torso. The girls' games when contrasted
with those for boys affirmed our impotence in speed, attack and
defence, leaving us with feminine dexterity and an eye for detail. While
our school song acknowledged the greater restrictions on noise from
girls, it strove to assert an equality which we couldn't achieve, which
couldn't exist:

> So we jog day by day
> On our life's pleasant way
> And although we don't
>   make such a noise,
> There are things I can name
> Such as playing the game,
> We can do them
>   as well as the boys.

Success was circumscribed, for to be truly female, we were not to
develop masculine muscles. In any case, we knew that hockey, lacrosse
and netball, unlike football, rugger or boxing, rarely penetrated the
adult sports pages and radio. Tennis, being a mixed game, and one we
could continue most easily after schooldays, was not systematically
coached unless, like dance lessons, we paid for it above the main fees.
Generally we were trained in games we could neither continue, nor
identify with, when grown.

We also marched: daily at roll-call and as the major event of Sports
Day. For weeks of the summer term we practised on the hockey pitch,
while the games mistress gave orders through a megaphone. On the
final day we were decked in tunic and clean striped shirts, with white
ankle socks and tennis shoes. A hired van blared out recordings of
military bands, playing especially the compositions of J. P. Sousa. A
shape resembling the Union Jack was chalked on the pitch and we
travelled along its lines, dividing, redividing, crossing and regrouping.
The parents, staff and honoured guests (the prize-giver was usually the
headmaster of a boys' prep school) and the rejects from the marching
watched from a raised bank. This was all very exhilarating, but again
we were being exercised in an unfeminine accomplishment to be abandoned after leaving school. Only men did national service and marched
in the forces.[31] That straight-shouldered gait with swinging arms and
regular footwork would have to be discarded, indeed unlearnt, as feminine step took over. We would only need it for country walks and
following the hounds. Just as hockey hinted at impotence, so did the
mode of marching. Instead of thumping our heels first on the ground,
we had to point our toes; the feminised fall of the foot. Our attack was

gently broken. Moreover we landed on the sound-dead turf of the hockey pitch; no noisy thrill of tarmac. Beneath the military music we heard only the rustle of our skirts and starched sleeves.

Conclusion

There are similarities between the girls' boarding-school and that for boys: the separation from urban life, from economic production and members of other social classes, from parents and home, and the separation by gender. In this preliminary analysis I have concentrated on some of the differences for girls concerning the choice of heroic models, the degree of control over pupils, the distribution of authority between adults and pupils, forms of punishment, the approach to the body and the types of movement permitted in the games curriculum and the like. For girls, important discontinuities may be found between school and what is realisable in later life. The presentation to girls of models of achievement generally associated with men undervalues any which might be associated with women, and conveys male dominance as inevitable. The girls' school, without corporal punishment, may paradoxically be stricter than that for boys, and allow its pupils less self-determination. Indeed, power may be exercised more completely over girls precisely because it is not visible as physical force. I suggest that in so far as alternatives are not emphasised, the girls are prepared mainly for economic and political dependence within marriage,[32] whether or not this is the intention of the authorities. The differences between the education of boys and girls are important indicators as to how within the same social class each gender is socially defined and culturally reproduced. In this paper, I have taken as an example a type of education usually regarded as privileged, but the analysis may be relevant to other girls' schools without such pretensions.

Notes

1 The terms 'public' and 'independent' refer to private fee-paying schools in the UK, in contrast to wholly state-maintained schools. In 1965 only 2 per cent of girls in the 13-year age group in the United Kingdom were in independent public schools (cited in Ollerenshaw, 1967, p. 13).
2 See Lambert, 1975, Honey, 1977, and Gathorne-Hardy, 1977.
3 See Blackstone, 1976, p. 199.
4 Wober's *The English Girls' Boarding School* (1971) is a pioneering study but limited in scope. The data are based on only 20 weeks of field-work in 23 schools, using questionnaires. It is significant that the terms of the original grant for the larger research project by Lambert on boys' schools specifically excluded girls' schools (1975, p. 5). Gathorne-Hardy's research is largely devoted to boys' schools (1977). His two chapters on girls' schools offer some imaginative, although sometimes erratic observations.

Recently there has been a revival of interest in the fantasy literature on girls' boarding-schools (Cadogan and Craig, 1976; Freeman, 1976). Angela Brazil, the major pedlar of illusion, never attended such an institution as a participant member. Inevitably crucial aspects of boarding-school experience do not surface.

5 When I delivered the first draft of this paper at the Oxford Women's Seminar, reactions were mixed. Those who had attended day schools were incredulous, while former boarders found many parallels or echoes of their own experience.

6 See also Okely, 1975.

7 A girl's academic ambitions will also depend on the extent to which she is encouraged by her parents off-stage. Wober notes in his questionnaires among the girls that 'Careers and professions seemed less common as a central focus: instead the emphasis was on "good jobs" . . . that would finance the gay pre-marital years, and thereafter serve for part-time or temporary occupation' (1971, p. 88).

8 Gathorne-Hardy has also found the concept of the *rite de passage* illuminating (1977).

9 Further research is necessary to explore the extent of permitted free movement by individuals beyond the school grounds. Certainly, some of the girls' schools are elaborately bounded by high walls, barricades or 'battlements' to prevent both intrusion by outsiders (Gathorne-Hardy, 1977, pp. 240, 258) and to reaffirm the enclosure of the inmates.

10 See Bateson, 1973.

11 The evening after a nine-year-old girl learnt of her father's death, she was told by the matron not to cry lest she keep the other girls in the dormitory awake.

12 Further research might confirm the impression from the literature and other sources that homosexuality is more explicit in boys' schools (see Gathorne-Hardy, 1977, p. 171). As in other areas, the differences would relate also to early socialisation, not merely the effects of schooling.

13 Public-school boys are literally prepared in 'prep' schools. Lambert notes that over 80 per cent of all boys in public schools had been to preparatory schools and that 85 per cent of his own sample had boarded in such institutions (1975, p. 126). Wober found that only 25 per cent of his sample of girls (the majority of whom arrived at boarding-school at 11 or 13) had previously boarded in a prep school (1971, p. 44). Many had attended coeducational schools.

14 See later section, Containment and powerlessness.

15 There are, by contrast, more persons of the opposite sex in boys' schools, namely the domestic staff, matrons and masters' wives. But 'boys and staff have learned to relegate women to marginal organizational and largely decorative roles' (Lambert, 1975, p. 116).

16 This dog was named after a day of the week, just like *Man* Friday. A colleague from another girls' boarding-school has noted a similar collection of males. Her headmistress had two male dachsunds.

17 Wober records that among his sample of girls' schools 'About one-third of the governors were women' (1971, p. 48).

18 In many schools, girls had to sing 'Forty Years On' which was written specifically for boys and included the inappropriate football chorus (Haddon, 1977, pp. 21–2).

19 Even in the late 1960s Wober found that the majority of teachers in the girls' boarding-schools were unmarried (1971, p. 38) and that only a minority had boarded (1971, p. 40). By contrast Lambert records that the

majority of staff in boys' public schools were themselves educated in such institutions (1975, p. 54).

20 Wober notes, 'In most cases, no matter at what time one arrived, the schools appeared quiet; girls, if seen, were scurrying about . . . whispering' (1971, p. 293). Gathorne-Hardy, during his visit to Cheltenham Ladies', noted 'a dead silence . . . a silence more awesome and more indicative of discipline than any bell, 800 girls swished in swift lines down the long, dim, tiled corridors towards the next classroom' (1977, p. 244).

21 I am grateful to Dr Peter Rivière for drawing my attention to this difference in social structure.

22 It is possible that the extent of authority allotted to girls in boarding-schools containing adolescents is similar to that for younger boys in their prep schools.

23 'No one could really call Patty pretty . . . she was neither dull nor particularly clever, only possessed of average abilities, able to remember lessons when she tried hard, and gifted with a certain capacity for plodding, but not in the least brilliant over anything she undertook. She was never likely to win fame, or set the Thames on fire, but she was one of those cosy, thoughtful, cheery, lovable home girls, who are often a great deal more pleasant to live with than some who have greater talents' (Brazil, 1909, pp. 20–1).

24 See also women's reluctance to speak or speak audibly at seminars where egoistic panache is demanded.

25 See also Foucault (1977, pp. 135–69) for his discussion of 'Docile Bodies'.

26 Stephen Spender has said of his prep school: 'They might as well have had me educated at a brothel for flagellants' (cited by Gathorne-Hardy 1977, p. 111).

27 The navy knickers and linings were a feature of many girls' schools (Haddon, 1977, pp. 75–6).

28 The matron's dominion over the girls' bodily health and sickness cannot be fully explored in this paper.

29 The various forms of these male sports depend also on the public school. Eton has also its own, like the Wall Game. There are also preferences according to social class and nationality within the UK. But the broad gender differentiation occurs in both public and state schools.

30 In the privacy of the gymnasium, the legs are opened when jumping over the 'horse' or when hanging on bars, but not raised in an aggressive kick. Some kicking motions are permitted when helplessly lying on the floor, with no target.

31 The single annual visit to London by the whole school was to the Royal Tournament; an all-male military display.

32 Since the 1950s the girl's biological virginity may be less important although her social virginity must still be protected. Moreover, greater sexual freedom may not alter a woman's economic and political dependence.

Bibliography

Bateson, G. 'Double Bind' in his *Steps to an Ecology of Mind*, Farnham, Paladin, 1973.

Blackstone, T. 'The Education of Girls Today' in J. Mitchell and A. Oakley, *The Rights and Wrongs of Women*, Harmondsworth, Penguin, 1976.

Bourdieu, P. *Outline of a Theory of Practice*, Cambridge, Cambridge University Press, 1977.

Brazil, A. *The Nicest Girl in the School*, London, Blackie, 1909.

Cadogan, M., and Craig, P. *You're a Brick Angela!* London, Gollancz, 1976.

Connolly, C. *Enemies of Promise*, Harmondsworth, Penguin, 1961.

Foucault, M. *Discipline and Punish*, London, Allen Lane, 1977.

Freeman, G. *The Schoolgirl Ethic: The Life and Work of Angela Brazil*, London, Allen Lane, 1976.

Gathorne-Hardy, J. *The Public School Phenomenon*, London, Hodder & Stoughton, 1977.

Goffman, E. *Asylums*, Harmondsworth, Penguin, 1968.

Haddon, C. *Great Days and Jolly Days*, London, Hodder & Stoughton, 1977.

Honey, J. R. de S. *Tom Brown's Universe*, London, Millington, 1977.

Lambert, R. *The Chance of a Lifetime?* London, Weidenfeld & Nicolson, 1975.

Marks, P. 'Femininity in the Classroom: An Account of Changing Attitudes' in J. Mitchell and A. Oakley, *The Rights and Wrongs of Women*, Harmondsworth, Penguin, 1976.

Mauss, M. 'Les Techniques du Corps', 1936, in his *Anthropologie et Sociologie*, Paris, Presses Universitaires de France, 1938.

Mitford, J. *A Fine Old Conflict*, London, Michael Joseph, 1977.

Okely, J. 'The Self and Scientism', *Journal of the Oxford Anthropology Society*, Michaelmas, Oxford, 1975.

Ollerenshaw, K. *The Girls' Schools*, London, Faber & Faber, 1967.

Pocock, D. 'The Idea of a Personal Anthropology', Paper given at the ASA Conference, 1973 (unpublished)

Pocock, D. *Understanding Social Anthropology*, London, Teach Yourself Books, Hodder & Stoughton, 1975.

Shelley, P. B. *Selections*, A. H. Thompson (ed.), Cambridge, Cambridge University Press, 1956.

Wilson, C. *The Outsider*, London, Gollancz, 1956.

Wober, M. *English Girls' Boarding Schools*, London, Allen Lane, 1971.

Part four
Education and qualifications

4.1
Schools, examinations and occupational attainment†

Anthony Heath and John Ridge

In 1972 a group of Oxford sociologists carried out a national sample survey of 10,000 adult men resident in England and Wales and aged between 20 and 64. Two main reports have appeared so far on the data thus collected. Together with A. H. Halsey we analysed the educational experiences of the sample, and this was published as *Origins and Destinations: Family, Class, and Education in Modern Britain* (1980). In addition John Goldthorpe has studied their occupational histories and achievements, as described in his monograph *Social Mobility and Class Structure in Modern Britain* (1980). But nowhere have we properly related the two. We shall make an attempt in the present paper to fill this gap.

To begin with, we must recapitulate some of the main characteristics of the changing educational system through which our respondents passed. The older members of the sample, who grew up before the Second World War, entered a complex and developing school system which clearly bore all the marks of its historical origins. There were the so-called Public Schools which were in fact private establishments which charged full fees for tuition and which in many cases provided, at a price, residential accommodation as well. Some were ancient foundations, but they had been given a new stimulus in the mid-nineteenth century when the abolition of patronage and the introduction of competitive examinations had thrown open careers in the Armed Forces and Civil Service for those with the requisite educational skills. They were thus geared to the aspirations of the rising bourgeoisie for elite positions in the administration of the British Empire. They were patronised by professionals, clergymen, businessmen and of course the landed gentry who had for so long provided England's ruling class. The Public

† Source: F. S. Capello, M. Dei and M. Rossi (eds) (1982), *L'Immobilità Sociale*, Bologna, Il Mulino, pp. 257–79.

Schools were perhaps crucial in welding together these 'old' and 'new' groups into a new, socially and culturally united ruling class.

At the other extreme were the Elementary Schools which had grown up to provide a minimal level of free education for the masses. The Education Act of 1870 had established universal education for children aged between 5 and 11 in these Elementary Schools, but the period of compulsory education was gradually extended and by the time our older respondents were at school the minimum leaving age was 14. They received a basic instruction in literacy and numeracy, but were prepared for no public examinations and left school for the labour market without any formal academic qualifications. This was before the age of 'credentialism'.

In between the Public and Elementary Schools came a complex array of secondary schools – Central Schools, Junior Technical Schools, Direct Grant Schools, minor private schools, and of course the Grammar Schools. By the twentieth century the latter were managed by Local Education Authorities. Some pupils were charged fees, but even the fee-payers were heavily subsidised, and under the 1907 free-place regulations at least a quarter of the places had to be allocated on the basis of competitive examination to pupils who had previously attended the Elementary Schools. The proportion was often much higher than a quarter, and so even at the beginning of the twentieth century the Grammar Schools enabled substantial numbers of children from relatively humble backgrounds to obtain a 'superior' education without having to pay tuition fees. Once admitted, these pupils were prepared for the Ordinary School Certificate – the principal educational credential available before the war and one that would usually be obtained at the age of 15 or 16. This in turn gave access to higher education or white-collar employment.

After the Second World War the state sector of education was further reformed, and it was through this new reformed system that the younger half of our respondents passed. The minimum school-leaving age was raised to 15. The Elementary Schools were abolished (at least in name) and all pupils had to transfer at the age of 11 to a distinct secondary school. They took a competitive examination (the now notorious 'eleven plus') and on the basis of this were allocated either to a Grammar School (now made wholly free), a Technical School, or one of the new Secondary Modern schools. The examination system was reformed too and the School Certificate replaced by the General Certificate of Education, which could be taken either at 'Ordinary' or 'Advanced' Level. But it was still only the Grammar and Technical Schools which were geared to these new examinations. It was felt at first that, without the constraints of a formal examination system, the Secondary Modern Schools would be freer to cater for the individual needs of their pupils. But this admirable ethos gradually broke down and by the 1960s the popular demand for educational credentials meant that many pupils at these schools were taking either the 'Ordinary' level of the GCE or a new, lower-level examination called the Certificate of Secondary Education.

The tripartite system, as the division into Grammar, Technical and Secondary Modern Schools was usually called, survived for twenty years, but was gradually abandoned in the 1960s and 1970s. Neighbourhood comprehensive schools replaced the three different types of secondary school, the leaving age was raised again to 16, and virtually all pupils began to take some kind of public examination at the end of their school careers. But most of our respondents had already left school by the time of these reforms. We cannot, from our material, usefully say much about comprehensive schooling. Instead we can compare the experiences of our older respondents (those born between 1913 and 1932) who were educated before and during the war with those of the younger respondents (born between 1933 and 1947) who went through the tripartite system. Indeed, a lot of the interest of our research derives from our ability to monitor the effects of these post-war reforms which lay behind the tripartite system. By introducing universal, free secondary education and a nation-wide competitive selection system, the authorities were avowedly attempting to make education more meritocratic and to increase equality of opportunity between the classes.

The main conclusion of *Origins and Destinations* was that Britain had made little progress towards meritocracy over the years covered by our study. The educational reforms had had little efficacy. And in *Social Mobility and Class Structure* John Goldthorpe showed that while upward mobility had increased this was largely a result of the great expansion of higher-level administrative and managerial posts in the post-war period. The *relative* chances of men from different class origins, however, showed little change. Economic growth gave an illusion of social progress; more people went to Grammar School; more people got secure and well-paid jobs. But the gains went to the privileged as well as to the disadvantaged and so inequalities of opportunity continued unabated.

However, while the lack of movement towards greater openness was disappointing, this does not mean that throughout the century Britain has been a rigid society in which position in the class structure has been fixed at birth. There has been a substantial degree of fluidity both in the educational system and in the labour market; it simply has not increased over time. True, class differences permeate the schools. Both before and after the war the Public Schools drew their pupils overwhelmingly from what Goldthorpe has called the 'service' class (composed of administrators, professionals and managers). At the other extreme Elementary and Secondary Modern Schools were heavily populated by children from working-class homes, but they were also leavened by the '11 plus failures' from the other social classes, and there were perhaps more of these failures than one might have imagined. Just over a quarter of the boys from service-class homes ended up in Elementary or Secondary Modern schools.

The Grammar Schools, furthermore, were much more mixed in their intake. They were never the preserve of the privileged strata. More than a third of their pupils came from the working class and two-thirds of them were what we have called 'first generation grammar school boys' – ones, that is, whose parents had only attended Elementary Schools themselves. This predominance of 'first generation' boys in the Grammar Schools led us to question the usefulness of the concept of 'cultural capital' in mid-century Britain. As we wrote in *Origins and Destinations*:

> Our evidence does not dispose us to accept any exaggerated claim for the concept of cultural capital as an exclusive means of cultural reproduction of the social classes. The concept is useful as an umbrella term for a set of mechanisms through which families influence the formal educational experience of their children. But the twentieth-century history of secondary-school expansion, at least in Britain, draws attention to the accumulation and dissemination of cultural capital as much as to its preservation and concentration. Our figures show the large volume of upward intergenerational educational mobility and the overwhelming feature of the [Grammar and Technical] schools throughout our period was the presence in them of a dominant element of first generation novitiates into the 'national cultural heritage'. (p. 88)

Instead, our view is that free or subsidised secondary education, coupled with ostensibly 'meritocratic' selection tests like the scholarship examination and the eleven plus, although undoubtedly retaining class bias, did open the way for many boys from less-privileged backgrounds into the academically superior Grammar Schools. They got their foot on the bottom rung of the ladder at least.

Did the Grammar School thus provide a channel for upward mobility throughout the twentieth century in Britain? Or was the opportunity that success in the scholarship examination gave an empty one? We might have expected that the mechanisms of cultural reproduction would have operated more strongly *within* the Grammar Schools rather than at the point of entry, with the 'first-generation' boys faring much less well in the School Certificate and the General Certificate of Education than their second-generation rivals. But there was little evidence of this. Rather, the striking feature of the British educational system was the *similarity* in the fortunes of those who attended a particular type of school, irrespective of their class origins. The intake into the Grammar Schools was highly heterogeneous in its social origins; it appeared to be much more homogeneous in its educational destinations. True, class differences persisted; working-class boys were more liable to drop out before sitting School Certificate or the General Certificate of Education than were their service-class peers, but, as we observed in *Origins and Destinations*, this should not 'blind us to the considerable assimilative capacity of the grammar schools. The working-class boy at grammar school still has a superior chance to the service-class boy at a technical school or non-selective school of an extended school career' (p. 133).

This led us to refute Boudon's* claim that 'the secondary effects of stratification on inequality of educational opportunity are, other things being equal, probably much more important than their primary (cultural) effects' (Boudon, 1973). Until the advent of the comprehensive school Britain had, in Turner's famous phrase, a sponsored rather than contest system of educational ascent (Turner, 1960). The primary effects of stratification influenced one's chance of being sponsored in the first place, but once selected for Grammar School education less scope was allowed to the secondary effects of stratification.

But what happened at the end of full-time schooling? Did class differences, held in abeyance by the rigid character of the secondary schools, reassert themselves? Or were those sponsored for educational success able to capitalise on this in the labour market? Conversely, did educational failure leave a legacy of occupational failure, or were the 'eleven plus failures' from service-class backgrounds able to climb back to their fathers' levels? In short, how fateful was success or failure at the age of eleven in the selection examinations for secondary school for subsequent occupational as well as educational fortunes?

To answer these questions we shall make use of the fact that our social mobility survey gives us occupational data on our respondents for three points in their career. We know what the *first* job was on leaving full-time education, what job they held *ten years* after that, and what job they held at the time of the survey (that is, in 1972). We also know what job their fathers held when they (the respondents) were aged 14. These four pieces of information give us a rudimentary outline of our respondents' biographies.

There are two different ways in which we shall classify these occupational data. First, we can place jobs on a continuous, hierarchical scale,

---

* [Boudon's 'primary' effects of stratification are differences between people, e.g. the lower the social status, the poorer the cultural background, hence the lower the school achievement. (These are generalizations about broad tendencies, not universal statements about each and every individual.) The secondary effects of stratification are the costs and benefits deriving from the position of an individual in a social network, and attaching to particular courses of action. A more prestigious curriculum may have both higher benefits and lower costs for a middle-class than for a working-class child, even where both children are identical in terms of primary effects (cultural ability, educational achievement, etc.). For example, middle-class children may stay with their friends if they choose a prestigious curriculum, working-class children may lose their friends. It appears from Heath and Ridge's account that the 'sponsorship' provided by grammar schools protected their pupils against Boudon's 'secondary effects', perhaps because by the time they were at the grammar school, they had already broken with their circle of childhood friends – eds.]

ranking them according to their prestige or general social standing. We prefer to interpret these scales as measures of the general desirability of the jobs in question, that is as measures of the net advantages, both monetary and nonmonetary, which accrue to them. The particular construction which we shall employ is the Hope-Goldthorpe scale which ranks 124 occupational groups. It is an appropriate one to use when we are considering, as we are in the present paper, the 'life chances' of different groups. (See Goldthorpe and Hope, 1974.)

Second, we can adopt the classification used in *Origins and Destinations* and in *Social Mobility and Class Structure*, grouping occupations according to their market and work situations to produce discrete social classes with their own distinct interests. This is an appropriate one to use when we are thinking of classes as broad socio-cultural formations variously located in the social structure. We shall follow our earlier practice and distinguish three classes, the 'service' class, the intermediate class and the working class. Goldthorpe describes the service class as 'the class of those exercising power and expertise on behalf of corporate bodies – plus such elements of the classic bourgeoisie (independent businessmen and 'free' professionals) as are not yet assimilated into this new formation, (Goldthorpe, 1980: 40). It contains both higher and lower grades of professionals, administrators, officials and managers together with large employers. The intermediate class consists of a rather mixed bag of marginal occupations which do not properly belong to either of the other two major formations. It includes the white-collar labour force of routine clerical and sales personnel; the petty bourgeoisie of shopkeepers and small employers; farmers, smallholders and self-employed artisans; and those classic marginal men of industry – the foremen. Finally, the working class consists of industrial manual workers, both skilled and unskilled, together with the small number of agricultural workers which remains in Britain.

How we are going to employ these data and classifications will, we hope, be clear from Diagram 1. The diagram covers men born between 1913 and 1932 (namely those who were educated pre-war) and it divides them according to their social class origins. Thus the upper curve gives the occupational profiles of men with service-class origins (that is, those whose fathers held service-class jobs when the respondents were aged 14); the middle curve represents men with intermediate-class origins; and the lower curve men with working-class origins. We have then computed the average rank on the Hope-Goldthorpe scale of these three groups of respondents at the four stages of their lives on which we have data. (For the detailed definitions of service, intermediate and working classes see Goldthorpe, 1980, ch. 2.)

Consider, for example, the respondents from service-class origins. Service-class jobs have a high rank on the Hope-Goldthorpe scale, and so they start off towards the top. As one might expect, they then enter the labour market at markedly lower levels but over the next ten years receive relatively rapid promotion bringing them back towards their

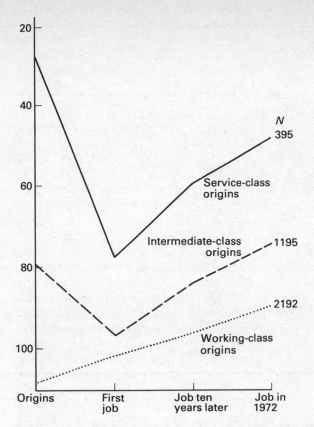

Diagram 1 Class origins and occupational career (men born 1913–32)

fathers' levels, illustrating the well-known phenomenon of counter-mobility. Observe, however, that even by the end of their careers these men have not, on average, fared quite so well as their fathers, and this is despite the fact that, unlike their fathers, they had lived through a period of expanding opportunities for occupational advance. Rather, what we see is something akin to regression towards the mean: children tend to be closer to the overall average than their parents were.

The same phenomenon is demonstrated by the boys from working-class homes. Theirs was, on average, a steady progression upwards, showing none of the counter-mobility of the other two classes. It was also a progression which continued right through the life-cycle not, as is often thought, one which petered out after the first few years in the labour market. True, they do not in general actually reach the overall mean; most men from working-class origins still hold working-class jobs at the ends of their careers, but some of them will have achieved long-range upward mobility into the service class while others will have skilled jobs instead of the unskilled ones of their fathers.

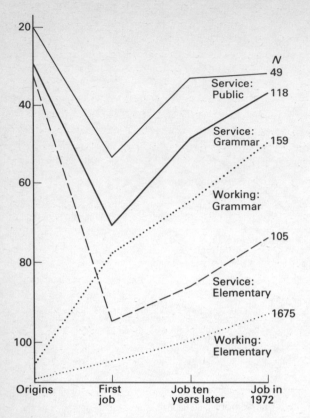

Diagram 2 Class, schooling and career (men born 1913–32)

But to what extent did schooling aid or shape these processes?
Diagram 2 begins the answer. It is again restricted to the older members of our sample, the men born between 1913 and 1932. It shows the
career profiles of men from service-class origins who attended the
major Public Schools, Grammar Schools and Elementary Schools
respectively, and of men from working-class backgrounds who attended
Grammar and Elementary Schools. (So few of the latter attended Public
Schools – only two in this cohort in fact – that they can safely be
ignored.)

The broad outlines of the diagram are clear and striking. The service-
class boys who were sent to Public and Grammar Schools managed
overall to avoid any very substantial regression towards the mean. Elite
schooling did not ensure elite occupation (for there was quite wide
variation around these average scores in Diagram 2) but did at least
give these boys a high probability of returning to those privileged
positions in society in which they had been brought up. Here is a
good example of social reproduction via the educational system. By

exploiting the private sector of education and the subsidised Grammar Schools the service class could protect its children against the downward mobility that regression to the mean might otherwise have caused.

But those who missed out educationally missed out occupationally too. The service-class children who went to Elementary Schools (and as we have observed they were not a negligible number) suffered dramatic downward mobility on leaving school, and while they managed to recover somewhat thereafter, it is clear that the legacy of their schooling stayed with them throughout their careers. The upward movement during their working lives was little more than the normal progression which was to be expected as men grew older in a time of expanding opportunities. There is no sign that privileged origins managed to rescue men from the sentence passed on them at the eleven plus.

In contrast the working-class boys who had climbed the scholarship ladder into the Grammar Schools had indeed embarked on the first stage of an extraordinary ascent. And we should again remember that there were quite large numbers of these boys; indeed they actually outnumbered the service-class boys in Grammar Schools. Success in the scholarship examination thus opened the door to upward mobility for the bright boy from the working class. Whatever his initial cultural and social disadvantages may have been, he clearly could reap at least an occupational pay-off from the academic education that he was offered. Sponsored mobility really did seem to operate.

This first part of the occupational analysis, therefore, clearly confirms the educational picture painted in *Origins and Destinations*. The kind of secondary school that boys attended before the war was indeed fateful for their careers in the labour market as well as at school. The educational opportunities offered by the Grammar School to working-class children were indeed a prelude to occupational advance. But those who missed out at school had no easy road to recovery. Just as *Origins and Destinations* showed the homogeneity of the educational experience of boys from different backgrounds who attended a given type of school, so Diagram 2 emphasises the homogeneity in their work careers. The typical working-class boy at Grammar School ended up much closer to his service-class school-fellow than to his working-class neighbour who attended the local Elementary School. True, class differences remain even within school categories, but the within-school differences are much smaller than the between-school ones. The pre-war British educational system did not merely reproduce the social division of labour but performed important functions of redistributing the personnel from the different social strata.

What effect, then, did the post-war reforms have on this? We have already noted that they did little to increase equality of educational opportunity, but the expansion of the Grammar Schools and the spread of credentials may have changed the link between school and work in other ways. Expansion might conceivably have led to dilution as children of lower ability were admitted to the Grammar Schools; credentialism may have increased the competition from ambitious boys in the Secondary Modern schools. Either of these processes might have reduced the between-school differences and increased the within-school variation.

Before we move on to the post-war data one minor difficulty should be dealt with. The younger men whom we are now dealing with (men born between 1933 and 1947) had necessarily spent a shorter time in the labour force by 1972, the time of the survey, than their elders in the pre-war cohort. Their careers were in this sense unfinished, and we might have expected them to have reached lower occupational levels by 1972 than the 1913–1932 cohort. Surprisingly, this is not the case. At each stage of their career the younger cohort held, on average, slightly higher-level jobs than the older cohort, and this applies to their 1972 jobs as well. This is, perhaps, another example of the way early days influence the later ones. Thus people who grew up and entered the labour market during the pre-war depression years lost out at that point of their lives, and while they benefited from the post-war expansion, they did not benefit to the same extent as those whose start in life had not been so blighted. Once you have missed out at one stage you are not so well placed to take advantage of new ones. In this way generational inequalities are added to class and educational ones.

To be honest, however, these generational differences are fairly small, as can be seen by comparing Diagrams 1 and 3. But what of the much bigger school differences which we saw in Diagram 2? Diagram 4 takes up the story. As before, we see powerful school differences, but within the Grammar School class differences have greatly increased. Thus among the older cohort the service-class Grammar School boy had an occupational advantage of 7 points on the Hope-Goldthorpe scale at the point of entry into the labour market, but among the younger cohort the advantage has increased to 20 points. There is no corresponding change among the Secondary Modern School boys, but for Grammar School boys the change is marked and reappears at each stage of working life.

There is an important paradox here for social policy. Reforms designed to improve the chances of the bright boy from a disadvantaged home seem to have had the reverse effect. Their relative handicap instead increased. Was this perhaps due to dilution? Bantock, for example, has argued that many working-class children were 'for cultural reasons likely to be inhibited from gaining the best of what is offered them even if they were to be offered "chances" in these terms; and this because they have already been formed by historical socio-cultural forces which make the segment of "high" culture for them pretty meaningless' (Bantock, 1965: 150–1). He could interpret the present finding by claiming that most of the working-class children who could profit from the Grammar School and make effective use of their education were already doing so before the war. The newcomers admitted after the war, he might be tempted to assert, were not so well equipped

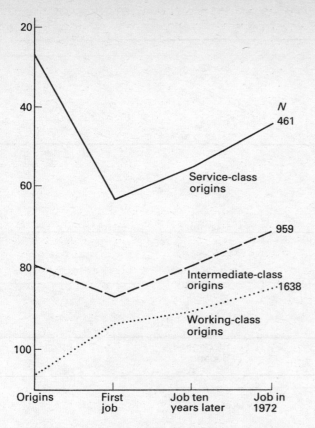

Diagram 3 Class origins and occupational career (men born 1933–47)

to cope. This argument implies that there were definite limits to the dissemination of cultural capital to which we alluded earlier, and that the limits were already being reached before the war.

An alternative explanation might rest on the concept of credentialism. One of the most striking features of post-war education has been the spread of formal qualifications, both in variety and in the kinds and numbers of students acquiring them. It is quite possible that, before the war, employers were more concerned with the kind of education potential recruits had received; to have spent several years in a Grammar School, even without obtaining School Certificate at the end of them, might well have been sufficient to differentiate such pupils from the Elementary-School-educated masses. The working-class 'early leaver' from Grammar School may thus have been in an advantageous position in the labour market even if financial circumstances had forced him to leave school before he had had a chance to sit the School Certificate. But after the war, perhaps, it would not have been so easy for him. There would have been more competitors from the Secondary

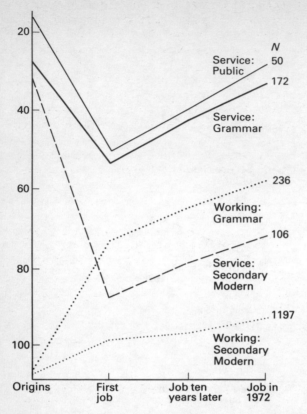

Diagram 4 Class, schooling and career (men born 1933–47)

Modern schools with some kind of certificate, either GCE or CSE, which he could not offer himself. If employers increasingly used formal credentials in selecting and promoting staff, and there is some evidence that they did, the balance of advantage may have swung back in favour of those pupils from privileged homes who could afford to stay on at school long enough to secure the requisite pieces of paper. Credentialism, although nominally universalistic and meritocratic, may in fact have involved a greater class bias than its forerunner.

The dilution argument can be tested relatively easily. Table 1 shows the proportion of respondents from different class backgrounds obtaining School Certificate before the war and the General Certificate of Education at Ordinary Level after the war. There are certainly class differentials in the acquisition of credentials, but there was no tendency among the Grammar School boys for these to widen in the post-war period. If anything the reverse occurred and the gap narrowed slightly. It could be argued that Ordinary Level was rather easier than School Certificate, and so the general increase in percentages does not in itself disprove dilution. But it is clear that if there was any dilution it occurred at least as much among the service-class pupils as among the working-class. So working-class dilution cannot explain the increased occupational advantage of the service-class Grammar-School boy which we saw in Diagram 4.

Table 1 does, however, provide some support for the notion that there was increased competition in the post-war period from qualified school-leavers from the Secondary Modern Schools. It is notable that it was the service-class boy who was the most likely to take advantage of the new opportunities for obtaining qualifications, but their numbers were not very great and could hardly, on their own, account for the relatively worsened occupational chances of the working-class Grammar School boy.

Table 1 Social origins and educational qualifications

School attended	Father's class	Percentage obtaining School Certificate or Ordinary Level GCE	
		men born 1913–32	men born 1933–47
Grammar	Service (118)	71.2	86.4
	Intermediate (191)	63.4	72.2
	Working (159)	50.9	68.8
Secondary Modern or Elementary	Service (105)	6.1	19.6
	Intermediate (728)	2.7	5.7
	Working (1675)	2.1	3.1

To test the credentialism thesis properly, however, we must look at the occupational fates of qualified and unqualified boys from different school and class backgrounds. Diagrams 5 and 6 give the pre- and post-war pictures for Elementary and Secondary Modern School boys. They show that in both periods the service-class boy who obtained some qualification was able to avoid the adverse consequences of an Elementary School education. His typical career path demonstrates almost exactly the same pattern of counter-mobility that his Grammar School contemporary enjoyed. But, in line with the credentialism thesis, the gap between qualified and unqualified increased in the post-war period. At entry to the labour market the gap increased from 17 to 24 points in the case of the service class and from 11 to 18 points in that of the working class. In this way the Secondary Modern Schools were producing a less homogeneous output than their predecessors, the Elementary Schools. Not only were more of their pupils obtaining qualifications, but the qualifications they obtained were also more consequential for their subsequent careers. Failure in the 'eleven plus' was thus not quite so fateful after the war as failure to take the scholarship examination had been before the war.

But when we turn to the Grammar Schools we find that the credentialism thesis does not account quite so well for the various changes. Before the war things were much as we might expect. The qualified

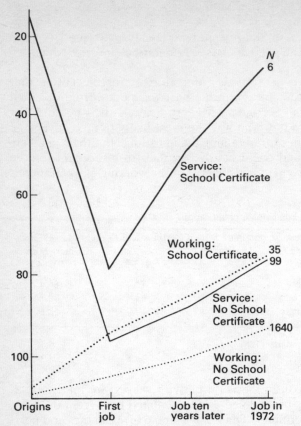

Diagram 5 Schooling, qualifications and career (men born 1913–32 who attended Elementary Schools)

men with their School Certificates fared markedly better than the unqualified, but even the working-class boy who left without School Certificate was likely to experience marked upward mobility and his service-class equivalent, although downwardly mobile compared with his father, none the less achieved definite counter-mobility. After the war it is more complicated. True, the working-class boy who failed to get any Ordinary-Level passes at the General Certificate of Education had relatively poor prospects, but in general the gaps between the qualified and unqualified are reduced rather than increased. At entry into the labour market the gap is reduced from 23 to 15 points for the working-class boys and from 25 to 18 in the case of the service-class.

It could be claimed that this post-war reduction was due to the fact that Ordinary Level was of a lower standard than its pre-war equivalent of the School Certificate. The *educational* gap between the qualified and unqualified, it might be argued, really was smaller than it had been before and the *occupational* differences merely reflected this. Of course,

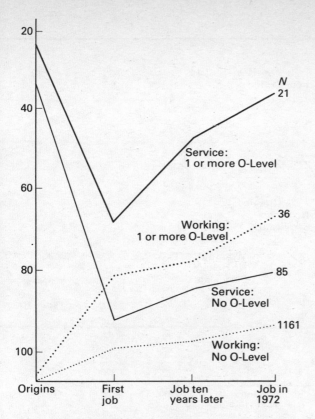

Diagram 6 Schooling, qualifications and career (men born 1933–47 who attended Secondary Modern Schools)

this makes the widening gap among the Secondary Modern School boys which we saw in Diagrams 5 and 6 rather puzzling. But there are some other difficulties too. After the war there is an astonishing level of occupational success for the service-class Grammar School boy who had not managed to obtain any Ordinary Level passes at all. He actually fares better than his qualified working-class contemporary – something quite the reverse of the pre-war pattern. And even if we object that there were relatively few of these respondents on which to base any strong conclusions, we also see that the gap between *qualified* boys from the service and working classes has also increased. This widening gap also appears if we restrict ourselves to respondents who obtained five or more Ordinary Level passes. And so whichever way we look at the results it still seems to be the case that service-class boys at Grammar School increased their advantage over the working-class ones. Credentialism provides no easy answer to our findings.

We are left, then, with a curious puzzle. In a period when there were government reforms aimed at making education more meritocratic and

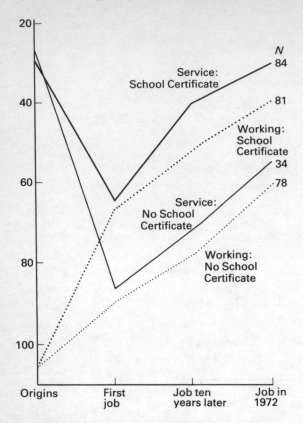

Diagram 7 Schooling, qualifications and career (men born 1913–32 who attended Grammar Schools)

when formal educational credentials might have been expected to become more important stepping-stones to occupational success, old-fashioned class bias seems to have reasserted itself. One is tempted to agree with Goldthorpe's concluding remarks in *Social Mobility and Class Structure*. He wrote:

> The implications of [our] findings . . . therefore count as rather grave ones for the general strategy of egalitarian reform that has been widely adhered to among liberals and social democrats in modern Britain: briefly, the strategy of seeking to attack social inequalities via legislative and administrative measures of a piecemeal kind that can be carried through without venturing too far beyond the limits of 'consensus' politics. What our results would suggest . . . is that this strategy grossly misjudges the resistance that the class structure can offer to attempts to change it; or, to speak less figuratively, the flexibility and effectiveness with which the more powerful and advantaged groupings in society can use the resources at their

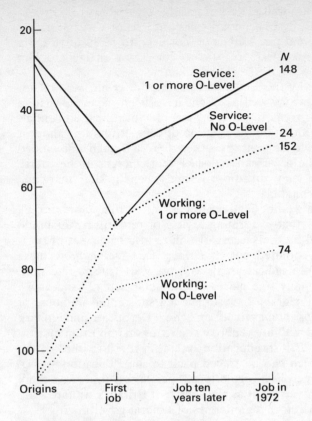

Diagram 8 Schooling, qualifications and career (men born 1933–47 who attended Grammar Schools)

disposal to preserve their privileged positions. . . . Consequently, we would add, *the main function of economic growth can then best be regarded as being not that of facilitating egalitarian reform but rather that of obscuring its failure.* (p. 252, my emphasis)

But Goldthorpe is, we think, too pessimistic. True, our evidence forces us to agree with him that the post-war economic expansion did not facilitate the egalitarian reform sought by the social democrats. It was one of the hopes of the reformers that expansion would enable benefits to be distributed to the underprivileged without having to provoke social conflict by depriving the privileged of their accustomed advantages. And we would agree with Goldthorpe that the reformers failed to see that under this strategy *relative* inequalities might actually increase. Indeed, we would go further than Goldthorpe and suggest, in the light of the present findings, that expansion so far from facilitating reform might actually make it easier for the dominant class to strengthen its hold. In a period of expansion there are many easy pickings to be gained by those who are well-placed in society. The rigours of competition are less. There is, as an economist has put it, more organisational slack. Appointments and promotions do not need to be justified quite so carefully and there is less pressure to get rid of an incompetent colleague who belongs to one's own social circle.

This may explain why the credentialism thesis does not account for the post-war data quite as well as might have been expected. There may be an underlying trend towards the use of educational credentials in selection and promotion but in a period of competition for labour it may often be easier to appoint an 'acceptable' although unqualified candidate. In short the organisational slack that emerges in the course of economic growth may disproportionately benefit the 'marginal' members of the dominant class.

But why, then, are we not even more pessimistic than Goldthorpe? Our answer to this is that in forming a view of reformism we should not be too influenced by the success or failure of a single set of post-war reforms. As we pointed out in *Origins and Destinations* these reforms did not mark a radical break with pre-war British education. There were already many free places in Grammar Schools and as we saw in Table 1 and Diagram 2 these enabled substantial numbers of boys from working-class homes to obtain School Certificate and embark on a career of upward mobility. There was already an important merito-cratic element in the British education system in the first third of the twentieth century which can be traced back to the Education Act of 1902 and the 1907 free-place regulations. Sociologists too often think of the 1945 Labour government as the source of Britain's welfare state and forget the earlier reforming energies of Liberal governments.

We cannot of course show from the data at our disposal that these early twentieth-century reforms actually increased equality of educational opportunity and in turn social mobility. All we can do is point to the dramatic upward mobility through free places at Grammar School that got under way at a time of economic depression and contraction. That educational opportunities can be a prelude to social ascent cannot be denied whatever the lack of success achieved by later attempts to expand these opportunities.

References

Bantock, G. H. (1965), *Education and Values*, London: Faber.

Boudon, R. (1973), *Education, Opportunity and Social Inequality*, New York: Wiley.

Goldthorpe, J. H. (1980), *Social Mobility and Class Structure in Modern Britain*, Oxford: Clarendon Press.

Goldthorpe, J. H. and Hope, K. (1974), *The Social Grading of Occupations: A New Approach and Scale*, Oxford: Clarendon Press.

Halsey, A. H., Heath, A. F. and Ridge, J. M. (1980), *Origins and Destinations: Family, Class and Education in Modern Britain*, Oxford: Clarendon Press.

Turner, R. H. (1960), 'Sponsored and contest mobility and the school system', *American Sociological Review*, 25: 855–67.

4.2

Evenings at the ivory tower: liberal adult education†

David Jary

I am aware of what is going on in the world but I do not yet get a chance to discuss with other people these problems. I hope to do this at the class.

I am seeking insights into man's relationships with man . . . the study of existing patterns and future trends.

Another attraction is the possibility of meeting a kindred spirit, an eligible man, who shares common interests.

The words are those of students in non-vocational adult education classes talking about their reasons for attending their courses.[1] In any winter week in Britain one in every twenty-five adults will spend one of their evenings at a local college or university attending a non-vocational adult class. Over a longer period a much larger proportion, possibly in excess of 30%,[2] will attend a class. Adult education is a considerable leisure-time activity. In terms of numbers of participants and their regularity of commitment it is roughly on a par with the watching of professional association football. Yet, when even a glance at the quotations above suggests the importance of intrinsic gratifications, adult education is too often analysed as *education* producing extrinsic effects rather than as *leisure* yielding immediate gratifications. Adult education often fails to live up to narrow educational criteria employed in evaluating it. But as leisure it may perform functions for which no other forms of leisure are a substitute. This article describes and explains adult education, giving special attention to its under-emphasized aspects as leisure and play, and argues that the under-valuation of leisure functions is a typical, even growing, feature of

† Source: M. A. Parker, S. Smith and C. Smith (1973) (eds), *Leisure and Society in Britain*, London, Allen Lane, pp. 263–77.

general educational thought. Although important in its own right, adult education will also serve as a case study in educational and leisure purposes.

The shape and goals of liberal adult education

We shall be analysing in detail only a part of adult education, the sector specializing in the provision of courses in academic subjects at or near university level. Usually this is referred to as Liberal Adult Education. While the Local Education Authorities provide the bulk of classes in adult education, those in liberal academic subjects are mainly, and often jointly, provided by two organizations, a voluntary body – the evocatively named Workers' Educational Association – and the Extra-Mural Departments of universities. Annual enrolments in their courses are around 200,000. [. . .] In many ways liberal adult education exists at one end of an extreme typology of adult education. Of all adult education liberal adult education presents perhaps the highest psychological barriers to participation and its course content is demanding. For an evening its students enter the ivory towers of academic subjects and confront the fundamental and potentially transforming issues these subjects raise.

It might seem simple to ask the organizations of liberal adult education what their students are striving for, but organizations' views of their goals are notoriously poor indicators of actual results. There is in any case a particular reason for not accepting their views about the functions of adult education for, in response to what has been called their great 'institutional insecurity',[3] the adult education organizations' own claims for their purposes have been grandiloquent rather than descriptive. Nevertheless, these claims must be our starting point. Much of the distinctive style and content to be found running through the claims of liberal adult educationalists can be traced to the founding father of contemporary adult education, Albert Mansbridge, who started the W.E.A. in 1903 to encourage universities to provide classes for those denied opportunity of full-time higher education. Writing soon after the W.E.A.'s first decade, Mansbridge saw its classes as

> incontestably proving that the workers of England . . . are alive and responsive to the finer creations of the mind and spirit . . .
> [possessing a] divine spark which the slightest breeze will fan into flame, lighting up with joy unspeakable the way of knowledge.[4]

His conception of the W.E.A's goal was dualistic; it would bring individual development and social harmony. He looked to the liaison of the universities and the W.E.A. to help bring workers more fully into the political life of the community. Mansbridge's mixture of individual and social functions has remained the core of adult education's public expressions of purpose.

There have been other organizations some with less consensual, even revolutionary, goals[5] but it was the W.E.A.'s work that attracted government financial support. In one of the early reports about adult education which Hobhouse and Headlam made to the Board of Education, they described the W.E.A. as

> accustom[ing] the student to the ideal of work familiar at a university . . . aimed not so much at filling the mind of the student with facts and theories as at calling forth his own individual . . . [and at enabling him] to distinguish between what may be called a matter of fact and what is certainly a matter of opinion.[6]

This kind of report led to the W.E.A. and the universities receiving public funds in support of their adult education work. The organizations also won the sympathy and the time (as class tutors and guides) of numbers of very eminent academics.[7]

Although there was room in Mansbridge's view of adult education for individual enjoyment, this was usually accompanied by a puritanical alter ego, by a tendency to deep mistrust of immediate pleasures, and a preference for obviously 'self-developing' and 'socially purposive' forms of adult education. That this remains the basic ingredient of liberal adult education's idea of itself can be illustrated by a recent policy document of the W.E.A., which states:

> Adult education has a positive role and it seeks to encourage informed discussion and study of the problems facing society in the belief that it is vital to the health of the democracy. It seeks to develop *serious and sustained* study.[8]

Education for social purpose continues as the core ideology. Any suggestion that leisure *primarily* for its own sake may have priority over other purposes is likely to be attacked by the movement's spokesmen. Certainly it will be handled with caution. One telling tract states that adult education 'is liable to be regarded . . . as a resort of those who are casually seeking diversion for their leisure time.' Instead its author wished to see it 'as an essential expression for those who would enjoy their lives to the full and *shoulder their responsibility* as persons and citizens', claiming that the goals of adult education should be to produce a 'sense of values and the self-discipline of the people'.[9]

Without denying that these ideologies have had *some* effect on the shape of adult education, my central argument will be that, *contrary to its ideologies*, liberal adult education is primarily a leisure-centred activity. Rather than 'sustained study' or 'social purposiveness', informal teaching methods, extensive class participation and particularly lengthy discussion periods are a typical feature of its classes. Many classes seem centred on immediate gratifications, even – dare I say it – on 'fun'. The actuality of what, in adult education, is sometimes weightily referred to as the 'grand tradition' of earnest study, is often a group obviously enjoying an admittedly rather different from everyday intellectual interaction, but with obvious wider social purposes little evident. Although classes are usually organized around subjects like English literature, history or sociology, these subjects are treated in a very different manner from their treatment in undergraduate education. They are mined for their general relatedness to life, and above all for their personal relevance. They are used as promptings for generalized reflection and discussion. But rather than education with a core of sustained private study, the heart and life of the whole activity of liberal adult education is the immediate pleasure of the class.

My conclusion is that this leisure-centredness of liberal adult education ought not to be hidden or apologized for; it should be recognized and its gratifications elaborated. This will not be to accept that liberal adult education is an 'irrelevant casual diversion'. Far from it, liberal adult education will be seen as a highly distinctive form of leisure. That such leisure functions are often missed or played down indicates the strength of the forces at work in sociology, in adult education, and in society at large, against taking leisure seriously.

Sociological theories of adult education and leisure

Perhaps the most systematic attempt to outline the main functions of adult education is that of Floud and Halsey, although they admit that their suggestion is little more than a preliminary framework.[10] They divide adult education's functions into five. There are 'remedial' and 'mobilizing' functions, involving processes of *occupational and political differentiation* – i.e. equipping people to occupy specialist 'roles' – which the institutions of full-time education did not, but might have performed. There are 'assimilative' functions, where integration is the focus. Again these *might* have been performed by full-time institutions. Floud and Halsey see the contact which British liberal adult education provided with university 'élite culture' as an assimilative function. Only their final two functions, referred to as 'compensatory' and 'recreative' are continuous leisure functions. However, since compensatory educa tion is seen by them as arising from the emotional and intellectual deprivations associated with narrow and routinized work, and because their recreative function remains an unexplicated residual category, Floud and Halsey's schema must be regarded as biased towards extrinsic effects, and limited in its treatment of adult education as leisure. This we must remedy by utilizing general theories of leisure.

Sociologists, like Dumazedier and Giddens, have provided basic conceptual distinctions.[11] 'Obligatory' leisure activities (e.g. church-going, lawn-cutting) and 'instrumental activities' (into which remedial adult education clearly falls) must be distinguished from leisure in its 'pure' forms. Pure leisure occurs when obligation and *extrinsic* instrumentality are absent and when only more immediate affectivity and *intrinsic* leisure gratifications are involved. But the absence of extrinsic instrumentality does not imply what Floud and Halsey's schema might suggest, that leisure functions cannot be further specified. Much non-obligatory leisure is spent in purely 'restorative' relaxation, but some leisure has more ramifying implications. 'Play', for example, is often distinguished from restorative leisure by its latent potentialities for personal transformation. It is just these play aspects of adult education as leisure that are often neglected. At least two sets of play elements seem likely to be involved. First there are affiliative needs for physical contact and for other forms of intimacy and interaction. Secondly, there are needs for self-esteem, self-consistency and an ordered world view.

If, as in animal play, there was a direct functional relationship between play and organic and societal survival, it would be a simple matter to move from the above analysis to an adjustment of Floud and Halsey's functional schema. However, because this is not so, their stress on assimilation and integration – with its neglect of human creativity – misses the individuation of 'identity' and enlargement of self that human play and therefore adult education can provide. Their category of compensatory education, which gets closest to capturing these effects of education, nevertheless finally remains shackled within a perspective assuming a norm in which 'central life interests' are in work. It suggests that adult education is needed only to satisfy groups who are deprived of more normal gratifications, mainly from work. Neither this category nor Floud and Halsey's recreative category can adequately elaborate adult education as leisure, *sui generis*. I suggest that liberal adult education as leisure provides for two overlapping kinds of play. These are:
(a) sociability – interaction primarily for its own sake and –
(b) self-expansive play, involving self-display, self-expression and self-insight, but stopping short of (or in addition to) Floud and Halsey's extrinsic functions.

Sociability, as I will use it here, is (approximately) Simmel's term. All social activity involves sociability, but sometimes, as at parties, sociability 'exists for its own sake and for the sake of a fascination, which in its own liberation from [social] ties, it diffuses'. Simmel actually refers to this as a 'play form'. It need have 'no extrinsic results', and 'entirely depends upon the personalities among whom it occurs'. Thus on the whole it grows freely, but it must always avoid (a risk it always faces) breaking down into the 'naturalism' of basic drives. Although it is not seen by Simmel to possess extrinsic purposes, sociability is not without seriousness and it does have wider effects, for it involves play with serious aspects of life. Simmel sees in it a capacity for transferring the 'seriousness and tragic to a symbolic shadowy play form', which reveals reality obliquely. He also suggests that it is 'the more serious person who derives from sociability a feeling of liberation and relief' and that he does 'so because he enjoys [in sociability] . . . a concentration and exchange of effects that present all the tasks and all the seriousness of life in a sublimation and at the same time dilution'.[12]

The liberal adult education class can be best considered as providing a *specific* form of sociability situation. The *class* is the centre of liberal adult education far more than it is in almost any other form of education. Members of classes demand precisely the mixture of structure and flexibility required for successful sociability; gratification through conversation is pursued in a way that is typical of sociability – many an adult education tutor has come to grief in failing to notice that. We noted that the typical subject-matters of liberal adult education are the social sciences and the humanities. These contain the topics of human concern and dilemma which are the same stuff of more spontaneous sociability situations. Automatically raised are the serious and tragic sides of man. But the presence of a tutor and a subject focus takes the sociability of the adult class beyond the 'usual'. Moreover, as we will later see, its students may well be just those kinds of people for whom Simmel felt sociability yielded most. Finally, as well as people well known to each other – 'familiars' as Potter calls them – the liberal adult education class also brings contacts with 'casuals', whom Potter regards as a creative ingredient of sociability situations contributing 'insight' and 'fresh' behaviour.[13]

Sociability is also involved in our second form of play, the self-expansive. Riesman and Watson regard sociability as having 'a special contribution to make both to the development of unique individual identities and the development of shared norms and identities which facilitate social integration.'[14] But the development of identity and the development and display of self are not *only* found in sociability. In liberal adult education they can stem from the more formal exchange of orthodox teacher-student roles as well as from reading, thought and creative expression connected with the class, rather than from sociability as such.

Social recruitment

Unfortunately research on all kinds of adult education has been by survey method and little related to explicit functional discussions.[15] The information most frequently yielded by these surveys is about the age, sex, marital status and occupation of participants. In all types of non-vocational adult education the majority and, it seems, an ever-increasing proportion of students, are female. [. . .] In general the unmarried have higher rates of participation, and the married with young children, who have the lowest quantities of pure leisure time, lower than average rates. The proportion of students from manual occupations has fallen over the years [. . .]

The low support from manual workers has been the source of much soul-searching by liberal adult educationalists. Most sociological studies of working-class leisure reveal a predominance of recuperative activities, often closely connected with kinship, locality, and perhaps work groups. Adult education, as a specialized individual activity, normally housed in urban centre institutions, is markedly incongruent with work-ing-class life. If entered into, it is capable of creating tensions in rela-tionships with family and friends and dissatisfaction with work. There are several studies, notably one by Trenaman, showing the 'reinforcing' character of education.[16] Attitudes towards education established in schools either inhibit or encourage further involvement.

In general the more educated a person the more he continues to seek education. It certainly could be argued that liberal adult education does remarkably well in recruiting working-class students. Especially does it do so in those courses which it arranges in conjunction with industrial firms and trades unions – courses which incidentally *do* display clear extrinsic purposes.[17] It is also true that adult education's own usual modes of recording the occupations of its students – with its separate entries for housewives, the retired, etc. – tends to underestimate the extent of working-class participation.[18] Furthermore, much of the 'middle-class' enrolment, at least in the classes, would appear to be concentrated in the lower rather than the upper reaches of that class. In all this, the W.E.A.'s names and ideology may be a valuable property.

In arguing above that adult education would be better seen as leisure, it is not my intention to argue for it to drop all its remedial concerns. What I am arguing against are attempts to hide the manifest fact that it is not *mainly* an agency of remedial education, and against the great feelings of guilt about its remedial failure which periodically sweep adult education.[19] My argument against such guilt feelings must rest on further elaboration of my sketch of the positive qualities of the leisure-oriented adult education class and student.

The purposes of liberal adult education students

Broad analyses of social recruitment give little guidance on the precise motivations and gratifications of the students. Precisely because social class, and especially education, explain differential participation in a whole range of leisure activities, general characteristics of socio-econ-omic status groups and occupational categories fail to explain particular activities which involve only a minority of *any* socio-economic group. A more direct analysis of motivations and gratifications is required, and other research may be of assistance here.[20]

The *Adequacy of Provision* survey examined the whole range of adult education and found that one sixth of the students saw themselves as most interested in 'personal contact within the class', one half in 'self-development' for its own sake, and a few who regarded their adult education as 'merely recreational'. All these responses would seem to constitute intrinsic rather than extrinsic purposes. At the other extreme, only 10% mentioned 'work-related' motivations, and a somewhat smaller percentage 'family relatedness'. In relation to liberal adult education primacy of leisure was even more striking. 'Self-development' (around 70%), and 'social contacts through the class' (nearly 20%) far outweigh instrumental orientations, although family, work or community-relatedness are mentioned by a few.

A more sophisticated American inquiry by James Davis of one kind of American liberal adult education – the Great Books Programme – confirms this picture.[21] Davis's methodology involved him in the cluster analysis of participants' selections from a check-list of twenty-four reasons for joining the programme. The analysis yielded four clusters. The first consisted of predominantly vocational items – 28% of respondents checked one or more of these items by Davis. Next the analysis suggested a 'self-help' cluster, from which 51% chose at least one item. In it were brought together items concerned with improving taste and gaining self-confidence with people of higher intellectual background, and reading skills. It was Davis's opinion that this cluster included the most superficial of the motives, a concern with the externals of social status, for example. The third cluster, 'content', involved deeper intellectual and abstract concerns and a desire for self-insight, rather than gimmicks. In Davis's opinion, this cluster, from which 68% selected one or more item, came closest to the official ideology of the programmes. Finally, the analysis gave a cluster which Davis labelled 'cosmopolitanism'. It was made up of the items 'escaping the intellectual narrowness of my community', 'talking with people who have more intellectual interests than my usual friends', and 'meeting people who are quite different from me'. This had the highest check-rate, 71% checking one or more items.

There is much in the Great Books survey that supports the outline of liberal adult education advanced in this chapter. The links can be made explicit by way of Table 1, categorizing forms of adult education. Where it is not self-explanatory, its content is explained earlier in the chapter.

Table 1

Societal functions	Individual needs – primacy of extrinsic instrumental	Individual needs – primacy of intrinsic play
Differentiation-Individuation	1 Remedial-Mobilizing	3 Self-expansive
Integration	2 Assimilative	4 Sociability

The categories of Table 1 correspond to Davis's categories as follows:
1. *remedial mobilizing*: 'stepping stone': items involve 'increasing ability to carry out my job through intellectual training or group discussion', yet making friends *per se* did not correlate highly with the cluster.
2. *assimilative*: 'self-help': items concerned with improving taste and

gaining confidence, but perhaps concerned with the veneer rather than the substance of status.
3. *self-expansive*: 'content': items display depth of concern with the 'basic issues of life' and gaining self-insight.
4. *sociability*: 'cosmopolitanism': items stressing opportunities to meet people with a wider range of interests than usual friends.

A survey of my own can be used to provide further confirmation and illustration of the leisure character of liberal adult education. The survey was part of an attempt to assess the motives of students in liberal adult education classes in sociology and social psychology. The following distribution of orientations was found:

3	clearly self-expansive	10%	
4	clearly sociability	15%	80%
3 & 4	a combination of the two	55%	
	(including a clear sub-category of 15% seeking solution to a specific personal problem)		
1	vocational	15%	20%
	plus 5% with clear social purpose		

10% of the respondents were placed in category 3 because they showed a definite and serious interest in a subject and little or no concern with the social interaction of the class. A further 15% gave heavy emphasis to the attractions of sociability offered by the adult class, but had little concern with anything wider. The classification of a further 15% who said that they were seeking help in handling *personal problems* is more difficult. Such orientations have sometimes been seen as threatening educational purposes. Where social science is the subject, this need not be the case. A few brief examples of students' reasons for attending classes will illustrate this claim.

> To reduce time spent in a less than happy home . . . shy, inhibited bachelor suffering from extreme social isolation of adolescence.

> My personality is best described in an article 'The Swing from Science', I am a 'converger' . . . but I am at a complete loss when dealing with people . . . I wonder should I divorce my wife.

> I do not like myself as a teacher. I want to learn enough to change my ways or my job.

With attitudes and expectations such as these, there is scope for self-insight to emerge both from the course content and from social interaction in the class.

By far the largest category of responses were the 40% who mentioned the sociability of the class but also stressed a broader band of interests and concerns, in people and society. While their very attendance at a class indicates their willingness to be at least a little more disciplined in their thought and talk about social life, they are not strikingly more focused on purposes extrinsic to leisure than people in more diffuse sociability situations. It is a serious discussion of things in general, coupled with some feeling of self-expansion that they seek from adult education. Again some brief quotations will convey something of this:

> Interested [because I read] semi-sociological works like Richard Hoggart, *Uses of Literacy* . . . now see the subject wider . . . feel that I am getting a deeper understanding of problems and more tolerance.

> I don't necessarily expect the course to provide answers to problems but to give clearer understanding.

> In old age one tends to become censorious, and sociology should broaden one's perspectives.

> As a technologist I consider that the social sciences have more relevance to present-day problems than natural science and technology.

In my survey 80% of liberal adult education students in social science showed little or no vocational purpose and few signs of the specific 'social purposes'. For the remaining 20%, however, these purposes were present. Fifteen per cent claimed a vocational purpose and 5% indicated a specific social purpose. None of these sought adult education for a remedial or mobilizing function. Adult education thus seems to provide an opportunity for reflection, self-expansion and sociability.

But do these personal statements of private purposes correspond to actual effects or functions? Earlier we concluded that an analysis of the socio-economic status of participants alone brought little insight to understanding the motives in adult education. But now the motivational analysis makes possible a reformulated occupational analysis, in which *specific* occupations rather than broader groupings of occupations are considered.

The idea of an opposition pattern of work and leisure (one of three suggested by Parker[22]) fits well what we earlier saw as the obstacles existing to working-class participation in liberal adult education. But it is Parker's idea of extension of work into leisure which is especially relevant. Gould's discovery that there are large differences in the levels of adult education participation *within* socio-economic groups (teachers and social workers and service occupations for example are over-represented; business and commerce under-represented) can be related to Parker's terms.[23] Although exclusively vocational purposes are not revealed by surveys, we do find some general vocational connectedness. Certain occupations, like social work and teaching, are especially compatible with the kinds of play and sociability which liberal adult education provides.

A useful analogy exhibiting this kind of compatibility of work and leisure can be made with those who are active in social movements.[24] Parkin shows that the support for movements like C.N.D. comes from the highly educated, but that there is a strong tendency for certain occupations, in particular the 'welfare and creative professions', to be heavily over-represented in C.N.D. and movements like it. Parkin's view is that it is not merely a matter of certain occupations producing leisure orientations, but that the occupations are themselves chosen by the activists as compatible with a whole style of life. Parkin outlines this style as involving an interest in the dynamics of interpersonal relationships, an ethical sensitivity and concern, and a relative lack of interest in economic goals. Parkin sees higher education as making a vital contribution to the formation of the integrated occupation and leisure style of the middle-class radical.

A similar life style may support liberal adult education. While it is unlikely that liberal adult education is as decisive as full-time education in creating styles (and certainly, as Bochel and others have shown, and consistent with what we earlier argued, it is relatively less associated with *specific* political activism[25]) there would seem strong parallels between the kinds of ethical sensitivity and interests mentioned by Parkin and the characteristics of liberal adult education students. At the very least, adult education participation appears to grow from a larger style of leisure. A kind of 'cultural activism' pervades its clientèle. Several studies, including my own, find students making a differentially large use of libraries, theatres, 'quality' newspapers and the like, and a much smaller than average usage of the *mass* media. Many students might fairly be described in terms similar to Riesman's notion of the inside dopester.[26] While he takes little part in active politics, the inside dopester knows 'a great deal about what other people are doing and thinking in the important "great issue" spheres of life, goes to great lengths to keep from looking and feeling like an uninformed outsider'. He is 'politically cosmopolitan rather than parochial'. He is sensitive, flexible in social situations, and although morally concerned, he does not 'moralize'.

Types of liberal adult education class

It is not my intention to argue that every liberal adult education class is dominated by intrinsic leisure rather than by extrinsic goals. Nor would I wish to claim that a 'serious' sociability pervades all classes. There are clear exceptions to both patterns. Particular classes reflect the styles of their membership. We can construct the following provisional *ideal* typology of classes:

	Strong, clear motives	Weaker motives
	Individual recruitment	Collective (i.e. industry-based or communal) recruitment
	City-centre location	Suburban or smalltown location
Preponderance of occupational relatedness; social science emphasis	Extension	Specific
More general social science and far greater arts and humanities emphasis	General	Discursive

The 'extension' type (we are employing this term in Parker's, rather than the adult education administrator's sense) and the 'general' type are those in which are to be found the kind of sociability, self-expansion purposes and life and leisure styles we outlined. The other two are contrasted exceptions to our suggested pattern. 'Discursive' classes, because they are based upon pre-existing groups, lack strong subject motives and contain students who would not enter adult education but for group pressure upon them, and consequently have little of the styles of those recruited individually. The frequent choice of local history as a subject in small-centre classes can be seen as a device for moulding a viable class from locality interests when other strong common interests are lacking. Another solution in those circumstances is for a class to develop as a coterie revolving around a particular tutor's weekly performance, a state of affairs labelled 'spell-binding' inside the adult education profession.

Liberal adult education for what?

Tyrrell Burgess has recently asserted that the W.E.A. provides 'ornamental knowledge mainly to middle-class people'.[27] I hope I have demonstrated that his verdict should not be accepted. His error would seem to be that if liberal adult education does not attract the working class, then it is merely a 'casual diversion'. But there is more reason for quoting Burgess's views than the remarks he directs at the W.E.A. His remarks can be seen as part of a currently modish, general philosophy of educational provision; a view which also finds the Open University wanting. Since it, like adult education, caters for those already possessing considerable educational advantage, it is seen as 'rather short on egalitarian purpose'. This view has also encouraged the expansion of full-time education in vocationally-oriented polytechnics rather than in universities. George Brosan puts this case bluntly – 'the main task of the system of higher education outside the universities is to deal with the matching sector, i.e. to provide a basis of manpower that the universities have not provided.'[28] His message is clear. Occupational differentiation, economic, mobilizing and remedial goals must be uppermost; the universities have failed; polytechnics must provide something different. These more general debates about tertiary education and leisure provision are very relevant to my thesis about liberal adult education and to current policy issues.

Some of the best liberal adult education has occupational relatedness but it is to do with occupational play rather than with the occupation *per se*; liberal adult education provides a sociability and an opportunity for self-development especially suited to particular roles. Occupational relatedness there may be, but participation is far from confined to a narrow band of occupations; individual life and leisure styles are the crucial causes and effects of participation in liberal adult education. Liberal adult education sometimes performs mobilizing and remedial functions. Doubtless it also has political repercussions and implications for social control, but these are not the individual purposes at its core; nor are they superior to such purposes. A recent policy survey of American tertiary education went so far as to argue that we have entered an era of 'cultural revolution'. 'More people are now seeking vocations or life styles outside the Horatio Alger syndrome than ever before . . . Higher education is built on the work ethic and we are now shifting to a more sensate culture.'[29] In such an age, when personal liberation and ethical exploration is becoming a watchword, and with the competitive work ethic questioned from many sides and now by 'ecologists', surely Brosan's and Burgess's assessment of adult education can't be right, either for adult education or for higher education as a whole.

Notes and References

1 The quotations are from a sample of social science adult students in fifteen W.E.A. and extra-mural classes which I made in Lancashire, Yorkshire and Cheshire in the winter of 1967–8. I record my gratitude to all the respondents, tutors and organizations involved.

2 These estimates are derived from the recent survey, *Adequacy of Provision*, published by the National Institute of Adult Education, March 1970.

3 Burton R. Clark, *The Marginality of Adult Education*, Chicago Center for the Study of Liberal Education for Adults, 1958, and *Adult Education in Transition*, Berkeley, University of California Press, 1956.

4 Albert Mansbridge, *University Tutorial Classes*, Longmans, 1913, pp. 2–3.

5 The most important was the National Council of Labour Colleges. For general historical accounts of adult education see T. Kelly, *A Short History of Adult Education in Great Britain*, Liverpool University Press, 1970, and J. F. C. Harrison, *Learning and Living, 1790–1960*, Routledge & Kegan Paul, 1961.

6 Mansbridge, op. cit., p. 145.
7 That men like R. H. Tawney have been involved shows that, although it has usually involved commitments to peaceful rather than revolutionary change, support for liberal adult education far from represents support for the *status quo*.
8 *Unfinished Business*, a W.E.A. Policy Statement, 1970, p. 3, my italics.
9 Mabel Tylecote, *The Future of Adult Education*, Fabian Society, 1960, p. 1, my italics.
10 Jean Floud and A. H. Halsey, 'The Sociology of Education', *Current Sociology*, vol. VII, no. 3, 1958.
11 A. Giddens, 'Notes on the Concept of Play and Leisure', *Sociological Review*, March 1964; J. Dumazedier, *Toward a Society of Leisure*, Collier-Macmillan, 1967.
12 Georg Simmel, *The Sociology of Georg Simmel*, ed. Kurt H. Wolff, Glencoe, Free Press, 1950, pp. 41–57.
13 Robert J. Potter, 'Friends, Familiars and Strangers as they Converse at Parties' mentioned in P. E. Hammond, *Sociologists at Work*, New York, Basic Books, 1964, p. 238.
14 Hammond, op. cit., ch. 10; D. Riesman and J. Watson, 'The Sociability Project', p. 237.
15 e.g. W. E. Styler, *Who Were the Students*? National Institute of Adult Education, 1950, or *Aspects of Adult Education*, W.E.A., 1960.
16 J. Trenaman, 'Education in the Adult Population', *Adult Education*, vol. 34, 1962.
17 See A. H. Thornton and F. J. Bayliss, *Adult Education in the Industrial Community*, National Institute of Adult Education 1965, for one discussion of these.
18 Because of this some of the analyses of the social class participation made by analysts of adult education seem to have greatly miscalculated the proportions. For example see R. Pahl's *Adult Education in a Free Society*, New Orbits Group, 1962.
19 A recent bout can be read in *W.E.A. News*, Sept. 1971 and Jan. 1972.
20 W. E. Styler, 'The Motives of Adult Students', *Adult Education*, vol. 23, 1950.
21 J. A. Davis, *Great Books and Small Groups*, Glencoe, Free Press, 1961.
22 S. R. Parker, *The Future of Work and Leisure*, MacGibbon & Kee, 1971.
23 J. D. Gould, *The Recruitment of Adult Students*, Vaughan College Papers, no. 5, University of Leicester, no date.
24 Frank Parkin, *Middle Class Radicalism*, University of Manchester Press, 1968.
25 John Bochel, 'The Recruitment of Local Councillors', *Political Studies*, vol. 14.
26 David Riesman and others, *The Lonely Crowd*, New York, Doubleday, 1953, especially pp. 210–15.
27 Tyrrell Burgess, 'The Open University', *New Society*, 27 April 1972.
28 See George Brosan, in Brosan and others, *Patterns and Policies in Higher Education*, Pelican, 1971. Eric Robinson, in *The New Polytechnics*, Turnstile Press, 1968, voices similar arguments to Brosan and to Burgess.
29 The Carnegie Commission on Higher Education, *New Students and New Places*, 1971, p. 3.

Index